PATHWAYS TO TEACHING SERIES

Practical Strategies for Teaching English Language Learners

ELLEN M. CURTIN

Texas Wesleyan University

NATIONAL CENTER FOR EDUCATION INFORMATION

NATIONAL CENTER FOR
EDUCATION INFORMATION

Merrill
is an imprint of

Upper Saddle River, New Jersey
Columbus, Ohio

Library of Congress Cataloging-in-Publication Data
Curtin, Ellen M.
    Practical strategies for teaching English language learners / Ellen M. Curtin.—1st ed.
        p. cm. — (Pathways to teaching series)
    ISBN-13: 978-0-13-513059-9
    ISBN-10: 0-13-513059-X
    1. English language—Study and teaching.   2. English language—Study and teaching—Foreign
speakers.   3. Effective teaching.   I. Title.
    LB1576.C885 2009
    428.2'4—dc22

                                                                                    2008006020

Vice President and Executive Publisher: Jeffery W. Johnston
Senior Editors: Darcy Betts Prybella and Meredith Fossel
Editorial Assistant: Nancy J. Holstein
Senior Managing Editor: Pamela D. Bennet
Project Manager: Sarah N. Kenoyer
Production Coordinator: Vishal Harshvardhan, Aptara, Inc.
Design Coordinator: Diane C. Lorenzo
Photo Coordinator: Valerie Schultz
Cover Design: Jeff Vanik
Cover Image: Jupiter Images
Operations Specialist: Susan W. Hannahs
Director of Marketing: Quinn Perkson
Marketing Coordinator: Brian Mounts

This book was set in Palatino by Aptara, Inc. The book and cover were printed and bound by
Courier/Stoughton, Inc.

Photo Credits: Chapter 1: Courtesy of the Library of Congress, Chapters 2 and 3: Scott
Cunningham/Merrill, Chapter 4: Anthony Magnacca/Merrill, Chapter 5: Anne Vega/Merrill,
Chapter 6: PH College, Chapter 7: Silver Burdett Ginn, Chapter 8: Patrick White/Merrill,
Chapter 9: Scott Cunningham/Merrill, Chapter 10 David Mager/Pearson Learning Photo Studio

Pearson® is a registered trademark of Pearson plc
Merrill® is a registered trademark of Pearson Education, Inc.

Pearson Education Ltd., London   Pearson Education North Asia, Ltd., Hong Kong
Pearson Education Singapore Pte. Ltd.   Pearson Educación de Mexico, S.A. de C.V.
Pearson Education Canada, Inc. Ltd.   Pearson Education Malaysia Pte. Ltd.
Pearson Education–Japan   Pearson Education Upper Saddle River, New Jersey
Pearson Education Australia Pty., Limited

Merrill
is an imprint of

10 9 8 7 6 5 4 3 2 1
ISBN-13: 978-0-13-513059-9
ISBN-10:   0-13-513059-X

This book, *Practical Strategies for Teaching English Language Learners*, is dedicated to all teachers past, present, and future for their positive impact/difference in the lives of so many children, and to my husband, Bruce Wertz, for his love and support.

PREFACE

PURPOSE OF THIS BOOK

"Who is this English Language Learner? How do I communicate with him or her? How do I prepare him or her for state standardized tests? How do I teach him or her advanced reading skills when his or her vocabulary is so limited?" These are common concerns voiced by teachers in grades K–12 as they express their inadequacies about teaching English Language Learners in the regular classroom.

This text is designed to help answer these questions for all K–12 teachers by providing the necessary information and research-proven teaching strategies that are best for all learners including English Language Learners. The book addresses the specific role that regular classroom teachers now play in ensuring that English Language Learners are acquiring English through the content subject areas. No Child Left Behind (2001) raises the accountability level for all our students including English Language Learners. English Language Learners are no longer the sole responsibility of an ESL teacher, as all teachers must now teach English Language Learners English regular subject content.

This book is for pre-service and in-service (practicing) teachers who will be or are teaching English Language Learners on-grade-level subject content in the regular K–12 classroom setting. This text is a concise and practical resource book that combines current research in English language learning with teaching application strategies for pre-K–12 classrooms. The use of research-based instructional strategies like Sheltered Instruction that teach English through grade-level subject content provides the theoretical framework underlying the teaching strategies selected in this text. This book targets student teachers, experienced teachers new to English Language Learners, beginning alternative route teachers, and "career changers" who find themselves grappling with how best to teach English Language Learners on-grade-level subject content in the regular classroom setting.

The author presupposes that the reader is new to the field of English Language Learners and may be new to the educational profession in general. This book can be used independently by a practitioner in the classroom seeking strategies for English language teaching. This text can also be used by professors, mentors, and all instructional supervisors for use in programs or classes designed for pre-K–12 teacher preparation.

The goal of this text is to demystify English as a second language educational theory by presenting it in concrete and easy to understand terminology, and then connecting it to the actual classroom setting wherever possible. Many novice and beginning teachers are in what the literature terms "the survival mode." Teachers in the survival mode are more interested initially in the "how" (practice) of teaching as opposed to the "why" (theory). This book comprises specific "how to" teaching strategies for teaching the English language and provides survival strategies for use by the first-year teacher and beyond. It also serves as a useful introduction to the field of second language research and learning.

This text is for all teachers and their instructors who wish to learn teaching strategies that actually work; it is not just a book about English Language Learners. Teachers who utilize these strategies will improve the learning level for all their students and not just English Language Learners. The teaching strategies in this book work and are extremely effective.

ORGANIZATION OF THE BOOK

This book is comprised of 10 chapters. Chapter 1 provides the necessary historical background to English as a Second Language education from the beginning of the 20th century to No Child Left Behind (2001) and high-stakes testing today. It provides the teacher with the knowledge and understanding of the law pertaining to English Language Learners within today's educational context. Steps for identification and placement of English Language Learners are discussed here as well as an overview of commonly used terminology.

Chapter 2 provides the theoretical background to first and second language acquisition theory. An understanding of this theory is vital for the teacher of the English Language Learner. Knowledge of this theory equips the teacher with the necessary understanding of the process of second language acquisition and the developmental language sequences for English Language Learners.

Chapters 3 and 4 serve as an introduction to the world of English Language Learners and their specific cultural, psychological, and learning needs. Questions such as the following are addressed: "How do the needs of an English Language Learner differ from that of other students?" "How should instruction be planned with the unique learning style needs of these students in mind?" "What advance planning is necessary to prepare for these students?" This section focuses on the learning styles needs of the ELL students and how a teacher can appropriately plan in advance for those needs. Sheltered Instruction (SI) is the theoretical framework underlying the teaching strategies presented in this chapter and this book.

Chapters 5–7 deal with how to actually teach to the needs of English Language Learners in content subject areas while also teaching all other students. Chapter 5 addresses the specifics of the lesson cycle and teaching strategies that can be encompassed within it and addresses English Language Learners' needs. Chapter 6 addresses teaching strategies for the content subject areas with a heavy emphasis on making content understandable for the English Language Learner.

Chapter 7 addresses the specifics of teaching the content subject areas of reading, social studies, math, and science.

Chapter 8 deals with assessment of student learning and how to appropriately assess the English Language Learner using multidimensional assessment strategies. Preparation for state standardized tests is also addressed in this chapter.

Chapter 9 provides a host of motivational tips and additional teaching strategies to engage students in classroom learning, as well as keeping them involved and motivated in the lessons. Three discipline management models are provided with practical steps for choosing and creating a discipline model for any K–12 classroom situation.

Chapter 10 focuses on the world of the English Language Learner beyond the scope of the classroom. Here the importance of the school community as a whole, and school and home relations are addressed. Chapter 10 provides strategies for teachers to create communities of learning within the school and within the community. This section also serves as a useful guide for administrators or teachers charged with creating enhanced home-school relations with immigrant and culturally diverse families. Strategies and ideas for becoming advocates for the English Language Learning community are addressed here. The importance of the teacher and how to maintain positive relations with the family of students, how to deal with interpreters, and communication issues are addressed in this chapter.

CHAPTER FORMAT

Each chapter is organized as follows:

Introduction: This provides a brief overview and description of the content of the chapter.

Focus Questions: These questions are designed to stimulate discussion between instructor and teacher trainees. These questions can be used by the instructor to assess prior knowledge and understanding of the concepts of the chapter. These questions are designed to stimulate talk and discussion on the content of the chapter.

Classroom Scenario: Each chapter has a case study/vignette relating to the content of the chapter. Many of the scenarios are derived from the author's own research in classrooms with English Language Learners and their teachers. Voices and perspectives from actual students, teachers, administrators, and parents are used to demonstrate or highlight the content addressed in each chapter. *The scenarios are varied to include examples from elementary, middle school, and high school. The scenarios also represent a range of cultural diversity and classroom situations.*

Focus Questions and Author's Insight: Each classroom scenario analysis begins with discussion questions. These can be used by the instructor to facilitate discussion among teachers (pre-service or in-service), commentary, and sharing personal experiences in classrooms. The Author's Insight is a forum for the author to share her personal teaching experiences and research insights.

What Research Tells Us: This section presents research underlying the classroom application teaching strategies content in each chapter. The research is comprehensive but presented in an understandable format. The research is the most up-to-date and current in the field of English Language Learners and for teaching in general.

Classroom Application Strategies: This section provides the actual teaching strategies that can be practiced and applied in the classroom. These can be directly utilized by in-service teachers already teaching or can be practiced and rehearsed by pre-service teachers in a classroom simulation. Each strategy is clearly labeled. All these strategies can be adapted for any K–12 classroom setting.

Chapter Summary: Provided at the end of every chapter, it synopsizes the pertinent research points and classroom application strategies discussed in each chapter.

Reflective Chapter Questions: These questions are intended to assist the pre-service or in-service teacher to reflect on the content learned, and to ensure comprehension and understanding of the material presented in the chapter. The questions are designed to stimulate classroom discussion as many are evaluative in nature and ask teachers to connect to their own classroom experiences as applicable. Questions can be selected or modified by the instructor and can be incorporated as part of a portfolio or journal log for student-teachers or teachers.

Suggested Field-Based Activities for Pre-Service and In-Service Teachers: Included here are some suggested activities that can be used by the instructor as needed. These activities can be used as credit assignments at the university level, or as a means of practicing the concepts within the chapter. These ideas can be expanded and modified according to the needs of the instructor.

These activities are designed to be practical and do entail field experience. For an instructor in an alternative certification program, many teachers will already be in their own classrooms, and many of these activities are designed to provide the teacher in training with more practice and time for reflection on how the strategies actually work in the classroom.

For the pre-service teacher who may be in a university setting, there are some activities included that do not require direct access to a classroom. A teacher preparation program that combines field-based experiences with courses will find these activities useful.

References: References are provided at the end of each chapter for easy access. Many of these references can be used for further reading and more in-depth understanding of the concepts of the chapters. These references can be utilized by the student-teacher for further research and inquiry.

UNIQUE FEATURES OF THE TEXT

The Classroom Scenario is a special feature in each chapter. Many are authentic voices from the classroom and actual classroom descriptions from practicing teachers. The scenarios connect with the content of the chapter and exemplify unique challenges faced by real teachers and students. Many scenarios portray actual teachers teaching and implementing teaching strategies. The scenarios are designed to stimulate discussion and raise awareness for beginning and pre-service teachers. The scenarios represent a variety of cultural groups and can be easily adapted and used by an instructor or teacher in any geographic location in the United States.

Guiding Discussion Questions follow the classroom scenarios. They are designed to stimulate talk and discussion among participants in a teacher preparation program or staff development workshop. The questions encourage teachers to become analytical and reflective and to understand what goes on in a classroom.

Author's Insight is offered throughout the book. These are suggestions from the author's own teaching experiences and from other teachers in the field. These tips speak directly to the teacher and offer practical suggestions about things to look for, ask, or do. These tips guide the beginning teacher, provide knowledge, and actively involve the teacher in seeking and gaining professional knowledge and experiences.

What Research Tells Us: This section provides a comprehensive, all-inclusive, but short and concise synopsis of research in the field pertinent to the chapter content. The research is presented in understandable language and is divided into clearly identifiable segments. The research is current and provides the teacher with the theoretical rationale for the teaching strategies in the classroom application section that follows. This research is also contextualized within the parameters of No Child Left Behind (2001) and provides the pre-service or in-service teacher with very valuable content and understanding for state certification tests.

Classroom Application Strategies: This is the very practical and hands-on section of the book. Examples from the classroom scenario are explained here as are many of the practical teaching suggestions supported by theory. These are actual research-based teaching strategies that can be applied to a K–12 classroom setting. Each strategy or combination of strategies is clearly explained for use in the classroom. Although many of these strategies are specific to teaching English Language Learners in the subject content areas, all strategies provided are extremely effective for all K–12 learners. These strategies can be used by teachers in the field, student teachers, and pre-service teachers in simulated classroom situations. An instructor can easily model or demonstrate these strategies in the classroom.

TO THE INSTRUCTOR

It was my intention when writing this book to provide a comprehensible, all-inclusive, yet concise book to assist you in your work of preparing outstanding teacher practitioners, and to make a positive impact on student achievement. This book is appropriate for courses in ESL certification, general teaching methodology, and alternative certification preparation programs. The text provides necessary content and methodological theory needed for preparing teachers for state certification tests as well as their first year of teaching and beyond. The text was designed to cover the main areas of concerns for most beginning teachers.

The book utilizes research-based instructional strategies that are supported within the parameters of No Child Left Behind (2001). The book addresses teacher planning, actual teaching, assessment, classroom management, home-school relations, as well as English Language Learners. The text provides the foundational knowledge necessary to prepare or induct any beginning teacher.

TO THE PRE-SERVICE AND IN-SERVICE TEACHER

To you, a beginning teacher, returning teacher, or seasoned veteran teacher, I hope you will gain a greater understanding of the world of the English Language Learner. It is my hope that this text will enable you to acquire additional skills and strategies that will allay your fears and assist you in meeting the needs of your English Language Learners and assist you with all your students. Many teachers assume they have to do something different for English Language Learners. This book explains why this is a myth and that in reality a teacher who uses the strategies provided in this book will better meet the needs of all students, including English Language Learners. English Language Learners learn English best by learning on-grade-level academic content. English Language Learners no longer have to wait until they have attained adequate English; they can learn English and subject content together. This book shows you how. These are strategies that work. These strategies have been utilized by the author during her own sixteen years of teaching, and today by many teachers. These strategies are research-based, time tested, classroom proven, and they work.

ACKNOWLEDGMENTS

I would like to say a special thanks to Darcy Betts Prybella and her assistant, Nancy Holstein, for all their administrative help and support during the long process of making this book a reality. A special thanks to Sheryl Rose for her attention to detail and editorial assistance.

I would like to thank all the reviewers who provided me with very helpful feedback and suggestions. I appreciate all their suggestions; I've incorporated them to the best of my ability, and I sincerely thank them for taking the time to help me improve my manuscript: Rebecca Asel, Dallas ISD; Russell Irwin, San Joaquin County's Project Impact; Nancy Kaczmarek, D'Youville College; Cynthia G. Kruger, University of Massachusetts–Dartmouth; Marie Lassmann, Texas A&M University–Kingsville; Pennie Olson, National–Louis University; and Pamela Parkinson, Western Governors University.

I would like to thank the many teachers who have contributed to this text by sharing their ideas, sharing their classrooms with me, and expressing their frustrations that provided the idea for the creation of this text. A special thanks to my sister, Dr. Kathleen Curtin, who teaches ESL in France and provides me with many ideas and suggestions both personally and professionally.

Many thanks to all my teaching colleagues, past and present, that helped form me into the teacher I am today, and still keep teaching me.

Thanks to Dr. Allen Henderson, provost of Texas Wesleyan University, for his encouragement and support of my educational endeavors. Very special thanks to Dean of School of Education, Dr. Carlos Martinez, for providing me with the time and space to complete this project. Very special thanks to all my students, past, present, and future, at Texas Wesleyan University whom I admire for their dedication and love of teaching. You inspire me and help keep me going!

Finally, a special thanks to my husband, Bruce Wertz, who loves and encourages me always to grow spiritually and emotionally and to take on new challenges professionally. He provided me with much needed support and love during this project.

ABOUT THE AUTHOR

Ellen Curtin is an Associate Professor of Education and has taught at Texas Wesleyan University in Fort Worth since 2000. She teaches pre-service, in-service, and alternative certification teachers at the undergraduate and graduate level. She teaches courses in ESL and K–8 methodology, curriculum and instruction, multicultural education and diversity training, and psychosocial and second language acquisition theory.

Prior to teaching at the university level, Dr. Curtin spent sixteen years as a K–8 Gaelic/Irish language teacher in Ireland, and an elementary teacher in Kansas City and Hurst-Euless-Bedford in Texas. As an administrative intern at the Hurst-Euless-Bedford ISD she researched, designed, and obtained federal funding for an after school program as well as researching and developing a Foreign Language Education Program for the school district. Dr. Curtin is a native of Ireland who immigrated to the United States in 1989 and became a naturalized U.S. citizen in 1997. She is a native speaker of Irish/Gaelic and designed, developed, and taught the first university credit course in Irish/Gaelic in the state of Texas.

Dr. Curtin holds a Ph.D. in curriculum and instruction with a minor in educational administration from the University of North Texas, a master's degree from Texas Wesleyan University, and a bachelor's degree from the National University of Ireland. Her research interests include immigrant and second language education, culturally responsive teaching, Celtic languages, foreign language education, and early childhood education. She has published several articles and presents her research nationally and internationally. This is her first book for Merrill.

She lives in the Dallas/Fort Worth area with her husband, Bruce Wertz, and has three stepsons and one grandson. She likes to paint, loves to travel, and enjoys spending time with her family in Ireland and her sister in France.

BRIEF CONTENTS

CONTENTS

Chapter 10   Facilitating School, Family, and Community Involvement for the English Language Learner   229

NOTE: Every effort has been made to provide accurate and current Internet information in this book. However, the Internet and information posted on it are constantly changing, so it is inevitable that some of the Internet addresses listed in this textbook will change.

CHAPTER 1 Journey of English Language Learners, Past and Present

"Give me your tired, your poor,
Your huddled masses yearning to breathe free,
The wretched refuse of your teeming shore.
Send these, the homeless, tempest-tost to me,
I lift my lamp beside the golden door!"

*Source: Emma Lazarus, The Poems of
Emma Lazarus, vol. 1 (1889), 2*

INTRODUCTION

Immigrants both past and present have helped build the United States into the country it is today. They brought with them a diversity of languages, customs, cultures, and traditions, as well as the common goal of becoming an American. Immigrants still come to America from all over the world in the hope of finding a better future. It is that same diversity that immigrants bring to this country

1

that has continually sparked political and ideological debates on how to best integrate all Americans in a common ideology while still honoring the many unique cultures and heritages.

This chapter provides today's pre-service and in-service teachers with the background and knowledge needed to better understand the debates and changes that have surrounded the education of immigrant children over the past 60 years. Upon completing the chapter, readers will have a better understanding of how political ideology like the No Child Left Behind Act (2001) affects and propels educational policy in schools today, and the reason why it is now considered best for English Language Learners (ELLs) to learn English through academic content taught in the regular classroom. This current policy creates challenges for new and experienced teachers alike who find themselves teaching immigrants. Teaching English Language Learners no longer falls under the domain of the English as a Second Language (ESL) teacher because many states require all teachers to have knowledge of ESL teaching techniques and practices. English Language Learners are no longer confined to pullout programs but are expected to integrate as quickly as possible into the regular educational setting along with native speakers of English.

Pre-service and in-service teachers should gain the insight needed to accurately identify and place English Language Learners into varying levels of English language proficiency. Readers should also expect to gain a greater understanding of the terminology used in the various ESL programs. Ultimately, this chapter and the ones that follow it should help readers better understand the vital role played by regular/mainstream teachers in the education of all English Language Learners.

FOCUS QUESTIONS

- ◇ Who is an English Language Learner?
- ◇ How is an English Language Learner tested and placed in public school?
- ◇ How does No Child Left Behind affect the teaching of English Language Learners?
- ◇ What challenges face teachers of English Language Learners?

CLASSROOM SCENARIO

A High School Teacher

It's the beginning of the school year; it's six weeks into her first year of teaching; it's the first semester, and Ms. Lockhart is feeling exhausted. If that's not enough, she is also completing her alternative certification program. Ms. Lockhart is teaching high school math in an urban school with a large percentage of English Language Learners. She spends all day teaching, and then all evening grading papers, working on lesson plans, or going to the regional service center to attend workshops and seminars that are part of her certification requirements. She finds all the teaching staff friendly; she loves her students and finds them quiet but responsive. She has learned how to do lesson plans, and she has learned how to properly structure her classroom, thanks to the help from her assistant principal, team coordinator, and teacher mentor.

After receiving the results of the district benchmark math tests she administered to her classes the previous week, Ms. Lockhart is shocked. Carefully reading the testing results and analysis, she discovers that more than 50% of her students failed to pass the district's benchmark test at the end of the first six weeks. She is devasted because the report cards she just sent out to parents reflected that overall her students did really well in math, and that no one had failed this semester.

Knowing she has students who are classified as English Language Learners, she checks the results again and realizes some of them had failed this benchmark test, but Ms. Lockhart does not understand exactly why they failed. She has been very pleased with their social skills because they talk up a storm, they are always chatting, and there is no apparent shortage of English. They are enjoying being in school and yes, while some seem behind in their reading and writing skills, they are making great progress in math.

Ms. Lockhart is upset and asks herself, "What happened? I've covered all these skills with my students, so what am I doing wrong?" Her team coordinator notices she's upset and asks, "What's the matter, Ms. Lockhart?"

"I have been working very hard to teach my students, but they scored badly on the first benchmark. My English Language Learners are *so quiet*, and appear to be doing so well in class, I just don't understand why they didn't pass that benchmark test."

"Welcome to teaching," cajoles her upbeat team coordinator. "What you have before you is students' current academic levels, and the good news is you will be able to chart their growth and progress from now to the end of the year. You now know who is struggling and what skills you need to work on in order to prepare them for the state standardized test. You still have several months in which to get them on grade level. You will just have to adjust how you teach and make the necessary modifications, but eventually you will get the hang of it."

Ms. Lockhart smiles. For the first time in her newly chosen profession she feels the heavy burden of responsibility. She must now begin the task of fixing the problem.

"I have to get all these students up to district and state standards by April," she says to herself, "but I have students in my classroom who have never even been to school in their home country. I've tried calling their parents to get them in for a parent-teacher conference but they *do not speak English* and I am unable to properly communicate with them. I wish I could speak their languages so I could teach them better.

"I am still figuring out how to teach and use the manuals, I'm barely one week ahead of my students, I have no personal life, I don't know if I'm meeting the expectations of my principal, and I certainly don't know if I'm meeting the needs of my English Language Learners. I keep hearing terms like LEP, ESL, ELL, and IEP, and I know full well that I must meet the needs of my English Language Learners, but I have no training or background in ESL, and I do not speak their native languages. What am I supposed to do? I'm beginning to realize there is much more to teaching than I thought. I don't seem to know where to start. I have over 120 students to teach. How can I be expected to do this?"

Guiding Discussion Questions

◇ What are the aspects of teaching English Language Learners that are challenging for Ms. Lockhart?
◇ How can Ms. Lockhart ask for support?
◇ What challenges do you anticipate or are you currently experiencing in your school?

Author's Insight

For teachers who have never had the benefit of traveling abroad, or the benefit of speaking other languages, the task of teaching immigrant and non-English-speaking students can be fraught with anxiety and fear. I have personally witnessed teachers' frustrations as they tearfully anticipated the arrival of immigrant and non-English-speaking students to their classroom. I have witnessed non-English-speaking students delegated to the backs of classrooms, cutting and pasting simple English words and letters and not included in the mainstream activities, as their teachers operated under the misguided assumption that these students could not begin learning until they had acquired the English language skills to participate in regular classroom learning. Researchers now know that *learning English through subject content* is best for English Language Learners.

Teachers have to trust that the process of English language learning is happening for students and that students are learning even though they may not always understand everything. Teachers can begin instantly communicating with a non-English-speaking student so that the student will "read" the teacher's body language and facial expressions and understand that they are welcome and part of a community of learners. Regardless of their age, students never have trouble befriending non-English-speaking students and love teaching them English.

Today's era of testing and accountability has raised the stakes for all teachers and the pressure to ensure that all students are prepared to take these tests. English Language Learners are required to take the same tests as native students after three years of residency in the United States. Teachers' fears are not unfounded, and more than ever, teachers need the staff development and administrative support necessary to teach all students effectively.

I hope this book will provide you, the pre-service or in-service teacher, the necessary tools and teaching strategies to meet the learning needs of all your students.

WHAT RESEARCH TELLS US

Immigration in the Past—Assimilationist

Annie Moore was the first documented immigrant to pass through the New York's newly opened Ellis Island on January 1, 1892. Annie was 15 years old when she stepped off the ship all alone. She was forced to leave Ireland during the period following 1845 when more than one million Irish people died of starvation due to the potato famine. Before Annie left Ireland, her family mourned her departure with an "Irish wake," as was the common tradition of that time, because they knew that they would never see her again. Immigration in the late 1800s was a process of upheaval, heartbreak, and survival. Many immigrants like Annie came from countries in Europe and many were poor and possessed few material possessions. Many rarely had the opportunity to return home to the "old sod." Many tearful songs and poems exist from that period depicting immigrants' eternal homesickness and longing to go home (Curtin, 2002).

Immigrants like Annie, having survived many weeks of travel by ship, often had to endure additional quarantine on Ellis Island and rigorous physical examinations. Some were denied entry to the "New World" and many died en route to the United States. Travel during that period was arduous and difficult at best. Many immigrants unwillingly had their names changed by immigration officers to facilitate bureaucratic record keeping. There were no interpreters available and certainly no provisions were made to ease the arrival of new immigrants to their new country (Curtin, 2002).

Immigrants in 1892 were expected to speak English, *assimilate,* and become American citizens as quickly as possible. History records that immigrants who attended school were not provided with English language assistance or special programs to ease the transition into the classroom, all of which must have seemed so alien and foreign to a non-English-speaking student. Immigrants and non-English-speaking children were expected to "sink or swim," which was the prevailing political and educational ideology at that time.

Although the first through Ellis Island, Annie was not the first immigrant to arrive on America's shores. Immigration began in the United States with the introduction of the European culture in the 1840s. Since the time of Christopher Columbus in the late 1400s, America had been a haven for immigrants fleeing the religious, cultural, and economic hardships of their native lands while at the same time longing for a taste of the American Dream. The United States is a nation of immigrants. "E Pluribus Unum," on the quarter coin, is Latin for "out of many, one." This term signifies the United States to be a country formed out of many nationalities and yet one nation. The great debate today still centers on how to unify so many culturally, ethnically, and linguistically diverse peoples into one nation (Cushner, McClelland, & Safford, 2002). In the past immigrants like Annie Moore were forced to assimilate, lose their native language, and adopt the customs of their new country.

The term *melting pot* was derived from a play written by Israel Zangwill (1909) and is still used today to express political ideology and the treatment of immigrants. This ideological term aptly describes the belief that immigrants and their children need to lose their ethnic identities and assimilate or "melt" into the one homogenous group known as Americans.

Immigration Trends Today—Cultural Pluralism

Today's immigrants are vastly and ethnically different from those who came to the United States at the start of the twentieth century. Immigrants today are more likely to be non-European in origin. The 1965 amendment to the Immigration and Nationality Act (Hart-Celler Act, PL 89-236) has resulted in more than 85% of all immigrants today coming from Asia and Latin America (Center for Immigration Studies, 2007).

In 2002, the U.S. Census count of foreign-born population from the 2000 census revealed that more than 31.1 million immigrants resided in the United States, which was triple the 9.6 million in 1970 and more than double the 14.1 million in 1980. The data reveal that 7 million births to immigrant women in the 1990s accounted for over 60% of the U.S. population during the last decade. More than 60% of this group was of Mexican or Mexican American origin. The others came from Central and South America, Puerto Rico, Cuba, and other Spanish-speaking countries. The Asian–Pacific Islander population comprised over 10 million and constituted more than 4% of the population (Center for Immigration Studies, 2007).

Nationwide since 2001, 18% of the population speak a language other than English at home. Forty percent of the population of California speak a language other than English at home, as do 36% in New Mexico and 32% in Texas. Other states like Illinois, Florida, and New Jersey have experienced sharp increases in immigrant populations. These numbers only take into account those documented workers entering the country legally. These figures increase dramatically when we consider the estimated 15 million illegal and undocumented immigrants residing in the United States.

Cultural pluralism, an ideology that emerged in the United States in the early 1970s, is the most prevalent one in today's schools. The analogy of a salad bowl is used to describe the benefits that immigrants bring to our society. The cultural pluralism ideology views immigrants with their diversities of languages and cultures as being an asset to society and differences are not discouraged (Banks, 2006).

It is the tensions between these two opposing ideologies, cultural pluralism and assimilationist, that best describes the political and social tension surrounding immigration today. Most people's political views on the subject of immigrants fall into either one of these categories.

Reality of Classrooms Today

Demographic and Population Shifts

It is the teachers of America who meet the daily challenge of teaching both immigrant and nonimmigrant students. The classroom scenario presents very realistic pictures of the challenges facing teachers today in our urban classrooms created by the high influx of English Language Learners. Statistics reveal that more than 20% of all new teachers find employment in schools with high numbers of English Language Learners (Wirt et al., 2003). Additionally, many beginning teachers have little pedagogy or strategies for working with English Language Learners (Curtin, 2002).

In the past immigrant and non-English-speaking students simply dropped out of school or just never came to school. This is not the case today. With compulsory education and changes in federal law, the education of immigrant children is a contentious issue among legislators, educators, and the public. Public schools have become the "battleground" for this debate and teachers are part of this struggle.

During the 1991–1992 through 2001–2002 school years, the numbers of children with limited-English-speaking skills rose to 95% in the K–12 grades in public schools, while the total enrollment increased by only 12% (National Clearinghouse for English Language Acquisition, 2007). In 2001–2002 almost 4.7 million children were English Language Learners, which represented more than 10% of the school-age population. Although the numbers of immigrants are increasing, the *academic achievement* levels are decreasing on standardized tests of reading and math, particularly at the high school level (Faltis & Coulter, 2008).

Another reality of classrooms today is that *dropout rates* are higher among the immigrant groups than any other school-age group. The dropout rate for immigrant Latinos is the highest rate at 44%. In 1998, 30% of all Latinos aged 16 to 24 dropped out of school (Latinos in Education, 1999). Today those figures continue to rise (Orfield, 2004).

Educational Accountability

In the past, immigrant and non-English-speaking children were not expected to receive an education through high school. In the past, immigrants were expected to drop out of school, and many did. However, this is not the case today. Today federal law states that all immigrants are entitled to an equal educational opportunity regardless of their legal status (Plyer v. Doe, 1982, p. 219), which must be accommodated linguistically by teachers. Immigrant youth can no longer drop out of school due to compulsory education laws.

School failure is not acceptable to the federal and state governments. All states must now conform to the mandates of the No Child Left Behind Act

(2001) and must have assessments in place to show yearly academic growth for all students including English Language Learners. How a teacher accommodates the needs of immigrant students is a critical issue today and for the future of our educational system. As the increasing population of school-aged children is becoming more culturally and linguistically diverse, the necessity of teaching these students to compete academically is more important than ever. Today, teachers and school personnel are accountable for the test scores of immigrant students (NCLB, 2001).

No Child Left Behind–Implications for Teachers

Teaching English Language Learners is no longer the responsibility of the English as a Second Language teacher. In the past ESL programs were concerned with teaching basic conversational English. It was the norm that immigrant students stayed in a pullout program learning basic conversation until such time as they could be mainstreamed into a regular classroom. This resulted in what the literature terms "ESL Lifers" or those students who missed out on grade-level skills while acquiring conversational English in a segregated setting. For this reason this process is no longer used today. All children must be accounted for, especially with regard to their academic progress. Education is now in an era of accountability that legislatively mandates that "no child" be "left behind" (NCLB, 2001).

No Child Left Behind requires that only proven, *research-based instructional practices* be used in the classroom. "Research-based" means the effectiveness of a model has been tested by the National Center for Research in Education, Diversity and Excellence before being used.

According to O'Malley and Valdez-Pierce (1996), "standards" are defined as benchmarks for accountability. Standards and expectations for progress are articulated in No Child Left Behind. These standards apply to all students from pre-K to twelfth grade, but also of these student in to and teachers how they use teaching methods to increase student achievement. The thrust of this book will address teaching strategies and research that have been proven in the classroom to increase student achievement.

By law, English Language Learners must be included as early and as quickly as possible in the *mainstream* classroom. All English Language Learners must, in their third continuous year in the United States, take the same on-grade-level standardized tests and must make "adequate yearly progress" (No Child Left Behind, 2001). This ensures that no child will be left behind and is the foundational cornerstone of the federal act passed by Congress in 2001. Many mainstream teachers are now required to seek English as a Second Language (ESL) certification or professional development to better meet, teach, and reach the academic and learning needs of English Language Learners.

Challenges Facing Teachers of English Language Learners

The numbers of English Language Learners are increasing every year. Based on current demographic indicators, the highest concentration of English Language

Learners in the near future will be located in New Mexico, California, and Texas. It is estimated that by the middle of this century, more than 50% of the U.S. population will be non-white and will be increasingly diverse. According to the National Clearinghouse for English Language Acquisition (2007), English Language Learners represent the fastest growing segment of the school-age population. English Language Learners can no longer be ignored; they are becoming an increasing reality for many teachers who never dealt with them in the past.

Researchers demonstrate that there are many challenges facing mainstream teachers. Some English Language Learners come to school with academic gaps in their own native languages. Some come to school unable to read or write in their native language; and many have had very little schooling or even access to education in their home countries (Ruiz-de-Velasco, Fix, & Clewell, 2000). Some English Language Learners come as refugees and with their own set of unique separation and emotional needs. Many English Language Learners may be involuntary immigrants and had no choice in the matter (Ogbu & Simons, 1998). Other children and youth may be reluctant to talk about their immigration experiences or previous home country if they are innocent victims of illegal immigration by their parents. Many of these children may tell stories of "coyotes" and their experiences of being smuggled across the border into this country (Curtin, 2002).

Some children and youth may be sojourners, here only as legal guests in the country for a few years because of a parent's job or transfer. Some English Language Learners may be children of migrant workers who are here on a temporary status (Urban Institute, 2006).

These are only some of the variables that are beyond the control of the classroom teacher and make teaching these children more complex than what meets the eye. In the classroom scenario Ms. Lockhart realized that while teaching may be fun and rewarding, there is now accountability involved, and that clear academic progress must be measured and tracked for each student. This places increasing pressure on teachers who feel unprepared to deal with or cope with English Language Learners.

What makes the teaching of English Language Learners more complex is the *attitude of the teacher,* which must be positive and favorable toward immigrants and non-English-speaking students. There is a xenophobic climate that is prevailing in our society today as anti-immigrant, and "English only" debates occur throughout the country. Although teachers possess their own set of ideas and philosophies concerning immigration, they must be careful to set high expectations for all students. Otherwise, teachers risk exposing students to the "self-fulfilling prophecy," which occurs when you set low expectations for students, or possess the belief that they will never learn English or do well academically. When that happens a teacher sets the stage for failure. Teachers are ethically and legally obligated to educate all children and must do everything in their power to teach all students no matter how complex or difficult the task.

CLASSROOM APPLICATION STRATEGIES

What follows is some fundamental knowledge that will be beneficial for all teachers to understand with regard to the identification of and placement of English Language Learners.

Steps for Identification of English Language Learners

Many terms have been used in the past and are currently being used to identify non-English-speaking students. The term used for non-English-speaking students has varied from Limited English Proficient (LEP) to English as a Second Language (ESL) to English Language Learner (ELL). The term LEP is rarely used because of its negative connation. The term English as a Second Language (ESL) is not accurate because many immigrant children may already speak two or more other languages; English may be their third or fourth language. Today, the term English Language Learner (ELL) is more commonly used and more widely accepted. This term is considered more comprehensive and accurate in its description because it describes a learner learning.

A beginning teacher needs to be aware of the school district's policies and procedures in relation to English Language Learners as well as the appropriate terminology used to identify English Language Learners and their placement in classrooms. See Figure 1.1 for a summary of the following steps.

STEP 1: All students entering a school district are required to fill out certain paperwork and must be registered. Upon registration, parent's or guardians are asked to fill out a Home Language Survey in which they must state the dominant language that is spoken at home. If that language is other than English, then school personnel must inform the ESL teacher in the school, if available, an administrator, or appropriate district personnel, and specific procedures must be followed. *Each district has clear procedures already in place.*

AUTHOR'S INSIGHT: Check with your school district. Ask for the procedures and policies that pertain to your district and keep them for your own records. Find a copy of a Home Language Survey and keep it with your records.

STEP 2: Once it is determined that English is not the language spoken in the home, the ESL teacher or designated school district official in charge will administer some tests to determine the English Language level of the student. There is a different test for each grade level, including an *oral language test*, as well as basic *reading and writing tests*. Check with your school district and familiarize yourself with the testing processes used.

Testing by district personnel (ESL coordinator) will vary from district to district and state to state but will usually be similar to one of the following. With pre-K there is usually some kind of oral language proficiency test. With second graders it might be the reading section of the Iowa Test of Basic Skills

FIGURE 1.1　　Possible Identification and Placement Procedures Checklist for School District

YEAR 1

- Home Language Survey
- Newcomers Center for intensive English language instruction
- Placement with ESL teacher for intensive English instruction
- Placement in regular classroom with ESL teacher and specific English language instruction in regular content
- Bilingual classroom with 50% instruction in native language
- LPAC meeting with placement decision for coming year

Language Level of Student

Beginning–Intermediate

- BICS (Basic Interpersonal Communicative Skills)—Developing social language

YEAR 2

- In regular school in mainstream classroom with English language support
- In bilingual classroom with 40% instruction in native language
- LPAC meeting with placement decision for coming year

Language Level of Student

Intermediate to Advanced Level

- BICS/CALP (Cognitive Academic Language Proficiency)
- LPAC meeting with placement decision for coming year

YEAR 3

- In regular classroom all day
- Preparing for state content exams
- May be tested to exit ESL program—decision of LPAC committee

Language Level of Student

- Transitional and ready to exit ESL or sheltered English classroom
- In a mainstream/regular classroom for all or most of day

YEARS 4 & 5

- Monitored by LPAC committee but spending all day in regular class with ESL sheltered English language support

Language Level of Student

Transitional

- Still need a lot of CALP (Cognitive Academic Language Proficiency) support by regular/ mainstream teacher

(ITBS). With third to sixth grade it might be that section of the ITBS, which may also be used with older students.

STEP 3: Test results will determine the student's English language level. After testing, the ESL teacher or administrator arranges a Language Proficiency Assessment Committee (LPAC) meeting to determine the best placement for the student. The committee generally includes an administrator (principal, assistant principal, counselor), homeroom teacher, parent of record (there might be an interpreter also who speaks the student's native language) or a representative for the parent, and the ESL teacher or designated official for the school district in charge of ESL education.

STEP 4: There are criteria that determine the student's placement from complete ESL services, to partial services for some of the day, or regular classroom with ESL monitoring or support. These criteria determine if the student is at a beginning, intermediate, or advanced level of English language proficiency. These language proficiency levels will be explained in more detail in Chapter 4.

If the student tests at any of these levels, then an *ESL schedule* is established, which includes the amount of time the student will be in the ESL program as well as exemptions from state standardized tests. All necessary forms are completed and signed at that time by appropriate personnel, including the parent or parent representative. Parents are notified in writing of the LPAC decision and written parental consent must be obtained before the student can receive ESL language instruction.

STEP 5: The student is tested again later in the year to determine progress and placement for the coming year. In some districts, a student must score 40% or more on the ITBS and be functioning on grade level to exit the program. In many states, results of state standardized tests may determine this final exit score. The ESL teacher or appointed administrator is responsible for monitoring student progress for two years after the student exits from the ESL program.

English Language Learners exiting the program still require continuous academic support and monitoring. Students will be mainstreamed into a regular classroom for most or all of the day. In this situation, the regular classroom teacher becomes responsible for the academic progress of the student. However, the ESL teacher is available for support and monitoring as needed.

 AUTHOR'S INSIGHT: Check the *cumulative folder* (it won't exist if the student is new to the country) to learn about the student's previous time in school, duration, and as much as possible about his or her early literacy development. Use Figure 1.2 as a guideline for questions to ask a parent, or through an interpreter as necessary, in order to glean as much information as possible about the student. The more information gathered ahead of time, the more complete the knowledge gained by the teacher about the academic and linguistic needs of the student. Fill in any additional questions or information you feel could be helpful.

Placement Possibilities for English Language Learners

Placement possibilities will vary widely throughout the country and different terms may be used to describe the placement setting. Federal law mandates

FIGURE 1.2   Gaining Background Knowledge and Information

- Tell me about school in your home country.
- Did you go to school every day?
- How many hours each day did you attend?
- What subjects did you study in school?
- Did you learn to read and write?
- What was the language used by the teacher in school?
- Did you have to take any tests or exams?
- Other possible questions:

Ask for following:

- Any documentation or records that verify regular attendance in a school in home country.
- Check out the home country's national educational system for equivalency or similarities with school in United States.
- Other:

that all English Language Learners must be provided with a program that assists them in (1) assessing the core curriculum, and (2) English language development support. The federal government does not mandate how these programs are to be organized as long as there is a definite support system for English Language Learners in place. Individual states govern more specifically in this regard. As a teacher you will be responsible for knowing what your respective district does and how they do it. The following are general descriptors of available programs that can be found in a school district.

 AUTHOR'S INSIGHT: Do not be afraid to ask your colleagues, principal, counselor, or school personnel for help. You can use ESL teachers or someone in your building as a resource. You may be required by your district to acquire additional training in ESL techniques or you may be required to become ESL certified. Many districts now require that a minimum of at least one teacher per grade level be ESL certified. This ESL-certified teacher provides the support for the rest of the team and may have more ESL students in his or her classroom than the other teachers on the team. You may find yourself in a district that is only beginning to have an influx of English Language Learners, which means your district may not yet have a clearly developed system.

Total ESL/Language Centers/ Newcomers Center/Welcome Center

Description. This is usually an intensive program of instruction designed to teach new immigrants to speak English as soon as possible. The newcomers may spend anywhere from 6 to 9 months in such a center, being acclimated linguistically and culturally to life in the United States. The program is meant to provide a lot of support for the family, who may still be dealing with the shock and the emotional trauma of the immigration experience.

If the Newcomers Center is located within a school, it is likely that the regular homeroom teacher will have the student for some or part of the day, including recess, lunch, and so on. The newcomer maintains a connection with a teacher and a group of students in the mainstream classroom. In many large urban school districts, the Newcomers Center may be located strategically in the center of the district to facilitate busing needs. In a smaller district, such a center may not exist; it depends entirely on whether funding and/or grants are available at the time. Ultimately, it is the school that has the responsibility for creating a warm and welcoming school environment for the newly arrived student and family, regardless of the facilities available.

Educational Goal for English Language Learners. Time spent in this Newcomers Center is meant to be brief as possible because the goal is to get the newcomer to the regular campus as quickly as possible. During this period a developmental sequence of four language skills is followed. These are listening, speaking, reading, and writing. The educational goal during this time is to keep students on grade level in skills and competencies, while at the same time transitioning them into the mainstream as quickly as possible. This is all done simultaneously with the development of their basic communicative English language skills.

Partial ESL

Description. Here the student is assigned to a regular homeroom teacher but may spend part of the day with an ESL teacher in an ESL classroom during language arts. This period of time is used to teach English language skills. This however, is becoming less the model for use in many districts as more regular mainstream classroom homeroom teachers are required to attain ESL certification.

Educational Goal for English Language Learners. To teach basic language skills using regular content classes.

Maintenance Bilingual Education Program

Description. Students are taught in their native language. It is necessary to have a fully certified teacher who is also competent in the targeted native language of students. This model is based on research that supports the development of reading and writing skills in the native language and then transferring those skills to English. Beginning with kindergarten the teacher starts by using more of the student's native language and gradually reduces teaching in the native language until 50% of the instruction is in English and the other 50% is in the native language.

Educational Goal for English Language Learners. The goal is to maintain competency in two languages. Very few districts in the United States actually support this model through high school. Most districts only maintain this model until third to fifth grade. This model, however, is common in Europe and French-speaking Canada. The educational goal is do develop bilinguals.

Transitional Bilingual Program

Description. Instruction in the native language is provided from 1 to 3 years with a gradual increase of instruction in English. The goal is to transition completely to English. No more instruction in native language occurs after third to fifth grade. This model is most common in Texas.

Educational Goal for English Language Learners. The goal is to teach English as soon as literacy develops in the student's native language. Once the student exits the program, no more native language support is provided.

Immersion

Description. Originally developed in Canada and Europe, the goal is to immerse students in a new language. Students speak the native language at home and are immersed in another targeted second language in school. This is the old "sink or swim" model and is not considered appropriate for English Language Learners unless a lot of additional ESL and teaching scaffolding supports are provided by their teacher.

Educational Goal for English Language Learners. The students acquire competence in a second language. Little or no academic support is provided for the first language.

Two-Way Immersion

Description. This is where native and non-native speakers are combined in a single classroom. Half of the students speak the native language and the other half speak the targeted second language. Half of the day is devoted to teaching in one language and the other half of the day is devoted to the other language. Students benefit from socializing with each other and learning from each other.

Educational Goal for English Language Learners. Develop a child with bilingual skills.

ESL Pullout

Description. Here the student is placed in the mainstream classroom for most of the day, but for a period of time each day will be pulled out for intensive English language support.

Educational Goal for English Language Learners. Provide concentrated and intensive English language support and development.

English Language Development (ELD)

Description. The English Language Learner is taught all subject matter in English by a teacher who has more knowledge, training, and techniques in English as a second language.

Educational Goal for English Language Learners. The teacher uses specific teaching strategies to ensure that the student comprehends the content and is learning English language skills at the same time.

Sheltered English or SDAIE

Description. (Specially Designed Academic Instruction in English). This is the model supported by researchers as being most effective for English Language Learners. This model is also referred to as "sheltered instruction" and "content-based ESL." The terms vary depending on the geographical location within the United States (Ovando, Collier, & Combs, 2003). The terms *ESL content* and *content ESL* tend to be used in the eastern half of the United States, while the term *sheltered instruction* is used more often on the West Coast. Currently, the term *Specially Designed Academic Instruction in English* or SDAIE is more prevalent nationally (Ovando et al., 2003).

Educational Goal for English Language Learners. Here the emphasis is on teaching subject matter entirely in English, teaching on-grade-level material, with lots of English language support. This is most effective with students who have an intermediate level of English language development.

Structured English Immersion

Description. This is when English language learners are taught regular content with sheltering techniques. Language is taught within the regular classroom but by a teacher who is trained in using these types of sheltering techniques.

Educational Goal for English Language Learners. Keep students on grade level with academic content while they learn English concurrently.

Mainstreaming English Language Learners into the Regular Classroom

Description. Here students are taught by a certified teacher or a teacher who is trained in using scaffolding techniques for English Language Learners. This teacher should have ESL certification or be fully trained in second language techniques.

Educational Goal for English Language Learners. Teach students English using grade-level content.

TESOL Compliance

Programs for English Language Learners may vary widely and may use different terminology when referring to programs and students. The No Child Left Behind Act of 2001 demands that academic content must now be used to teach the English language.

The programs offered by school districts across the country vary widely but most of the key elements described in this textbook are common throughout programs created for English Language Learners. These programs generally support the teaching of English language skills by means of academic content. These programs must also comply with the suggested standards issued by TESOL (2006) (Teachers of English to Speakers of Other Languages). TESOL advocates that specific characteristics be visible in all programs for English Language Learners. For a full list of standards visit the Web site listed in the references at the end of this chapter.

TESOL standards encourage the provision of programs for English Language Learners that keep students challenged and abreast of on-grade-level academic content. Programs should promote and encourage English Language Learners to develop their native languages. Finally, TESOL encourages ongoing professional development opportunities for all teachers so they can learn to better meet the linguistic and academic needs of all English Language Learners (TESOL, 2006).

Commonly Used Terminology

The following are some common terms still being used in literature for English Language Learners.

 AUTHOR'S INSIGHT: Make a list of the terms for future reference by combining these with the ones currently being used by your district but not described here.

- ◇ **Refugee:** Granted political asylum in United States to escape political situation in home country.
- ◇ **Sojourner:** Visitor to United States for a short period and plans to return to home country of origin.
- ◇ **Immigrant:** Legally permitted to live and work in United States. May have a visa, green card (resident alien), work permit.
- ◇ **Migrant Status:** Temporary legal status to work in country.
- ◇ **Native:** Born in United States but home language is not English.
- ◇ **ELL:** English Language Learner.
- ◇ **ESL:** English as a Second Language.
- ◇ **NEP:** Non English Proficient.
- ◇ **NES:** Non English Speaking.
- ◇ **LEP:** Limited English Proficient.
- ◇ **LES:** Limited English Speaking.

◇ **FEP:** Fluent English Proficient.
◇ **FES:** Fluent English Speaking.
◇ **OLPT:** Oral Language Proficiency Test.
◇ **Mainstream:** Regular classroom for native speakers.

Identifying English Language Levels of Students

Figure 1.3 provides descriptors that identify the language level of students. These descriptors provide an efficient means of documenting language behaviors. Additionally, Figure 1.3 provides a checklist for recording and documenting teacher observations in the classroom. This documentation provides anecdotal evidence of new language behaviors or patterns observed by the teacher in the classroom. This or a similar checklist can be a valuable source of documentation as well as providing an initial assessment of students' English language level.

No Child Left Behind and the Classroom Teacher

The following are the main tenets of what the beginning teacher needs to understand about the No Child Left Behind Act (2001) and how it impacts the teaching of all students, but more specifically English Language Learners.

Tenet 1

School administrators and teachers alike are now accountable for student achievement at all levels. Students must make measured progress in learning, which has to be demonstrated on state tests that are objective and standardized. All teachers must be "highly qualified," meaning they must be certified by the state and be able to demonstrate subject area competency. The act now requires that after two years, overall improvement must be shown or the administration must act by (1) replacing staff that are contributing to student failure, (2) changing the curriculum, or (3) reorganizing the school. A school that fails to improve student achievement over a given period of time can be closed down and then reopened as a charter school, or it can be taken over by the state or a private company that has a proven track record of effective instructional teaching. Annual assessments are made in grades 3–8 at all schools.

Impact for Teacher of English Language Learners. English Language Learners in their third continuous year in the United States must take the test and must make "adequate yearly progress" in measurable objectives. This is significant in that it ensures all students are properly accounted for. As a result English Language Learners are now showing yearly academic gains.

ELL students are expected to become proficient in English-speaking abilities as well as attain high academic standards in reading and language arts and in math. When English Language Learners have been enrolled in a U.S. school for three consecutive years they must be assessed in English, reading and language

FIGURE 1.3   Descriptors for Documenting Language Levels of Student

GRADES K-3		
Beginning **Behaviors of Student**	**Observed** ☑	**Supporting Teacher Documentation**
Unable to speak or communicate in English; should nod or respond		
Responds with gestures or 1–2 word answers		
Reads environmental print (labels); recognizes some letters or words		
Reads Language Experience Approach (actions and mime provided) charts and stories		
Reads along with predictable books		
Records thoughts through scribbles, pictures, and invented spelling		
Intermediate **Behaviors of Student**	**Observed** ☑	**Supporting Teacher Documentation**
Requires some pictures or props for comprehension		
Initiates and sustains a social conversation		
Responds with short phrases and sentences		
Reads simple stories		
Records thoughts through writing short phrases and sentences		
Advanced **Behaviors of Student**	**Observed** ☑	**Supporting Teacher Documentation**
Initiates and sustains conversations without a classroom topic		
Responds with elaborate language		
Reads quality children's literature		
Uses story and poetry patterns in writing		
Edits own writing		

(Continued)

FIGURE 1.3 Continued

Transitional **Behaviors of Student**	**Observed** ☑	**Supporting Teacher Observation**
Presents ideas to others in a formal manner		
Expresses thoughts in literary language		
Applies reading comprehension strategies to state-adopted basal textbooks		
Reflects artistic expression in writing		
Edits own writing		

GRADES 4–12

Beginning **Behaviors of Student**	**Observed** ☑	**Supporting Teacher Observation**
Unable to speak or communicate in English; should nod or respond		
Responds with gestures or 1–2 word answers		
Reads environmental print; recognizes some letters or words		
Reads Language Experience Approach (actions and mime provided) charts and stories		
Reads along with predictable books		
Records thoughts through scribbles, pictures, and invented spelling		

Intermediate **Behaviors of Student**	**Observed** ☑	**Supporting Teacher Observation**
Requires some pictures or props for comprehension		
Responds with short phrases and sentences		
Initiates and sustains a social conversation		
Reads a variety of literature		
Expresses thoughts through invented and/or standard spelling		
Writes with a variety of literary styles		
Edits own writing		

Advanced **Behaviors of Student**	Observed ☑	**Supporting Teacher Observation**
Initiates and sustains conversations about a content-area topic		
Reads quality adolescent literature		
Writes in a broader scope of literary styles		
Writes for a variety of purposes and audiences		
Edits own writing		
Transitional **Behaviors of Student**	Observed ☑	**Supporting Teacher Observation**
Presents ideas to others in a formal manner		
Expresses ideas in literary language		
Reads more advanced quality literature		
Applies reading comprehension strategies to state-adopted basal textbooks		
Reflects artistic expression in writing		
Edits own writing		

arts, and math. During assessment, English Language Learners must be provided, as may be appropriate and feasible, a copy of the testing material in their own native language. States must annually assess the English proficiency levels of all English Language Learners in oral language, reading, and writing skills in English (NCLB, 2001).

Tenet 2

All teaching and instruction used in schools must be research-based. Title I money is used to fund ESL programs in public schools. Title I money supports the education of economically disadvantaged students by providing free and reduced-cost lunches and other services. Strategies and pedagogy used by teachers must be proven to be effective and research-based. All plans to improve schools, professional development activities for teachers, and technical assistance to low-performing schools must be based on effective research-based strategies and techniques that are proven and that work.

All paraprofessionals must have a minimum of two years of postsecondary education. Paraprofessionals (aides and instructional support personnel) fall under the direct supervision of a certified teacher and may not provide direct instructional support services without this direct supervision. Furthermore, states must close the learning and achievement gap to ensure that all students are making academic progress. To accomplish this task there will be biennial National Assessment of Educational Progress assessments in both reading and math for fourth through eighth graders. The purpose will be to ensure that state standards are rigorous and competitive with those of other states. In time, more interstate standardization will occur to ensure continuity in education for all states (NCLB, 2001).

Tenet 3

Parents Have More Options.   If their children are attending low-performing schools, parents can now request a transfer to a higher-performing school and take advantage of afterschool tutoring programs and summer school, for which transportation must also be provided. Parents must now be notified of their right to choose supplemental education programs such as tutoring, summer school, and remedial classes for reading and language arts and math (NCLB, 2001; U.S. Department of Education, 2005).

Tenet 4

More local control has been transferred to individual schools and districts. School districts are permitted to make their own decisions about the use of money in order to offer programs that will bring about improvements within the district. This can range from increasing teacher salaries and hiring more personnel, to more staff development and training programs (NCLB, 2001).

 AUTHOR'S INSIGHT: Check the current ranking of your school to see if it meets the requirements of NCLB. Find out if your school is making adequate yearly progress. Ask your principal to see the disaggregated test scores from the previous school year. Your principal is required to formally present these results to the parents in your school. Find out how this was done in the past.

CHAPTER SUMMARY

This chapter provided extensive background information on the treatment of English Language Learners in the past and today in the United States. This history was explained using the two opposing ideologies of assimilation (melting pot) and cultural pluralism (salad bowl). Extensive demographics were provided pertaining to the continuing influx of non-English-speaking immigrants today and the challenges for classroom teachers.

Classroom application strategies focused on the steps for the identification and placement of English Language Learners. The varied placement possibilities for English Language Learners available in many school districts were described.

Identification of language levels of students was discussed as well as the need to refer to TESOL standards and guidelines for ensuring the appropriate educational provisions for all English Language Learners.

Finally, the tenets of No Child Left Behind (2001) were discussed in depth, including the implications for teachers of English Language Learners as well as the new rights and provisions for parents.

REFLECTIVE CHAPTER QUESTIONS

1. Trace the history of immigration to the United States from the beginning of the 1900s to today. What are the characteristics of immigration today that differ from immigration in the past? Discuss this in terms of technological advancement, ease of travel, communication, the Internet, and so on.

2. What are the unique challenges facing teachers today in areas that have high numbers of immigrants? Research your own geographic area using the Urban Institute (2006) Web site and learn more about the immigrant influx in your area of the country. What provisions are in place in your local area to deal with the influx of these immigrant groups? What are the implications of this data for you as a beginning teacher?

3. What are the steps and guidelines generally used by school districts to identify and place English Language Learners? Conduct some research on your local school district and find out more about its identification and placement procedures for English Language Learners.

4. Using the TESOL Web site provided in the References at the end of this chapter, read the standards and guidelines. Write a summary of the expectations and standards. Visit your local school district or arrange to interview an ESL coordinator or administrator. Find out more from this individual about the provisions for English Language Learners in your district.

SUGGESTED FIELD-BASED ACTIVITIES FOR PRE-SERVICE AND IN-SERVICE TEACHERS

1. Which political ideology (assimilationist or cultural pluralist) do you subscribe to and why? Which one is more prevalent in society today and what are the reasons for this? Is it possible for both to exist simultaneously in a society?

2. In light of recent immigration policies and the tightening of U.S. borders since September 11, 2001, find two newspaper articles that address the topic of immigration with opposing viewpoints. One article should favor lessening the number of immigrants entering the United States and the other should favor more lenient immigration laws. Present both sides of the argument and explain how each position affects public schools in the United States.

3. Using Figure 1.1 as a guide, research the policies in your local school district for the identification and placement of English Language Learners. Find out as much as you can about the process for a newly arrived immigrant, the testing protocol, and the path to the classroom. Create a graphic organizer or a flowchart similar to Figure 1.1 indicating the route taken by immigrant children through the school system from entry level, ESL placement, and mainstreaming into the regular classroom. Interview as many people as possible. Did you discover anything that surprised you?

REFERENCES

Banks, J. (2006). *Cultural diversity and education: Foundations, curriculum, and teaching* (5th ed). Boston: Allyn & Bacon.

Buchanan, P. (2006). *State of emergency: The third world invasion and conquest of America.* New York: Thomas Dunne Books.

Center for Immigration Studies. (2007). Available online, http://www.cis.org/articles/1995/back395.html.

Curtin, E. M. (2002). *Students' and teachers' perceptions of culturally responsive teaching: Urban middle school case study.* Dissertation, University of North Texas. Electronic dissertation available at http://www.unt.edu/library.htm.

Cushner, K., McClelland, A., & Safford, P. (2002). *Human diversity in education: An integrative approach* (4th ed.). New York: McGraw-Hill.

Faltis, C. J., & Coulter, C. A. (2008). *Teaching English language learners and immigrant students in secondary schools.* Upper Saddle River, NJ: Pearson Merrill Prentice Hall.

Latinos in Education. (1999). *Latinos in education: Early childhood, elementary, undergraduate, graduate.* Washington, DC: White House Initiative on Educational Excellence for Hispanic Americans. Retrieved on July, 2007 from http://www.ed.gov/offices/oila/hispanic/rr/ecl.html.

National Center for Education Statistics. (2007). *Schools and staffing survey, 1999–2000: Overview of the data for public, private, public charter, and Bureau for Indian Affairs elementary and secondary schools* (NCES No. 2002–313).

National Clearinghouse for English Language Acquisition. (n.d.). *In the classroom: A toolkit for effective instruction of English learners.* Retrieved July, 2007, from www.ncela.gwu.edu/practive/lessons/schcomprehesnible.html/.

New York State Education Department. (2003). *Report on the status of limited English proficient/English language learners.* http://www.nysed.gov.

No Child Left Behind Act. (2001). 107th Congress of the United States of America. Retrieved December 1, 2002 from http://www.ed.gov/legislation/ESEA02/107-110.pdf.

Ogbu, J. U., & Simons, H. D. (1998). Voluntary and involuntary minorities: A cultural-ecological theory of school performance with some implications for education. *Anthropology and Education Quarterly, 29(2),* 155–188.

O'Malley, J. M., & Valdez-Pierce, L.V. (1996). *Authentic assessment for*

English language learners. Menlo Park, CA: Addison-Wesley.

Orfield, G. (Ed.) (2004). *Dropouts in America: Confronting the graduation rate crisis.* Cambridge, MA: Harvard Education Press.

Ovando, S. J., Collier, V. P., & Combs, M. C. (2003). *Bilingual and ESL classrooms: Teaching in multicultural contexts* (3rd ed.). New York: McGraw Hill.

Plyer v. Doe (1982). 457 U.S. 202,102 Supreme Court 2382.

Ruiz-de-Velasco, J., Fix, M., & Clewell, B. C. (2000). *Overlooked & underserved: Immigrant students in U.S. secondary schools.* Washington, DC: The Urban Institute.

TESOL. (2006). Available online: http://www.tesol.org.

Urban Institute. (2006). *The new neighbors: A user's guide on data on immigrants in U.S. communities.* Available online: http://www.urban.org/immigrants/index.cfm.

U.S. Department of Education (2005). No child left behind: What parents need to know. Available online at: http://www.ed.gov/nclb/overview/intro/parents/index.html/.

Wirt, J., Choy, S., Provasnik, S., Rooney, P., Sen, A., & Tobin, R. (2003). *The condition of education 2003.* Washington, DC: National Center for Education Statistics. (NCES No. 2003-067).

Zangwill, I. (1909). *The melting pot.* New York: Macmillan.

CHAPTER 2

Foundations of English Language Learning—Theory to Practice

INTRODUCTION

Chapter 2 will provide you with basic theoretical background and information underlying language acquisition. An overview of first and second language acquisition theories will be presented here.

This chapter provides pre-service and in-service teachers with a better understanding of the linguistic issues facing English Language Learners as well as basic comprehension of the second language development process. Understanding how second language acquisition occurs and recognizing the language development stages provides teachers with valuable knowledge for classroom instruction of English Language Learners.

FOCUS QUESTIONS

◇ What were the factors that aided or impeded your second language development process?

⬥ Why is it easier to acquire a second and subsequent language at a younger age than in high school or college?

⬥ How long does it really take to become proficient in a second language?

CLASSROOM SCENARIO

Mr. O'Malley was very concerned. On the first day of the school year Maria, a non-English-speaking student, arrived in his classroom. He had felt frustrated because he didn't speak her native language and regretted that he was unable to communicate with Maria or make her comfortable in her new environment. He wasn't sure how Maria was going to acclimate to a sixth grade classroom, if at all. It is now February and Maria has been in his class for five months. He is concerned about her language proficiency.

Mr. O'Malley is empathetic by nature and is caring and personable. He assures Maria by means of smiles and nods. He always makes sure that Maria has a classmate to assist her and that she is included in all activities. Maria responds to him nonverbally with her smiles, but Mr. O'Malley is concerned that she is not yet speaking English. In fact, she's not speaking much at all.

Several days ago, some of Maria's classmates ran up to Mr. O'Malley and with great excitement explained how Maria had asked them questions during recess and had spoken with them for a little bit. Mr. O'Malley was relieved to know that she is talking and wonders if perhaps he should have tested her for a speech disability, just in case. She is well behaved and she nods and shakes her head a lot; but he's still concerned that she is not expressing herself verbally in the classroom.

Conversely, Mr. O'Malley's other English Language Learner is quite comfortable speaking. Mikhail has been in school in the United States for two years. He speaks conversationally and does not have a problem communicating in class. Although Mikhail makes grammatical mistakes, that does not deter him from talking, and he has become very popular in the class. The girls love him and for a sixth grader Mikhail is doing well socially. However, Mr. O'Malley is concerned because Mikhail's writing ability is very poor and it does not match Mikhail's level of English speaking.

Mr. O'Malley has in his hands a sample of Mikhail's writing from a class assignment entitled "My First Day in School." Mikhail wrote:

> It was good because my teacher talks Russian and English so I could communicate better and I start learning the colors also my first day of school in America, I was so nervous when I came here. I saw my teacher, an old lady, who spoke Russian and she give me a notebook and colored pencils, crayons and I feel well. And all the people talking in English and I feel, "How am I going to talk like that?

Mr. O' Malley shakes his head in concern and wonders what to do next.

Guiding Discussion Questions

◇ Using Figure 1.3 in Chapter 1, and based on the anecdotal evidence provided in the classroom scenario in this chapter, what is your assessment of the language levels of each ELL student?
◇ What other supportive strategies can Mr. O'Malley employ to develop Maria's verbal language skills?
◇ What other steps can Mr. O'Malley take to support Mikhail's writing development?

Author's Insight

Maria and Mikhail are clearly at two different levels of English language development. Maria is definitely in the silent stage where her language comprehension exceeds her production. She can understand a lot more than she speaks. She is happy and she is interacting with the students. Although it appears that she is not talking, she does in fact comprehend much of what she hears. She nods and smiles, which is positive; she is talking with the other students at recess, which allows her language skills to continue developing. Maria is in the first stage of language development, which is quite similar to that of a baby during the first two years when it only makes noises and says a word or two but is capable of understanding more than it can produce.

Mikhail, on the other hand, has great conversational speech and is well acclimated to the classroom. Closer examination of his writing sample reveals he does not write as well as he communicates, he makes grammatical errors, he uses simple syntax, and in many ways he is not writing at a sixth-grade level. Following are the kind of questions teachers should ask about students like Mikhail:

◇ Why does speech develop before written skills?
◇ Why is Mikhail not able to use more adjectives and complex sentence structures to make his writing more complete or more interesting?

The answers to these questions are connected to Basic Interpersonal Communication Skills (BICS) and Cognitive Academic Language Proficiency Skills (CALPS), which will be discussed in more depth later on in the chapter. Simply put, although Mikhail has developed nicely in conversational English, he still requires substantial academic support with his writing development, vocabulary development, and syntactic writing structures.

These are the challenges that Mr. O'Malley must face in order to properly support each of his English Language Learners at their respective stages of English language development.

WHAT RESEARCH TELLS US

A Brief Overview of First Language Development from Birth to Eight Years

We all acquire our first language (native language) skills during the first eight years of life. In fact, we acquired our first language naturally by moving through *predictable stages*. We went from babbling and gurgling in our first few months of life to the ability to communicate and be understood soon after the age of 2. Many second language acquisition theorists believe that the process of acquiring a second language can be best understood by comprehending the process of first language development. The process of language development from birth to 8 years is outlined in Figure 2.1.

This process takes an extensive period of time in order to properly develop, regardless of race, native language spoken, or geographical location. Full speech and language development occurs throughout a period of eight years. During the first two years of life babies are negotiating sounds (*phonemes*); then they develop simple sentences that are not always comprehended by adults around them. It is not until the age of two and a half years or so that a toddler can communicate fluently. Nativist theorists ascertain that language development is an innate ability that we are born with. Given the right environment and adults around us, language develops slowly and naturally (Chomsky, 1965).

Assuming the individual is totally immersed in the language, learners of a second language will pass through the silent phase within a period of 12 months; and during this stage comprehension exceeds language production. (This is very similar to what happens to an infant during its first two years.)

Theorists like Cummins (2001), Krashen (2004), and Krashen and Terrell (1983) refer to language immersion as the natural approach to language learning. They contend that acquiring a second language takes a minimum of 6–8 years and that it develops naturally if the environment of the learner is appropriately structured. However, the length of time for this acquisition period varies by individual and by many variables such as length of time in a country and how much time is spent using one's first language. This is the reason why many students who take multiple years of foreign language classes in high school are never able to speak it fluently. They were never able to spend enough continuous time with the language, and they were not immersed completely in the language (or culture) for an extensive period of time (Pray & MacSwain, 2008).

The Connection Between First and Second Language Literacy Development

There is a connection between language and literacy. Reading and writing skills develop during the first eight years of a child's life. Oral language skills must

FIGURE 2.1   Approximate Stages in First Language Development from Birth to Eight Years

Language Characteristics

Birth to One Year

- Crying, babbling, gurgling, cooing—infant learns to communicate specific needs by using different cries (one for hunger, one for pain, etc.).
- By 6 months babbling is more sophisticated—use of consonant sound with vowels ("ma," "da"). Positive reinforcement by parents encourages child to use more sounds.
- From 8–12 months child's comprehension exceeds production.
- Use of holophrases—one-word utterances that express an entire sentence (Au, Depretto, & Song, 1994).

From One to Two Years

- Use of telegraphic speech (use of nouns and verbs but omitting function words such as nouns and verbs), e.g., "doggie fall," for "The toy dog fell off the table."
- Child begins to combine words.
- Child can pronounce four-fifth of English phonemes.
- Child can use between 20 and 50 words.

From Two to Three Years

- Most dramatic in terms of language development.
- Vocabulary expands from 300 to 1,000 words.
- Child can comprehend 2,000–3,000 additional words.
- Child uses telegraphic sentences of 2–3 words.
- Child begins to use function words such as pronouns, conjunctions, prepositions, articles, and possessives on occasion.
- Child actively plays with language by repeating new words and making up nonsense words.
- Child enjoys rhyme, pattern, and repetition (Bloom, 1990).

From Three to Four Years

- Use of regular verbs and plurals.
- Child seems to have acquired all the elements of language but many adult words are unknown and child has only acquired the basic foundations of language.
- Child still makes grammatical mistakes, e.g., "I runned away," understands the grammatical structure but will invent to make it fit for language need at time.

From Five to Six Years

- Possesses vocabulary of over 2,500 words and is articulate.
- May still have difficulties pronouncing sounds at ends of words, especially "l," "r," and "sh."
- Aware that a word has more than one meaning.
- Embarrasses easily.
- Child will supply own word if he or she is missing one.
- Uses bathroom talk and curse words and enjoys shocking others (particularly adults).

From Seven to Eight Years

- Grammar is almost equivalent to that of adults.
- Incapable of using difficult grammatical transformations.
- Does not possess adult vocabulary yet.
- Can talk a lot.

From Eight to Eighteen Years

- Ability to analyze develops.
- Ability to abstract develops.
- Academic speech develops in accordance with schooling and education.

Source: Adapted from Mandel Morrow, 2001.
Note: These stages are universal and are true for any child in any language

develop first, followed by reading, and finally writing (Krashen & Terrell, 1983; Mandel Morrow, 2001). Writing is the skill that takes the longest to develop and that requires formal educational and academic support for many years after a language is acquired (Cummins, 2001).

Literacy must be fully developed in the first language in order for it to transfer to a second language (assuming that the native language is based on the Roman alphabet, like Spanish and English). With a language that uses non-Roman characters, this transfer will not be as automatic, but children will understand that the printed word has meaning and is a form of oral communication in symbols to be deciphered.

However, if literacy (reading and writing) is not fully developed in one's native language, then the process of literacy development (reading and writing) will be more complex and may take longer than expected (Cummins, 2001).

Language Differences

Research clearly indicates that some English Language Learners come to school in the United States with academic gaps that occurred in their native countries. Some English Language Learners never learned to read and write in their native language, and this does affect their abilities to acquire literacy in the United States (Pray & MacSwain, 2008). In addition, their parents' socioeconomic levels and level of education have an impact on language and literacy development for all students (Orfield, 2004). These academic and literacy gaps can also apply to children born in America who speak nonstandard English, because the English spoken at home is slang or it is a dialect that is not similar to English spoken in school.

The language a child brings to school must be honored. Language differences should not be seen as a deficiency, and teachers must learn to respect these differences (Nieto & Bode, 2007). The purpose of school is to teach all students formal and informal language registers. The *formal register* (CALPS) is the academic language all students need to be successful in school and to gain entry into college. The *informal register* (BICS) is the language used between friends and in the home (Cummins & Hornberger, 2001).

An Overview of Second Language Development Theory

Why is it that after taking a foreign language in high school or college for two to perhaps even five years, people lose their ability to speak that language? Brown (2006) answers this question by using the following example to illustrate why learning a foreign language must occur in a natural context that requires interaction with native speakers as opposed to the isolation of a classroom setting.

Francois Gouin (1880), considered to be one of the first reformers of foreign language teaching and the precursor to Charles Berlitz (now a household name in tapes and foreign language teaching), described in his book his efforts to learn German and what he discovered about the process of learning, acquiring, and eventually teaching a second language.

Gouin describes how he went to Germany for a year and, rather than interacting with native German speakers, stayed in his hotel and memorized verbs and vocabulary for a period of 10 days. He then tested his progress by going to the local university, where to his dismay he discovered that he could neither utter nor understand a single word of German.

He returned to his hotel and continued the memorizing process, and after a year he had memorized 30,000 German words, verbs, and phrases, all learned in the isolation of his room. After going back out into the German community he discovered he was still unable to communicate or understand German, so he returned to the United States. Upon his return he discovered that his three-year-old nephew had developed great linguistic and communication skills. What Gouin (1880) learned and what Berlitz later expanded upon was the notion that language is *not learned in isolation*. Language is acquired through social interaction and conversation. *Trial and error and making mistakes is a common process in the development of first or second language.* Vocabulary is best learned in the context of communication with other people. Newly acquired words and phrases are best applied in actual real-life situations communicating a need or desire rather than in isolation in one's head (Brown, 2006).

The lesson to be learned from Gouin's experiences helps answer the question why many people never are successful acquiring a second language in the isolation of a classroom or by just taking a course in college. Teachers of English Language Learners must allow students to make errors, to interact, to work in groups with native speakers, and also must provide students academic support via vocabulary and academic content (Brown, 2006). This research substantiates just how a second language develops and the need for adequate time for the process itself. Figure 2.2 provides an overview of some approximate language

FIGURE 2.2 Stages of Second Language Development

GRADES K–12

Beginning/Preproduction/"Silent Period"/Early Production/BICS

Observed Language Limitations	Time Frame
Silent Period: Unable to speak or communicate in English; should nod or respond	**0–6 months**
End of silent period/Early production	**6–12 months**
Responds with gestures or 1–2 word answers	
Reads environmental print (labels), recognizes some letters or words	
Reads Language Experience Approach (actions and mime provided) charts and stories	
Reads along with predictable books	
Records thoughts through scribbles, pictures, and invented spelling	

Intermediate/Speech Emergence/BICS

Observed Language Limitations	Time Frame
Speech emergence/Intermediate fluency	**1st–2nd year**
Requires some pictures or props for comprehension	
Initiates and sustains a social conversation; will make grammar and pronunciation errors; will not understand subtle jokes or idiomatic phrases; limited vocabulary; learning new vocabulary daily; limited academic writing skills	
Responds with short phrases and sentences	
Reads simple stories	
Records thoughts through writing short phases and sentences; limited vocabulary; learning new vocabulary daily; limited academic writing skills	

Advanced/BICS–CALPS

Observed Language Limitations	Time Frame
Advanced fluency	**3rd–5th year**
Initiates and sustains a conversation without a classroom topic (near native); will make occasional grammatical errors	

(Continued)

FIGURE 2.2 Continued

	Time Frame
Responds with elaborate language	
Reads quality children's literature	
Uses story and poetry patterns in writing	
Edits own writing but still requires academic support in writing	
Transitional/CALPS/Native **Observed Language Limitations** **Varies with each student**	**Time Frame**
Native	**6th–8th year**
Presents ideas to others in a formal manner	
Expresses thoughts in literary language	
Applies reading comprehension strategies to state-adopted basal textbooks	
Reflects artistic expression in writing	
Edits own writing	

development expectations from BICS to CALPS. Figure 2.2 attempts to provide an estimate of language development throughout an eight-year period. This is only an example, and individuals will vary within this process of language development. Some individuals may develop faster or slower than others.

Research by Cummins (1979) and his analogy of the iceberg (more below the surface than above) is still the most comprehensive and possibly best explanation for understanding the difference between social language (BICS) and academic language (CALPS) development. Figure 2.3 helps to illustrate his theory.

This image also helps us to better understand Mr. O'Malley's dilemma in the classroom. As we saw earlier in the chapter, Maria demonstrated only beginning conversational proficiency (BICS) in the classroom, and Mikhail demonstrated only beginning-level CALPS.

Basic Interpersonal Communicative Skills

Cummins (1979) defines *BICS* as Basic Interpersonal Communicative Skills. This occurs when contextual supports for the English Language Learner assist with and ease understanding and comprehension. These include face to face conversations and interaction, nonverbal cues (smiling, nodding, pointing, laughing) during the conversation. These help provide sufficient cues and clues to help the English Language Learner to more easily comprehend what the other person is saying. With respect to critical thinking, BICS requires a lower level of skills like knowledge, comprehension, and speaking.

FIGURE 2.3 BICS and CALPS

Above the surface

BICS →

Below the surface

CALPS →

Above the surface and visible
BICS, Conversational Proficiency (1–2 years to develop)
Pronunciation
Vocabulary
Grammar

Cognitive Processes
Knowledge
Comprehension
Application

Below the surface and invisible
CALPS, Academic Proficiency (4–7 years to develop)
Semantic meaning
Functional meaning

Cognitive Processes
Analysis
Synthesis
Evaluation

Source: Adapted from Cummins (1979).

Cognitive Academic Language Proficiency Skills

Cummins (1979) defines *CALPS* as Cognitive Academic Language Proficiency Skills. These skills, as shown in Figure 2.3, lie below the surface. These skills are more intricate and much deeper, causing this part of second language acquisition to be a longer and more in-depth process.

CALPS entails using the higher processing skills of analysis, synthesis and evaluation. This entails, for example, the ability to decipher or understand subtle meanings of poetry and creative composition. This is the level of language required for the successful completion of high school and college. Even some native English speakers never reach this level of academic language competency. CALPS is a developmental process and is maintained by the continuous deciphering of content and the development of knowledge, which usually occurs throughout high school, college, and continuous, lifelong learning and reading.

It is important for teachers to understand that academic language takes at least five to seven years to develop completely, and this development can take even longer for students who are not literate in their own native language before attending a school in the United States (Thomas & Collier, 1997).

Transitioning from BICS to CALPS

How does the transition occur for English Language Learners from basic conversation to cognitive academic language support?

Much research has been conducted on how best to support English Language Learners in this process. This will be the premise of the remainder of this textbook. There are many teaching strategies and techniques, but most are based on the principle that *English must be taught through academic content.* If English Language Learners are to develop cognitive academic language, they must be exposed to content in a manner that is supportive and scaffolded. This is the foundation for *comprehensible input,* which means English Language Learners must have an understanding of the academic content while also learning English language skills (Krashen, 1985). Academic content is made understandable or more comprehensible to English Language Learners when teachers provide a variety of visual cues and props during instruction. CALLA (Cognitive Academic Language Learning Approach) and SDAIE (Specially Designed Academic Instruction in English) are examples of research-based teaching models that will be used and explained further in this textbook. These teaching models support the development of cognitive academic language.

Cognitive Benefits of Knowing a Second Language

Brain research demonstrates the cognitive benefits of being bilingual. *It is critical for teachers of English Language Learners to understand that these are not students with language or cognitive deficits.* On the contrary, if their native language is properly developed and maintained while they acquire English concurrently, these students can reap many cognitive, professional, and personal benefits. Here are some of the many benefits of being proficient in a second language while maintaining one's native language:

- ◇ A distinct advantage in the competitive job market, given the ever-increasing growth of globalization
- ◇ Ease of travel in foreign countries

◇ Cultural awareness and sensitivity to others attempting to acquire a second language
◇ Increased creative and critical thinking
◇ Sharper mind and more developed intellect
◇ Expanded vocabulary
◇ Divergent thinking (Cummins, 1977)
◇ Communicative sensitivity (Brown, 2006), knowing when to speak a language and being aware of others around you

CLASSROOM APPLICATION STRATEGIES

Teacher Support Strategies during Language Development from BICS to CALPS

Figure 2.4 provides a list of teacher support strategies that may be used with English Language Learners during their predictable stages of language development. These strategies can be adapted for use with any grade level (K–12) ELL students. Understanding the difference between BICS and CALPS language levels enables the teacher to better know what to expect in the classroom. The remainder of this textbook provides specific examples and details to use with ELL students.

Literacy Gaps

It is important for teachers to understand that some English Language Learners, regardless of their age, may have academic gaps as a result of living in their native countries. Students may not have received any formal education or may have acquired only sporadic literacy in their native language. This will have a direct impact on their reading and writing levels (Ruiz-de-Velasco & Fix, 2000).

AUTHOR'S INSIGHT: Be cautious about rushing to test your ELL students. Language skills must develop before literacy can develop. Normal academic development occurs in the following order: oral language development first, then reading, and finally writing.

Comprehensible Input

Comprehensible Input (Krashen & Terrell, 1983) is the process whereby the teacher ensures that English Language Learners can comprehend academic content because the teacher provides them with enough language support. Teaching techniques are referred to as *scaffolding* and *sheltered English instruction*. To make content more comprehensible to English Language Learners,

FIGURE 2.4   Teacher Support Strategies for Stages of Second Language Development

GRADES K–12

AUTHOR'S INSIGHT: Adapt each to grade level. K–3rd grade is emergent literacy; reading and writing are developing with language. Older students, who have academic gaps in education, may be at the emergent literacy stage. However, it is important with older students to use teacher support strategies that are age-appropriate and appealing to that age group.

Beginning/Preproduction/"Silent Period"/Early Production/BICS

Behaviors of Student	Time Frame	Teacher Support Strategies
Beginning/Silent Period Unable to speak or communicate in English; should nod or respond	**0–6 months**	Smile and communicate with student, greet and address by name; assign a class buddy to accompany student. Include student in all classroom activities; do not isolate. Have student follow along with a partner or in a group while reading; point, mime, draw pictures to communicate; read aloud using books that are heavily illustrated, point and talk slowly.
Beginning/End of Silent Period/Early Production	**6–12 months**	
Responds with gestures or 1–2 word answers		Accept language errors and do not correct; encourage and praise student for speaking; ask simple questions.
Reads environmental print (labels)—recognizes some letters or words		Provide lots of books (illustrated) on interests for student to look at and read.
Reads Language Experience Approach (actions and mime provided) charts and stories		Use lots of mime and actions to explain what you are communicating.
Reads along with predictable books		Provide lots of books; have other students read to student; read aloud to student; have books on tape in a listening center.
Records thoughts through scribbles, pictures, and invented spelling		Have student write simple sentences; illustrate new vocabulary words; provide illustration with new words.

Intermediate/Speech Emergence/BICS

Behaviors of Student	Time Frame	Teacher Support Strategies
Speech Emergence/Intermediate Fluency	**1st– 2nd year**	
Requires some pictures or props for comprehension		Use lots of visuals and props to explain new words or concepts.
Initiates and sustains a social conversation		Accept grammar and pronunciation errors; avoid using idiomatic phrases. Teach new vocabulary daily. Encourage writing skills.
Respond with short phrases and sentences		Encourage student to speak in class; allow student to work in a group and share answer before calling on in class.
Reads simple stories		Provide books on reading level; adjust interest level to correspond with age of student; consider magazines, comics, books about native country, books on tape, books on CD.
Records thoughts by writing short phases and sentences		Be patient and encouraging of limited vocabulary. Teach new vocabulary daily to student. Provide alternatives to long writing assignments, e.g., shortened assignment; illustration; making models.

Advanced/BICS–CALPS

Behaviors of Student	Time Frame	Teacher Support Strategies
Advanced Fluency	**3rd– 5th year**	
Initiates and sustains a conversation without a classroom topic (near native)		Expect occasional grammatical errors and address one-on-one with student; do not embarrass or correct in front of class; target the grammar issue and provide practice exercises.

(*Continued*)

FIGURE 2.4   Continued

Behaviors of Student	Time Frame	Teacher Support Strategies
Responds with elaborate language		Always explain new vocabulary and allow student to practice and rehearse; do not assume that student is familiar with new vocabulary.
Reads quality children's literature		Provide opportunity and incentives for students to read daily in class and at home.
Uses story and poetry patterns in writing		Encourage writing and creative expression; teach the writing process (several drafts and edit last draft).
Edits own writing		Use peer editing in classroom and teach specific skill of editing and revision and checking final written work before turning in.

Transitional/CALPS/Native

Behaviors of Student	Time Frame	Teacher Support Strategies
Native	**6th–8th year**	**Will vary with each student**
Presents ideas to others in a formal manner		Encourage participation in debate and discussion daily in class.
Expresses thoughts in literary language		Encourage reading and vocabulary development; encourage use of new vocabulary and academic language depending on age, e.g., do not accept incomplete sentences or slang; develop "I agree with," "in consideration of the differences between the two positions." Teach formal language for use in classroom discussion.
Applies reading comprehension strategies to state-adopted basal textbooks		Reading and comprehension development should be at the analysis, synthesis, and evaluation stage.
Reflects artistic expression in writing		Expect high standards in writing; provide many examples of models; use a rubric (see Chapter 8) but accept student's own unique writing style.
Edits own writing		Consciously edits and knows where to find assistance independently (use computer, spell check, peers, dictionary, etc.); accept no errors in punctuation or grammar.

Krashen and Terrell (1983) suggest that the teacher's focus in each lesson should be as follows:

1. Communication, that is, the teacher is actively interacting and engaging students in communication. The teacher is speaking slowly and making sure that language used is neither confusing nor complex in structure.
2. Comprehension precedes production (silent period), that is, the teacher should expect students to listen more and say less while language is developing.
3. Production emerges in stages. Knowing the current stage of your language learner will help you determine how to present information. Remember, language emerges slowly and in stages. (See Figure 2.1)
4. The teacher must create a classroom environment that is psychologically safe and secure for students so that they are willing to take language risks to speak and communicate in English. Krashen (1985) refers to this component of second language acquisition as the *affective filter*. Negative emotions associated with learning (fear, anxiety) activate a filter that can prevent efficient processing of the learning input. Teachers must support students by ensuring that their learning anxiety levels are low so that optimum learning can occur. The teacher needs to ensure that native speakers in the classroom will not make fun of a student, and make sure there is plenty of opportunity provided for students to practice language. *A silent classroom is never beneficial or conducive to learning for ELL students.*

Communication, Not Perfection

Language is not about perfection. It is about communication. A teacher must be willing to accept mistakes and errors in speech before fluency can develop, or the student will be less likely to make progress.

No Teacher Left Behind

English Language Learners must be included in regular *academic content*. The reading level of regular classroom books may need to be adjusted, but the content must be similar to their current grade level. Regular academic content must be used in order to teach English.

English Language Learners *must not be ignored or isolated* from regular academic content while they are acquiring basic communication skills in English. English Language Learners must have access to the same curriculum as the other students. The teacher must provide a variety of visual cues and illustrations, and provide as much supportive teaching technique as possible to ensure that the English language learners can comprehend. Comprehension levels should be at least 50% while in the silent and early production stage of language and should increase progressively thereafter.

English Language Learners are no longer the domain of the ESL teacher. *All teachers are responsible* for teaching ELL students. Interaction, group work, and language communication are the standards expected in all K–12 classrooms.

English Language Learners must be *tested yearly* and must demonstrate adequate yearly progress in initial language acquisition, and then again in their third continuous year in the United States in their grade level academic content areas.

Understanding Linguistic Terms

It is important for teachers to have knowledge of language—phonology, morphology, syntax, semantics, pragmatics, discourse variations, formal and informal speech registers, and writing conventions. Specific knowledge of these will enable the teacher to identify where the student is on the continuum of second language development. Further, this knowledge will enable the teacher to support and plan accordingly for their ELL students. The following are some of the most commonly used terms and a brief definition of each:

Phonemes: "Sounds made by individual letters and combinations of letters that make a single sound" (Mandel Morrow, 2001, p. 394).

Phonics: "A strategy that involves learning the alphabetic principles of language and knowledge of letter-sound relationships. Children learn to associate letters with the phonemes or basic speech sounds of English, to help them break the alphabetic code and become independent readers in the pronunciation of words" (Mandel Morrow, 2001, p. 394).

Syntax: "The structure of language or rules that govern how words work together in phrases, clauses, and sentences" (Mandel Morrow, 2001, p. 395).

Semantics: "Meanings that language communicates" (Mandel Morrow, 2001, p. 395).

Discourse variations: Differences in how we communicate or use speech.

Formal speech registers: Used in class, giving a speech, in a formal situation like an interview, that is, the use of CALPS.

Informal speech registers: Language used in the privacy of one's home, with friends and loved ones; involves use of idiomatic speech and slang, that is, the use of BICS.

CHAPTER SUMMARY

This chapter provided a basic understanding of theory underlying second language acquisition. A simple overview of first language development from birth to 8 years was addressed. The connection between language and literacy development in the first language to the second language was then explored.

The reader learned that language differs among English Language Learners and that many have experienced academic gaps in their native language.

This means that some students may need a longer time to develop academic proficiency in English as a result of this academic gap. The difference between formal (Cognitive Academic Language Proficiency Skills) and informal (Basic Interpersonal Communication Skills) language was explained as was the importance for all students of developing formal language. It was emphasized that the development of Cognitive Academic Language Proficiency Skills is a lengthy process requiring anywhere from 6 to 8 years.

An overview of second language development was explored in this chapter. Language acquisition (first, second, and subsequent) never occurs in isolation but is a process of trial and error and making mistakes in socially interactive settings. The cognitive benefits of speaking more than one language were also highlighted in this chapter as well as the need for native speakers of other languages to maintain their mother language.

The classroom application strategies in this chapter focused on teaching techniques to support English Language Learners from BICS to CALPS. Strategies for identifying language levels of students within the BICS/CALP continuum were presented along with suggested teacher language support strategies.

Finally, the chapter closed with an explanation of one of the most significant directives embodied in No Child Left Behind for teachers of English Language Learners. English Language Learners must be included in regular academic content and must not be ignored or isolated from regular academic content while they are acquiring basic communication skills in English. English Language Learners must have access to the same curriculum as the other students.

REFLECTIVE CHAPTER QUESTIONS

1. What is the connection between language and literacy development in first and second language?

2. Explain the difference between formal and informal speech registers. What is the importance of developing a formal register for English Language Learner students?

3. Reflect back on your own experiences of learning a second language in elementary school, high school, or college or in your native country. Using the theory described in this chapter (BICS and CALPS), can you assess the success of that program? Can you provide a theoretical explanation for what occurred?

4. What are the key factors that need to be present for the successful process of second language acquisition?

5. Using the teaching strategies provided in this chapter in the classroom application section, discuss the teaching strategies for ensuring that English Language Learners can comprehend regular subject content.

Suggested Field-Based Activities for Pre-Service and In-Service Teachers

1. Using Figure 2.1 as a guide, choose a child who is between 1 and 8 years of age. Arrange to have a conversation with the child, or talk with his or her parents and observe the child's use of language. Discuss your results.

2. Describe a situation in which you are required to use formal language. On a chart, list the words or phrases you would be most likely to use in this situation. (Examples of formal language include an interview, giving a speech, meeting a dignitary, and so on.)

3. Interview an individual whose first language is not English. Ask the person to describe the process of acquiring English. How long did it take? How did the individual learn English, and how does he or she rate their level of English today? Discuss your findings in relation to the theories discussed in this chapter.

References

Au, T. K., Depretto, M., & Song, Y-K. (2001). Input vs. constraints: Early word acquisition in Korean and English. In L. Mandel Morrow, *Literacy development in the early years: Helping children read and write.* Needham Heights, MA: Allyn & Bacon.

Bloom, L. (1990). Development in express: Affect and speech. In N. Stein & T. Trabasso (Eds.), *Psychological and biological approaches to emotion* (pp. 215–245). Hillsdale, NJ: Erlbaum.

Brown, H. D. (2006). *Principles of language learning and teaching* (5th ed.). Upper Saddle River, NJ: Pearson Education.

Chomsky, N. (1965). *Aspects of the theory of syntax.* Cambridge, MA: MIT Press.

Cummins, J. (1977). Cognitive factors associated with the attainment of intermediate levels of bilingual skills. *Modern Language Journal, 61,* 3–12.

Cummins, J. (1979). Cognitive/academic language proficiency, linguistic interdependence, the optimum age question and some other matters. *Working Papers on Bilingualism,* No. 19, 121–129.

Cummins, J. (2001). *Language, power, and pedagogy: Bilingual children in the crossfire.* Multilingual Matters Limited.

Cummins, J., & Hornberger, N. (2001). In C. Baker and N. H. Hornberger (Eds.), *An introductory reader to the writings of Jim Cummins.* Multilingual Matters Limited.

Gouin, F. (2006). L'art d'enseigner et d'etudier les langues. In H. D. Brown, *Principles of language learning and teaching* (5th ed.). Upper Saddle River, NJ: Pearson Education. (Original work published 1880.)

Krashen, S. (1985). *The input hypothesis: Issues and implications.* London: Longman.

Krashen, S. (2004). *The acquisition of academic English by children, I. Two-way programs: What does the research say?* Paper presented at the National Association of Bilingual

Education Conference, February 2004, Albuquerque.

Krashen, S. D., & Terrell, T. (1983). *The natural approach: Language acquisition in the classroom.* Oxford: Pergamon.

Mandel Morrow, L. (2001). *Literacy development in the early years: Helping children read and write* (4th ed.). Needham Heights, MA: Allyn & Bacon.

Nieto, S., & Bode, P. (2007). *Affirming diversity: The sociopolitical context of multicultural education* (5th ed.). Needham Heights, MA: Allyn & Bacon.

Orfield, G. (Ed.). (2004). *Dropouts in America: Confronting the graduation rate crisis.* Cambridge, MA: Harvard Education Press.

Pray, L., & MacSwain, J. (2008). Different question, same answer: How long does it take for English learners to attain proficiency? In Faltis, C. J., & Coulter, C. A. (Eds.), *Teaching English language learners and immigrant students in secondary schools.* Upper Saddle River, NJ: Pearson Merrill Prentice Hall.

Ruiz-de-Velasco, J., & Fix, M. (2000). *Overlooked and underschooled: Immigrant students in the U.S. secondary schools.* Washington, DC: Urban Institute.

Thomas, W., & Collier, V. (1997). *School effectiveness for language minority students.* Washington, DC: National Clearinghouse for Bilingual Education.

CHAPTER

3

Getting to Know the English Language Learner

The photograph of my parents reminds me of where I am going. My parents came over here to the United States to give us a better way of life, and a better education. They did not speak the language, yet that did not stop them from pursuing their dream. I know their strength is in me too. I have not yet decided my career path however I know what it's like going to the moon. I will explore new things. I like to be challenged, expand my horizons, to soar to new heights, meet new people and be the best I can be. So some day I can say to my parents, I know who I am and stand up high with my head straight and proud.

English Language Learner
Western Heights Middle School
(Curtin, 2002)

INTRODUCTION

The first two chapters provided theoretical knowledge and background concerning second language acquisition and the process of identifying and placing English Language Learners. This chapter discusses the importance of getting to know and understand the English Language Learner. Understanding the student assists the teacher in creating a learning environment that is emotionally warm and comfortable so that the English Language Learner will take language risks, which are vital to the student's academic success.

This chapter orients the teacher in understanding how students learn best. This component is very important in planning lessons and learning experiences to ensure that students will remain motivated and interested in school. The concepts in this chapter are specifically designed for English Language Learners, but can certainly apply to many culturally diverse learners as well.

FOCUS QUESTIONS

◇ What should a teacher understand and know about English Language Learners?

◇ How do English Language Learners differ in their cognitive and academic needs?

◇ How can a teacher develop a relationship with ELL students while they are still limited in their abilities to communicate?

CLASSROOM SCENARIO

It is the first week of school and Ms. Stanley, who is a first-year teacher, is trying to get to know her students. She has several English Language Learners in her classroom who do not speak very much English. She is planning activities that will involve her English Language Learners.

Ms. Stanley asked her students to bring a picture of their family to school and to share as much about their family as they felt comfortable in doing. Several students responded well to this activity and proudly talked about their families. To ensure that her English Language Learners could participate, Ms. Stanley sent home a letter written in the student's home language explaining the purpose of the assignment. She arranged for an interpreter (a parent volunteer) to be present on the day that all students talked and shared about their families. Ms. Stanley displayed pictures and artifacts representing the cultures and backgrounds of her students. She has noticed her English Language Learners smiling and pointing to pictures and smiling a lot at her. Ms. Stanley already feels that her students are beginning to feel a sense of belonging in her classroom.

Ms. Stanley learned a lot about her students during this activity. She plans to get students to write a little more about their families and create a bulletin board display. She will plan lessons that incorporate the music and traditions of her students and will ask students to bring in things they would like to display in the classroom. Students have already brought her books written in their native languages as well as other artifacts. Every day she tries to include the ELLs in sharing about their experiences in their native countries. She is finding that her non-ELL students have no problems making friends.

Ms. Stanley is aware that some of her ELLs may be lonely. She makes sure to include a picture of different faces and emotions on the wall, and every day she checks in with each student to have him or her point to how they are feeling. If a student looks a little sad, she is sure to spend a little extra time with that student, have them draw a picture or communicate their feelings.

Ms. Stanley tries to send home all school communications in as many languages as possible. There are members of the immigrant community who volunteer their time and are glad to help her translate or interpret for her as needed. Her goal is to get to know as much as she can about all her students so she can incorporate their interests in their lessons. For example, one student was already telling her how much he missed soccer in his home country, and Ms. Stanley has decided that maybe she can find some reading material about soccer players that might be used as the basis for the reading lesson.

Guiding Discussion Questions

⬥ What is Ms. Stanley doing to connect with the background and experiences of her ELLs?
⬥ How is she culturally validating her students?

Author's Insight

English Language Learners do not want to be treated as remedial students and need to be cognitively challenged all the time. English Language Learners have high ideals and aspirations for themselves. Although they may not always be able to communicate that feeling, it is always there. It is important for English Language Learners to maintain a relationship with their teacher; to be liked and to be accepted. English Language Learners want to fit in and most of all want to be accepted into groups and the school culture.

WHAT RESEARCH TELLS US

What Teachers and Schools Need to Understand About English Language Learners

Adjustment to a new culture takes time. Predictable stages of acculturation take place. Figure 3.1 provides a model for the stages that occur for most people while adjusting to a different culture. This model can also apply to

FIGURE 3.1 U-Curve Hypothesis for Stages of Acculturation

Honeymoon   Home

Hostility   Humor

Characteristics of Each Phase

Phase	Characteristics	Time Frame Varies with Individual	Impact on Individual
Honeymoon	Excitement; newness; individual does not notice anything wrong in new situation	0–3 months	Physiological and psychological stress on body
Hostility (most critical phase)	Reality of finding a job; place to live; language frustration; disappointments; making comparisons with home country or previous situation; individual will feel hostility, anger, and may perceive prejudice and alienation	3–18 months	Homesickness; longing to go home; family discord; frustration
Humor (made the turn, hopeful)	Beginning to understand the new culture; individual can laugh at earlier experiences of frustration	18 months–2 years	Willing to adapt and learn new language; individual is feeling hopeful in new situation
Home	Less homesick; accepting, establishing roots and connections; willing to stay in new situation; appreciates differences in new culture	2–4 years	Acceptance; sense of belonging; ability to communicate and navigate new cultural norms

Source: Cushner, K., McClelland, A., & Safford, P. (2003). *Human diversity in education: An integrative approach* (4th ed.), p. 79. New York: McGraw-Hill. Reprinted with permission.

adjusting to almost anything new or different in life, not necessarily a new country (Lysgaard, 1955).

A cursory glance at Figure 3.1 reveals that for immigrants, the adjustment process into a new culture is extremely difficult during the first two years. Once individuals are able to successfully navigate past the "hostility" phase, then it should become easier. What is difficult for children and young immigrants, whether they are refugees, sojourners, or immigrants, is the fact that they are doing it involuntarily (Ogbu & Simons, 1998). We must remember that the parents of these children have made the immigration decision for them. It is important for teachers to understand where students are in the acculturation process and to be empathetic to their needs at each stage of their development.

Noddings (2005, 2006) believes that educators have an obligation to adopt an "ethic of caring" while educating all young people in America. The author argues that education is more than just training the intellect. Education should also teach students to understand themselves and others, so they can establish authentic relationships with those around them.

Zimmerman (2000) supports Noddings' "ethic of caring" by stating that programs and classrooms for English Language Learners should support a student's personal emotional growth by recognizing and validating where the student comes from. Zimmerman (2000) supports teachers and communities that strive to connect with the world of the immigrant child and youth, preserve and respect the child's and youth's home language, and in this way avoid cultural alienation.

Teachers must be empathetic and accepting of the native language of ELL students. Manning (2000) found that students can perceive intuitively and via nonverbal communication whether a teacher possesses negative or uneasy feelings about their cultural differences. Children and youth are sensitive to adults who are uneasy about differences in language, color of skin, cultural beliefs, and mannerisms. Teachers must positively validate students' native language and see it as an advantage and not a deficit.

Emotional/Psychological Needs

English Language Learners have a strong emotional need to belong and fit in. They are adjusting to a new school, a new culture, and a new language. All these adjustments create cultural shock, alienation, homesickness, and sometimes even anger, because the decision to immigrate was not theirs but that of their parents, and for this reason they are involuntary immigrants (Ogbu & Simons, 1998). The process of immigration and adaptation takes time. Teachers of English Language Learners need to be sensitive to this and need to create a classroom environment that is welcoming, safe, and psychologically secure (Igoa, 1995).

Abraham Maslow (1968) established a hierarchical structure of needs and belonging. According to Maslow, feelings of acceptance, belonging, security, and love must be present before any individual can learn. Many English Language Learners and their families are struggling to meet the most basic of needs: survival, belonging, food, shelter, acceptance; and the teacher must be empathetic to this. Ignoring English Language Learners or excluding them is going to negatively affect their ability to learn.

Cultural Needs

There are two components of culture, (1) objective and (2) subjective.

1. **Objective components** are tangible and visible aspects. The clothing people wear, the language that is spoken, and one's traditions are all visible and tangible aspects.
2. **Subjective components,** on the other hand, are the intangible aspects of culture. These include attitudes, values, norms of behavior, and social roles. These subjective and "hidden" aspects of culture are more difficult to understand and present the greatest challenges for immigrants adjusting to a new culture (Nieto & Bode, 2007).

Many people expect that they will be faced with unfamiliar behaviors and customs when coming in contact with a new culture. However, researchers in the field of intercultural relations demonstrate that immigrants are not truly prepared for the impact these interactions have on their feelings, anxieties, emotions, prejudices, and sense of belonging (Igoa, 1995; Cushner, McClelland, & Safford, 2002). This is known as *culture shock*, and contrary to popular belief, it is not a negative experience; but in fact it is a necessary prerequisite for successful adjustment to a new culture. Culture shock is the normal period of disorientation that occurs as a result of moving from known, comfortable surroundings to an environment that is significantly different and one in which many needs are not easily met. All immigrant children, youth, and adults experience culture shock.

Feelings of marginalization, loneliness, inferiority, and not belonging are very real for immigrant children (Igoa, 1995; Nieto & Bode, 2007). Alienation may occur when English Language Learners find themselves at the bottom of the class or placed in a grade level where they do not belong. Such actions can result in students eventually dropping out of school, and this particular phenomenon is all too common in the middle and high school levels (Orfield, 2004).

Many educational researchers recognize that English Language Learners excel academically if their learning process connects well with their background and culture. The multicultural movement of the 1980s and 1990s has infiltrated U.S. schools today in a conscious effort to make classrooms as culturally relevant as they are diverse, especially when it is based on the backgrounds and experiences of students (Banks, 2006; Nieto & Bode, 2007).

Public schools have their roots in the Greek tradition of education, and certain characteristics from those Greek traditions still exist in today's public school system. Schools in the United States are not designed to meet the needs of the individual, but instead the needs of the community. From their earliest days in school, children are taught that they must "fit in the group." As a result, the primary role of the teacher is to unify the individual students in a class (the group). For this to happen, the individual children must develop loyalties outside of their own family unit and transfer some of this loyalty to another authority figure, the teacher. This results in developing independence, which removes dependence from the child's primary social group, the family (Ladson-Billings, 2001).

To succeed in school in the United States, the student must learn to think and communicate by understanding abstract words and symbols that have been accepted as common knowledge. This knowledge constitutes the school curriculum and represents the values that are in many cases alien to immigrant and culturally diverse students, while at the same time more congruent with the middle-class white culture (Ladson-Billings, 2001). Many immigrant students, for example, may neither understand nor relate to Julius Caesar, Homer, or the Iliad; all of which, remnants of the Greek and Roman cultures, are a traditional part of education in the United States (Cushner et al., 2002).

For many English Language Learners their loyalties are solely with their families. Individual competition at the expense of their family is culturally incongruent with their traditional values. If an English Language Learner is to be successful in school, he or she must learn to compete within the evaluation and assessment measures utilized in public schools. Many immigrant and minority students value cooperation and family loyalty and choose not to compete. In many cases they fail in public schools because they are unable to abandon certain family traditions and cultural friendships rather than try to be competitive to attain academic success (Grant & Sleeter, 2007).

Cognitive Needs

English Language Learners need to learn and must be constantly challenged. Even though they may be acquiring a new language, they still need to be taught the English language though academic content. Using lower grade level materials for instruction can be demeaning and insulting. English Language Learners need to be cognitively challenged and may possess specific learning style needs.

Learning Style Needs: Field-Dependent and Field-Independent Learners

Numerous studies support the notion that immigrant and culturally diverse students may have learning styles that are not necessarily congruent with those required in public school. Additionally, research has shown that minority and ethnic groups are unsuccessful in many cases in school not because of lack of cognitive abilities but rather because of the inability of teachers to teach to the learning styles of their students. All students, including English Language Learners, are more likely to learn in an instructional setting that is consistent with their preferred learning style (Cushner et al., 2002).

Witkin (1962) devised the concept of *field-dependent* and *field-independent* learners. Hilliard (1976), in his final report to the California State Department of Education, defined distinct school-related behaviors for each of these learning preferences. Current publications instead refer to these same concepts as being the left brain and the right brain, or analytic and global. Students who are field-dependent (global/right brain) have very different learning needs than those who are field-independent (analytic/left brain). See Figure 3.2 for a comparative analysis and suggested teaching strategies to accommodate these preferences.

The learning preferences of field-dependent learners tend to be global in nature. These learners need context for better understanding, and they must

FIGURE 3.2 Learning Styles Checklist for Observing Learning Differences in Classroom

Left Brain/Analytic/ Field-Independent	Observed	Right Brain/Global/ Field-Dependent	Observed
Likes math and numbers		Likes words	
Prefers quiet and working alone, independently		Prefers working in a group and with others	
Likes to figure problems out by self before asking for help		Prefers to have someone else explain verbally what should be done rather than read	
Not very verbal/talkative		Very verbal/talkative	
Prefers to read directions over and over again		Dislikes reading directions and prefers verbal directions	

TEACHER SUPPORT STRATEGIES FOR LEFT-BRAIN PREFERENCE

Left Brain/Analytic/ Field-Independent	Teacher Support Strategies
Likes math and numbers	Student can create charts and Venn diagrams with words.
Prefers quiet and working alone, independently	Provide the option of working alone or in a group; establish quiet areas in the room—study carrels.
Likes to figure problems out by self before asking for help	Check in periodically with student; provide directions on board or on a separate sheet so student can work more independently.
Not very verbal/talkative	Instead of speaking in front of whole class let student choose to speak to a small group; encourage student to illustrate, create a diagram or graphic organizer to support his or her speaking skills.
Prefers to read directions over and over again	Provide written directions for student.

TEACHER SUPPORT STRATEGIES FOR RIGHT BRAIN PREFERENCE

Right Brain/Global/ Field-Dependent	Teacher Support Strategies
Likes words	Encourage students to write and describe.
Prefers working in a group and with others	Use cooperate groupings in class.
Prefers to have someone else explain verbally what should be done rather than read	Permit students to work in a group or with a partner to ask questions.
Very verbal/talkative	Allow time for group work and discussion.
Dislikes reading directions and prefers verbal directions	Allow student to ask for directions from peers or teacher without getting into trouble.

see the whole before they can understand the parts. They find meaning in personal and group relationships, and they devalue abstract and linear relationships. A field-dependent learner tends to exhibit more emotive behavior, has a shorter attention span, and more likely than not speaks loudly.

The learning preferences of field-independent learners tend to be analytical in nature. These learners do not need context in order to understand (they can extract information embedded in a text), prefer to see the parts upon which to build the whole, and they rely on linear relationships. Field-independent learners tend to have longer attention spans and concentration, prefer to work alone, and possess greater perceptual vigilance (Cohen, 1969; Hilliard, 1976).

English Language Learners may tend to exhibit a learning preference that is more field-dependent than field-independent (Grant & Sleeter, 2007). This is invaluable information for teachers of English Language Learners since instruction and teaching must be active, hands-on, interactive, and cooperatively grouped to best meet the learning preferences of ELL students.

Linguistic Needs

Competence and proficiency in the English language is essential for the academic success of English Language Learners in our schools. For this reason English Language Learners find themselves at a unique disadvantage when compared to their native counterparts. They must acquire not only second language skills but also content that may not be culturally congruent with their own backgrounds and experiences. This disadvantage can also result in alienation in the classroom, which may ultimately lead to their dropping out of school (Orfield, 2004).

CLASSROOM APPLICATION STRATEGIES

Caring for the Emotional Needs of English Language Learners

It is important for teachers to scaffold the emotional needs of English Language Learners by having an understanding of the U-curve hypothesis (see Figure 3.1), which gauges the emotional stages many immigrants and newcomers experience. Recognizing these characteristics in English Language Learners will greatly assist teachers in planning for and teaching them with their specific learning needs in mind. Teachers must be understanding of and sensitive to certain traits that English Language Learners might exhibit. They might be shy, scared, and feel inept; they may have been at the top of their class in their native country but now find themselves at the bottom academically; they might have low self-esteem; and because of the silent period, ranging from 1 to 6 months, they may feel isolated.

Teacher Support Strategies for the ELL Student

It is imperative for you to:

◇ Be patient and understanding.

◇ Smile and include the student in all activities at all times. Participation and interaction with other students is vitally important for language development.

◇ Assign a buddy (another student) to the English Language Learner.

◇ Observe and ensure that students are happy; watch for signs of withdrawal.

◇ Check on them regularly and call on them as often as you can when they raise their hand in class.

◇ Do not ignore these students and not call on them because you think they are too shy to speak yet (this is a common misconception and should be avoided).

◇ Find literature, picture books, and if possible music that represents the cultural origin of the student.

◇ Communicate with the parents as soon as possible, even if you have to do so through an interpreter. Consider sending home a translated copy of your procedures regarding homework, grading, attendance, and behavioral discipline. If time and funding permits, consider having this same information available on CD, DVD, or videotape in order to orient parents to your classroom. It may be a lot of work at the beginning but it is well worth it, since you'll only need to use an interpreter once for the master recording, allowing you to make as many copies as needed.

◇ Watch for eating preferences. Some children from other countries may not be familiar with the diet and food available in the school cafeteria.

◇ Watch for indicators of homelessness, abuse, or neglect. By law, you are obligated to report this to Child Protective Services.

◇ Make sure you are apprised of available community resources that might assist the family of the English Language Learner if they are in need.

◇ Use the language support strategies checklist in Chapter 2 (Figure 2.4) as a guideline.

◇ Immediately deal with issues of prejudice, exclusion, or unkind acts when they occur in the classroom.

Caring for the Cultural Needs of English Language Learners

Ovando, Collier, and Combs (2003) tell us how important it is for teachers to develop a set of questions to be asked privately, in order to get to know your ELL students. Some questions may be appropriate to ask in the classroom, and some are better asked by a church leader, community member, or a parent. Immigrants will proudly answer questions when asked about their home and native country. On the other hand, refugee children and their parents are not as inclined to speak out or answer the same questions.

The following information will be useful when getting to know your English Language Learner:

◇ Length of residence in the United States
◇ Country of origin (Is its language based on the Roman alphabet or not?)
◇ Ties with their home country (Do they go home for months at time and if so, how does this affect the attendance policies of the district?)
◇ The political and economic situation in their home country (Are they refugees, from a divided family, or plan to return home anytime soon?)
◇ Is their status legal or illegal? (If illegal, the parents will be less likely to be involved with school officials, and they will have an overall attitude of mistrust.)
◇ Reasons for immigrating to the United States?
◇ Are they voluntary or involuntary immigrants? (All children are involuntary immigrants and may resent their parents bringing them to the United States. If they're old enough, they may miss their home country and want to return.)
◇ What was the educational system like in their home country? Many have been educated in a second language other than their native one (this is quite common for students from African countries and certain European countries). Consider that English may in fact be their third or even fourth language and that formal schooling in their home country may have been in a second or third language and not their native tongue.
◇ Can they read and write in their native language?
◇ Ask the parents about their educational expectations. This is very important as it will significantly impact the motivation of the student and may be in direct conflict with the expectations of the school.
◇ Consider that English Language Learners face the pressures of prejudice in a climate of increasing accountability. Don't allow other teachers or parents to blame the student or to express negative views about English Language Learners.
◇ Find out their cultural orientation toward learning. Learning in the United States is based on the individual and being competitive, which may differ from the group or family-style orientation of many immigrant groups (Gay, 2000), for whom learning and school may not be as important.
◇ Find out the type of curriculum used in their home country, if any.
◇ Ask about health issues of the student and the parents, which could affect attendance.
◇ Ask if they've had a rural or an urban education.
◇ Ask their age upon entry into United States.
◇ Ask about previous schooling and classes they liked.
◇ Ask about any prior instruction in English.
◇ Determine the nature of the native language to see how closely it correlates with English.
◇ Ask about the family of the student and the habits of home literacy.
◇ How well do the families understand the principle of language acquisition discussed in Chapter 2?
◇ Determine the student's experiences with print.

Greeting Conventions and Introductions

Respect how your ELL students respond to you. In many cases it will be different from what you may be accustomed to, or they may have behavioral characteristics that differ from what you might consider normal. Different cultures have different customs when it comes to how they address you, whether they shake hands, gesture, or bow as a greeting. Some cultures consider use of the left hand as either unclean or disrespectful, and it can be taken as an insult. One needs to be sensitive to all these variations.

In some Asian cultures it might be considered disrespectful to address a person by the family name. The family name may not be used out of respect for ancestors. Instead they might use a term of endearment like "little sister" or "elder brother." In the classroom, Asian students might address you as "Teacher" and not be inclined to use your name. Many Asian students and many Hispanic students may not wish to maintain direct eye contact, which may be considered very disrespectful. Some Asian students may appear reluctant to ask questions or give answers in the classroom. These students may have come from cultures where giving a wrong answer can subject them to punishment. So volunteering a wrong answer could lose them the respect of the teacher or committing an error could cause them to lose face (honor) in front of other students (Whelan Ariza, 2006).

Physical Gestures

As mentioned, in some Asian and Hispanic cultures, making direct eye contact is considered very disrespectful. Touching another person is considered inappropriate. Showing someone the bottom of your shoe (i.e., while sitting with your legs crossed) is an insult. However, some Asians use eye contact and touching when giving or receiving an item or gifts. This shows both respect for the item and its giver, as well as respect for the receiver. The casual way people in the United States hand each other objects can be perceived as rude or impolite by other cultures (Whelan Ariza, 2006).

It is imperative that the teacher contact community resource people who are able to assist in translation or give insight into understanding different cultural traditions. Many of our students come from a variety of religious and cultural backgrounds. Beginning teachers must be prepared to teach students of many different nationalities.

 AUTHOR'S INSIGHT: Check to see if your local library subscribes to *CultureGram*, a tremendous source of information about the cultures, customs, and traditions of other countries.

Tending to Cognitive and Learning Needs of the English Language Learner

Learning Style Preferences

Figure 3.2 contains a checklist of learning style behavioral characteristics to observe and document in a file you should create for each of your students. The second half of Figure 3.2 also provides teaching support strategies for these varying learning styles.

Getting to Know the English Language Learner During the Silent Period

Many teachers, out of kindness, think that the best strategy is *not* to call on students so they won't feel embarrassed. This is not in the best interest of a student who is also learning English. Structure your classroom so that students have an opportunity to check their answers with other students and use their verbal skills (see the discussion of cooperative learning in Chapter 5). This way they will be more likely to be cooperative and to participate in class. Students who are not called on in class will feel ignored and will not feel a sense of belonging in your class (Curtin, 2002). It is important to have your students talking and not silent because it aids in their language development and growth.

Important Teacher Tips for the First Day and the First Week of School

These tips are universal. They are applicable and adaptable for grades K–12.

Surviving the Silent Stage

◇ Importance of *name:* Learn to pronounce the child's name correctly.
◇ Expect the silent period.
◇ Make the student *feel welcome* by showing the native country on a map. Prepare the other students. Find movie or pop stars, sports heroes, and the like that are of interest to your students. It makes the ELL students feel they are a part of your classroom. Be sure to include other students in the discussion as well.
◇ Assign a *buddy* to the student. Students are great at taking new students under their wing at recess, in the cafeteria, at the library, and so on.
◇ *Nonverbal communication*—The smile is universal. Give students an assigned seat, involve them in every activity, show and point to things, and get them books. Even if they cannot read, they can open the book and follow along. Language and learning is occurring all the while (heavy receptive skills are happening).
◇ *Teach greetings:* "Good morning, [student's name],". Verbalize simple commands, label your classroom (door, window, plant, desk, chair, etc.). It is a good idea to have a visual or pictures that explain the word as well.
◇ *Eye contact:* Look directly at your students to communicate with your eyes (unless this would be inappropriate).
◇ Use drawings and diagrams to communicate meaning.
◇ Use gestures.
◇ Get a picture dictionary in the students' native language so they can point, show, and begin the communication process if needed.

◇ Have all the children introduce themselves. Make a big production out of their presence; *do not ignore them*.

◇ Call on the students when they raise their hand (many well-meaning teachers don't think they should to avoid embarrassing students, but they want to be called on and should be given the option).

How English Language Learners Want Teachers to Teach: What Students Tell Us

Recommended Strategies

◇ Use thematic lessons and small groups to connect learning with a hands-on approach.

◇ Read aloud, a lot.

◇ Incorporate their cultural diversity into the lesson. As a part of social studies, display pictures that depict the home country, or show a travel video (students have tremendous pride in their home).

◇ Demonstrate what you mean—use visual examples.

◇ Develop a positive attitude—a smile is universal.

◇ Empathize by putting yourself in their shoes. Someone else brought them here (they are involuntary immigrants).

◇ Take the time to learn their customs and traditions.

◇ Use an interpreter (if available) in your school. Have lunch with them and speak through the interpreter. Remember that although students may be silent and noncommunicative, they are actually receiving and retaining a lot of information. In their early stage of learning, *receptive comprehension exceeds production*. Do not talk around students; they will quickly figure it out. *They are very adept at nonverbal cues for communication.*

◇ Use an encyclopedia or *National Geographic* for photos. Let students hang up posters of their homeland heroes (many love soccer). Write to the embassy or cultural information center, or contact a travel agent for other materials. Create a center of materials, or pictures, or a bulletin board for displays.

◇ Minimize lecture time.

◇ Include students in everything. Have them open their books and follow along.

◇ Assign them a buddy.

◇ Make it a goal to teach them something specific each and every day. Include the other students in the teaching process, because they usually enjoy a teaching role. The simplest starting example: "My name is _____."

◇ Watch your own language skills and speak slowly.

◇ Develop a notebook with pictures, words, and phrases. Have students act as buddy teachers. Make sure there is somebody accompanying them at all times (they get very anxious if they are stopped in the hall and do not have much grasp of English). Consider developing a special ID tag that says "My name is _____, I'm learning English" or something of that nature.

◇ See Figure 3.3 for additional strategies to use with your students. Modify each to fit the age of your students initially, and throughout the silent period, the emergent period, and the beginning language phases.

FIGURE 3.3   Suggested Activities for English Language Learners during Silent Period and Beginning Language Phase

LANGUAGE DEVELOPMENT	
Conversational Language Objectives to Develop with Student	**Activities to Consider**
Self and family; body parts and clothing; community helpers; shapes and colors; food; transportation; places in classroom; schedule—lunchtime, recess, etc.; asking for simple needs—restroom, lunch, etc.	Make booklets on self and family; play Simon Says; take tour of school; play memory game with pictures; color and shape bingo; draw personal silhouette and discuss interests
Animals; seasons; weather; money; time	Cut food pictures from magazine and label; animal match game; dress for specific seasons when asked to; paint pictures and label weather
Opposites; emotions; repeat simple directions (Language Experience Approach—follow teacher directives, e.g., stand up, sit down, open your book); use present tense; use regular verbs; answer yes/no questions; identify day of week; identify colors	Match different money combinations when asked; make clocks and tell time; memory cards; emotions; songs

READING DEVELOPMENT, K–3 (EMERGENT READERS) AND K–12	
Reading/Literacy Objectives to Develop with Student	**Activities to Consider**
Track from left to right; read daily using picture books; present vocabulary word with pictures; books on tape; reading buddy; introduce sight words daily	Play alphabet concentration game; dramatize story with flannel board; cut out pictures and sort into categories; make shapes and colors with corresponding word; take field trips; follow written directions in a recipe; write experience stories and illustrate; play clocks;

	play simple board games; make a This Is Me booklet; play total physical response game; play songs; go fish with colors and numbers; make community helpers workbook; have a tasting bee and make graphs of choices; make animals from clay; play opposites concentration on flannel board; develop a short story
Match letters with sounds; identify beginning sounds; on-set; rime; nursery rhymes; songs; rhyming words	Match picture opposites with picture on flannel board; match facial expression with corresponding emotions

Grades 3–12 **Reading Objectives to Develop with Student**	*Grades 3–12* **Activities to Consider**
Use word attack skills; recall details of a story; tell the sequence of events in a story; identify the main idea; draw conclusions and predict outcomes; understand cause and effect; understand graphic material; recognize and use reference material	Use story maps and graphics to organize main ideas and details; make an illustrated story board; Use picture books; use flannel board and sentence strips

WRITING DEVELOPMENT, K–3 (EMERGENT WRITERS) AND GRADES 3–12

Writing Objectives to Develop with Student	**Activities to Consider**
Recognize the relationship of sound with written symbol; recognize the use of conventions of writing using left-right, progression with spaces between words; use oral language in a variety of ways to generate writing; copy language experience sentences from the board; use basic phonetic spelling; expand basic sentences; use correct word order; recognize and apply basic conventions of capitalization and punctuation	Make letter with clay, paint, chalk, practicing and copying letters and word; student tells story and teacher writes; journal writing; copying simple sentences using dry erase board, paper; provide lots of writing media for students; students read aloud to class what they write

(Continued)

FIGURE 3.3   Continued

Grades 3–12 **Student Should Be Encouraged to:**	Grades 3–12 **Activities to Consider**
Recognize and apply basic conventions of written language expression, i.e., plurals, subject/verb agreement; narrate events in sequential order; develop paragraph using topic sentence and supporting details; edit and rewrite sentences and paragraph	Daily writing; allow student to write multiple drafts, to edit with a peer; write e-mails to another student; write simple stories to publish and read to other students; write for class magazine

CHAPTER SUMMARY

This chapter discussed the importance of getting to know and understand the many needs of the English Language Learner. Many English Language Learners are also newly arrived immigrants who experience culture shock and alienation. The U-curve hypothesis was highlighted as a teaching tool to understand the varying phases of cultural adjustment. Teachers need to understand that students who do not speak much English are very sensitive to the classroom environment. These students need a psychologically and emotionally safe environment with a teacher who displays an "ethic of caring."

Two components of culture (objective and subjective) were discussed in this chapter as well as the reason why many linguistically and culturally diverse students may find school culturally incongruent. Cultural incongruence may result in experiences of marginalization and isolation for some students.

The cognitive needs of all students were discussed and the importance of understanding two major learning styles (field-dependent and field-independent). The chapter also discussed how teachers can adapt their teaching to accommodate to the varying learning styles of all students. Classroom application strategies provided a host of strategies for scaffolding the emotional, cultural, cognitive, and linguistic needs of the English Language Learner.

REFLECTIVE CHAPTER QUESTIONS

1. Using Figure 3.1 (U-curve hypothesis), reflect on an experience in your life that was new to you (moving to a new country, moving to a new state, new town, college, new job, etc.) and that involved a period of adjustment. Reflect on that experience and, using Figure 3.1, analyze the phases you experienced. Share your experience with your classmates.

2. How does the understanding of cultural adjustment and phases discussed in Figure 3.1 assist a teacher in understanding students better?

3. What are the unique phases of cultural adjustment, and what signs should a teacher watch for in students? How can a teacher support a student who is experiencing the "hostile" phase of acculturation?

4. What is the significance of learning preferences, and how does this affect how a teacher teaches today?

SUGGESTED FIELD-BASED ACTIVITIES FOR PRE-SERVICE AND IN-SERVICE TEACHERS

1. Ask your students how they learn best in class. Conduct an informal interview similar to the scenario at the beginning of this chapter. Take note of what was significant from their discussion about their likes and dislikes. Devise a plan to incorporate their cultural backgrounds into your lessons.

2. Devise a lesson plan that incorporates the cultural backgrounds of all your students. Consider using music, stories, literature, songs, dance, and so on.

3. Interview a newly arrived immigrant and, using Figure 3.1 as a guide, ask questions that will help you understand the phases of acculturation they are experiencing. If a newly arrived immigrant is not available, find someone who immigrated at some point in their life and ask them to recall their experiences. Take note of what is significant from that interview and how their experiences fit in with the acculturation phases in Figure 3.1.

REFERENCES

Banks, J. (2006). *Cultural diversity and education: Foundations, curriculum, and teaching* (5th ed). Boston: Allyn & Bacon.

Cohen, R. A. (1969). Conceptual styles, cultural conflict, and nonverbal tests of intelligence. *American Anthropologist, 71* (5).

Curtin, E. M. (2002). *Students' and teachers' perceptions of culturally responsive teaching: Urban middle school case study*. Dissertation: University of North Texas. Electronic dissertation available at http://www.unt.edu/library.htm.

Cushner, K., McClelland, A., & Safford, P. (2002). *Human diversity in education: An integrative approach* (4th ed.). New York: McGraw-Hill.

Gay, G. (2000). *Culturally responsive teaching: Theory, research, and practice*. New York: Teachers College Press.

Grant, C. A., & Sleeter, C. E. (2007). *Turning on learning: Five approaches for multicultural teaching plans for race, class, gender and disability* (4th ed.). Hoboken, NJ: Wiley–Jossey-Bass Education.

Hilliard, A. (1976). *Alternatives to I.Q. testing: An approach to the identification of gifted minority children*. Final report to the State Department of Education, Sacramento, California.

Igoa, C. (1995). *The inner world of the immigrant child*. Mahwah, NJ: Lawrence Erlbaum Associates.

Ladson-Billings, G. (2001). *Crossing over to Canaan: The journey of new teachers in diverse classrooms.* San Francisco: Jossey-Bass.

Lysgaard, S. (2002). Adjustment in a foreign society: Norweigan Fulbright grantees visiting the United States. In K. Cushner, A. McClelland, & P. Safford, (Eds.), *Human diversity in education: An integrative approach* (4th ed.). New York: McGraw-Hill.

Manning, L. M. (2000). Understanding diversity, accepting others: Realities and directions. *Educational Horizons*, Winter, 77–79.

Maslow, A. H. (1968). *Toward a psychology of being* (2nd ed.). New York: Van Nostrand Reinhold.

Nieto, S., & Bode, P. (2007). *Affirming diversity: The sociopolitical context of multicultural education* (5th ed.). Boston, MA: Allyn & Bacon.

Noddings, N. (2005). *Educating citizens for global awareness.* New York: Teachers College Press.

Noddings, N. (2006). *Philosophy of education* (2nd ed.). Boulder, CO: Westview Press.

Ogbu, J. U., & Simons, H. D. (1998). Voluntary and involuntary minorities: A cultural-ecological theory of school performance with some implications for education. *Anthropology and Education Quarterly, 29*(2), 155–188.

Orfield, G. (Ed.). (2004). *Dropouts in America: Confronting the graduation rate crisis.* Cambridge, MA: Harvard Education Press.

Ovando, C. J., Collier, V. P., & Combs, M. C. (2003). *Bilingual and ESL classrooms: Teaching in multicultural contexts* (3rd ed.). New York: McGraw-Hill.

Whelan Ariza, E. N. (2006). *Not for ESOL teachers: What every classroom teacher needs to know about the linguistically, culturally, and ethnically diverse student.* New York: Pearson Allyn & Bacon.

Witkin, H. A. (1962). *Psychological differentiation.* New York: John Wiley & Sons.

Zimmerman, L. W. (2000). Bilingual education as a manifestation of an ethic of caring. *Education Horizons*, Winter, 72–76.

CHAPTER 4 Pre-Planning and Planning Instruction for the English Language Learner

INTRODUCTION

Chapter 4 will address the roles and responsibility of the teacher during the class planning and preparation phase. There are specific things that teachers need to include in their instructional planning if a lesson is to go well, particularly when planning for English Language Learners.

All teachers, even the most inexperienced, agree that *planning* and *preparation* are the keys to successful teaching. Gathering all your materials ahead of time, carefully planning your lessons, and organizing your thoughts must often occur after school, during your evenings, and on weekends. Avoid trying to plan ahead for one class while you're supposed to be working with students in another. Students will very quickly pick up on your lack of attention and may negatively perceive your teaching skills.

Although teachers are allotted planning time during the school day, in many cases this time is absorbed by parent-teacher conferences, committee meetings, ongoing training and staff development, and team meetings. The necessity for *time management* is critical for a teacher, and we will discuss it in more depth in this chapter. The importance of planning and preparation is discussed in this chapter, and how it instills in the teacher the professional confidence and the ability to deal with almost any set of unexpected circumstances that might occur in the classroom.

It is important to plan for each of the various academic levels—high, medium, and low—that you will encounter. It is important for a teacher to consider how to reteach a lesson if the planned lesson is not meeting the learning needs of your students. How do you plan for contingencies? How do you plan specifically for English Language Learners at varying proficiency levels? These issues are discussed in this chapter.

This chapter also addresses useful strategies for varying modalities (learning styles), planning for active learning, providing opportunities for using language and speech expression, and finally, planning with the interest of students in mind. This chapter specifically focuses on research-based strategies and emphasizes the Sheltered Instruction (SI) planning model, a necessary prerequisite for Specially Designed Academic Instruction in English (SDAIE).

FOCUS QUESTIONS

◇ What materials should I plan to use in my lessons?
◇ How can I plan lessons that are stimulating and interesting, plus cognitively challenging, while including my English Language Learners at the same time?
◇ How much time should I devote to planning?

CLASSROOM SCENARIO

Beginning and more experienced teachers were asked: "What was your greatest challenge during your first year of teaching?" Following are some of their responses.

High School Teacher Shares

Marie is a first-year high school teacher who attended a regular university-based undergraduate degree certification program. Marie tells me, "My heart feels broken most days. I bark like a drill sergeant, and when I do allow a smile to escape me, my students take this as a false signal to do anything they please with even more fervor than they were previously doing it. I realized my lessons were ill-thought-out and not very engaging, partly because of my lack of experience, but mostly because I spend my evenings calling parents and serving detentions instead of putting together materials for great lesson plans. Moreover, I am fearful of being my normal animated self, one of my greatest teaching assets; and I can't trust my students to perform experiments without ruining or stealing all of my equipment and supplies" (Curtin, 2006).

AUTHOR'S INSIGHT: The vicious circle of a new teacher and a misbehaved class:

1. Students refuse to follow simple instructions like reading their textbooks because they don't understand their purpose and the instructions don't seem to apply to them.
2. The solution is a more hands-on approach to better engage students and motivate them.
3. Hands-on activities require students to exhibit more responsible behavior and the ability to follow simple instructions, bringing us back to number one.

Elementary School Teacher Shares

Danny is a second-grade teacher. He changed careers after completing a university-based alternative certification program. He describes his greatest challenge during his first year of teaching: "For me it was coming up with lesson plans and then trying to follow an established timetable to get through those plans, when it was obvious the kids didn't understand. I was caught up in the dilemma of teaching to their needs or teaching to the schedule. If I stopped too often to help I could not devote enough time to the other subjects and that was very difficult to do. So lesson plans and scheduling were the biggest things for me . . . from the beginning we were told 'lesson plans are due' and I'm stuck asking myself, 'How do I do that?' I don't have an educational background, I didn't have any in-classroom training, and I was left to figure it on my own. Nobody helped, not my mentor teacher, not my lead teacher . . . nobody helped even though I would respond 'No' when asked, 'Do you know how to do that?' Mr. Chavez would shrug and say, 'Just try your best and good luck with that. We'll see what we can do to get you some help.' Then a month later he'd come back by and ask, 'How are you doing with your lesson plan?' Then he'd look at it and say 'Wow, you need some help with this.' Talk about really being frustrated, especially when I'm told, by the teacher who promised help and didn't deliver it, 'Oh you're doing it all wrong!'" (Curtin, 2006).

AUTHOR'S INSIGHT: Don't be afraid to ask for help when you need it. Remember, you are the person who is held accountable for the results in your classroom, and you have the right to expect help when you ask for it. So keep asking until you get it!

Middle School Teacher Shares

Denise is a sixth-grade teacher who's been teaching for almost five years. She confides, "I want to comment a little bit on lesson plans. One teacher always told me, 'It's only a plan or a guideline . . . you can't always cover everything in a class period. Sometimes you won't even get to certain lesson objectives, but that's OK, you can just focus more on those objectives the next day.' She always told me to consider it as a guideline and not something that I had to do.

"I moved here from another state and I worked in a school district that emphasized team planning and arranged for continuous help throughout my first year. We would plan things by the week and whatever our team leader was teaching in that grade level, we would all follow the same lesson plan so we could help each other with our lesson plan. It sure made both planning and my life a lot easier" (Curtin, 2006).

Time to Plan and Still Have a Life

"I would plan my day the morning of, and it was so stressful as I would get to school at six in the morning and I would go, 'Math, right, let's go,' now I've got reading and during SSR (Silent Sustained Reading) time while they were reading I was planning social studies, okay, and I'll plan science while they are in PE (physical education). It was so stressful," Josh, third-grade teacher, reflecting on his first year teaching (Curtin, 2006).

"How am I supposed to find time to do all that is expected of me in school and still have time to have a life . . . a family? I still want to do my best in the classroom but I still want a life . . . there is still a kid inside of me wanting to have fun in my life," Angela, high school teacher, reflecting on her first year teaching (Curtin, 2006).

Guiding Discussion Questions

1. How do these teachers differ in their challenges and experiences during their first year?
2. What other challenges do you believe these beginning teachers experienced, which were not discussed in the scenario?

Author's Insight

Teaching is a "live performance" and does not happen spontaneously. To the untrained eye, good teaching may look spontaneous, but in fact it relies heavily on the planning and preparation that occurs behind the scenes. Good teaching requires the ability to alter course from the written lesson plan and to adapt and change throughout the lesson. The ability to alter and change course is best achieved by a teacher who is adequately prepared and planned for all contingencies.

Each of the teachers in our classroom scenarios struggled with planning and preparation, in some cases not doing it at all; in other cases it was done at the last minute; but all mismanaged their time and did not do enough. Planning can be the hardest facet of learning good teaching methods, mainly because it requires knowing where the resources and materials are, and knowing how your students will respond to what you have planned. Very few beginning teachers have adequate knowledge about the needs of their students, so planning becomes just a "shot in the dark" without a sustainable mentoring program and reliable team support in place.

Proper planning is a teacher's imperative. Planning, whether good or bad, eventually impacts the classroom in many ways. Danny is stressed because he was never taught proper planning. Denise is stressed because she cannot teach everything in the allotted time (classroom management and pacing issues). But the common cause of stress for these three teachers stemmed from lack of help, and being thrust into what would appear to be a sink or swim environment during their first year of teaching.

How a teacher is inducted into the classroom or how he or she is mentored can vary dramatically from school to school and district to district. Some teachers are fortunate and find themselves in a supportive environment, while others are not quite so lucky, and beginning teachers can find themselves anywhere along this continuum. With or without help, a beginning teacher is expected to:

1. Take state standards and guidelines and translate them into meaningful learning experiences for their students, and
2. Prepare students for standardized tests and ensure that all students are receiving the best educational experience possible.

WHAT RESEARCH TELLS US

Plan for Teaching English to English Language Learners, Within Subject Content Areas

The premise underlying modern-day instruction for English Language Learners is the use of regular academic content to teach the English language. This is stipulated under No Child Left Behind (2001). No longer are English Language Learners confined to separate ESL pullout programs. The goal of ESL now is to teach English through content by using a multitude of supportive, scaffolding teaching techniques. This will be referred to as SI (Sheltered Instruction) throughout the remainder of this textbook.

Specially Designed Academic Instruction in English (SDAIE)

SDAIE is a collective body of research-based principles that are endorsed as appropriate teaching strategies for use with English Language Learners, and meet the requirements of No Child Left Behind. SDAIE is not one unique strategy, but rather a combination of specific instructional strategies that assist a teacher with making regular academic content understandable to the varying levels of English Language Learners (Echevarria, Vogt, & Short, 2004).

SIOP Model

The *SIOP model (Sheltered Instruction Observation Protocol)*, which was developed by Echevarria, Vogt, and Short (2004), is a research-based model that can be used by mainstream teachers to better instruct English Language Learners. This model has been modified into a system for lesson planning and instruction, and its effectiveness has been tested for more than six years by the National Center for Research on Education, Diversity and Excellence. "SIOP operationalizes sheltered instruction by offering teachers a model for lesson planning and implementation, providing English Language Learners with access to grade-level content standards. A research project through the Center for Research on Education, Diversity, and Excellence (CREDE) enabled these authors to engage in an intensive refinement process and to use the SIOP model in a sustained professional development effort with teachers on both the East and West coasts" (Echevarria et al., 2004, p. xi).

SIOP can be used by principals, lead teachers, and staff development personnel as a training instrument to observe a teacher's use of sheltered English instruction strategies, and it can also be used as a lesson planner by teachers for sheltered English instruction. It is a useful model used by many administrators when visiting classrooms with English Language Learners, as a way of assessing how well their specific learning needs are being addressed and met. This chapter will focus on using SIOP as a tool for planning.

Plan Lessons That Are Student Centered

The *Sheltered Instruction (SI) model* "is one key to improving the academic success of learners; pre-service teachers need it to develop a strong foundation in sheltered instruction; practicing teachers need it to strengthen their lesson planning and delivery and to provide students with more consistent instruction; site-base supervisors need it to train and evaluate teachers" (Echevarria et al., 2004, p. 13).

Sheltered planning instructional models are student centered because they *include English language target skills* for the immigrant student as part of the content for the lesson. In other words, English Language Learners no longer have to leave the classroom to go to special ESL pullout programs, and they no longer miss out on valuable grade-level academic content. Teaching English language skills is integrated within the teaching of actual content. Teachers present the regular grade-level subject curriculum to English Language Learners by planning ahead and using special techniques to support the English Language Learners who are trying to learn not only English but also new content in other courses like science or math.

Student-centered teaching strategies that comprise the Sheltered Instruction model entail techniques that must be incorporated in both planning and teaching. Some SI teaching strategies include ensuring that students are learning content by understanding the English language instruction with the addition and use of visual aids, demonstrations, graphic organizers, adapted texts with more understandable vocabulary, cooperative grouping, realia, actual materials, and so on. (Echevarria et al., 2004). Using the aforementioned supporting techniques provides scaffolding and support for English Language Learners.

All the teaching strategies used with ELL students must ensure that content is easily understandable, comprehension is taking place, while subject content learning is simultaneously occurring.

AUTHOR'S INSIGHT: When the English Language Learner is supported in a linguistically safe classroom environment, he or she will not get lost and will not feel overwhelmed by the mechanics of listening to a new language.

For maximum learning to occur for English Language Learners, teachers must plan lessons that enable students to make connections between what they already know and the new information being taught. In the past English Language Learners were exposed to adapted tests that strictly controlled the vocabulary used and in many cases limited the number of concepts given, thereby omitting critical pieces of information. Over time this resulted in a decrease of critical information being provided for English Language Learners and thus resulted in a widening of the achievement gap. "Therefore it is imperative that we plan lessons that are not negatively biased for students acquiring English and they include age-appropriate content and materials" (Echevarria et al., 2004 p. 21).

Including the cultural heritages and backgrounds of students is important when considering the planning for student-centered lessons. It is important for teachers to know the unique backgrounds and heritages of their students (Nieto, 2001; Nieto & Bode, 2007). Students' background and interests can help the teacher use applicable examples in lessons as the need arises. Many examples provided by student textbooks may not be congruent with the unique cultural backgrounds of some students. On occasion it may be necessary for a teacher to use an example, make an analogy, or simply make a comparative analysis with something from a particular cultural background that students can relate to. (Chapter 6 classroom scenarios provide good examples of this.)

What to Teach

Teachers must teach English Language Learners the same curriculum as they do other students. Under No Child Left Behind (2001), teachers must teach English using regular academic content. No Child Left Behind also stipulates that all states must have objectives and standardized measures for ascertaining student progress. Each year English Language Learners must make oral proficiency progress in English, and in each continuous year of residence in the United States, they must take regular *grade-level content-based* standardized tests.

No Child Left Behind makes it very clear that teachers are not free to teach anything they choose. Provisions call for clearly defined *state standards*, and *state assessments* that hold teachers and schools accountable for making adequate yearly progress. Choice of curriculum and instruction no longer exists. It is now clearly mandated at the state and federal levels.

How to Teach

No Child Left Behind mandates that research-based teaching strategies must be used by teachers in schools on a growth plan or by those failing to meet the minimum requirements.

Research shows that school districts that were successful in meeting the needs of immigrant and English Language Learners used *innovative teaching practices* (Grant & Sleeter, 2007). Teachers in these districts planned for and delivered classes in which the students were actively involved in learning rather than passively allowing the teacher to talk. These teachers relied on the experiences of their ELL students and a "theme-based" approach to planning instruction. Furthermore, students in these districts were encouraged to ask questions, and teachers carried on two-way dialogue with their students. Researchers observed in high-performing districts that teachers incorporated the cultural values of their students in lessons. A capacity-building model, rather than a deficit model, was evident in these high-performing districts. Conversely, the researchers found low-performing districts conducted business as usual, by lecturing, using worksheets, and spending time working on skill building and drills. Further, teachers in these low-performing districts also tended to rely heavily on achievement tests and used very few innovative techniques (Gay, 2000; Nieto & Bode, 2007).

In the past, passive learning constituted the mode of instruction in too many classrooms, resulting in many negative consequences for English Language Learners. In the past it was the norm to find classroom instruction that was teacher dominated with children treated as passive learners and assigned only cognitively simple tasks (Ramirez, Yuen, & Ramey, 1991). It was not uncommon to find English Language Learners isolated at the back of the classrooms, cutting and pasting letters of the alphabet and creating phonetic sound signs. They were isolated from classroom interaction until they were assessed as having enough English language skills to join in with the rest of the class (Curtin, 2002). Considerable research has been done to substantiate the positive correlation between active learning and academic success for English Language Learners (Marzano, 2004).

Research supports active learning as being more congruent with the needs of English Language Learners (Banks, 2006). Active learning is preferred for use with English Language Learners because they need to interact with language, and because there should be opportunity for discussion and conversation. English Language Learners need the opportunity to practice and access content that is comprehensible, that is, instruction that is supported with helpful pictures, illustrations, or mime. Lessons must be thoughtfully and thoroughly planned while at the same time anticipating difficulties that may arise. A well-prepared teacher must always have a backup plan that will allow for the modification of a lesson if the ELL students have too much difficulty or don't understand (Echevarria et al., 2004).

Lesson planning and implementation must eventually result in *tangible effects on student achievement* (No Child Left Behind Act, 2001). Teaching to different learning styles and using differentiating instruction so that multiple modalities are used are important components of active teaching for English Language Learners (Sleeter, 2005). The use of kinesthetic, tactile, and musical modalities should be considered also for English Language Learners. Too many classrooms in the United States tend to cater to the analytical verbal and the analytical learning styles. As discussed in Chapter 3, many English Language Learners are culturally diverse, tend to have a right-brain style of inquiry and learning, and are more global and holistic in their thought processes. This brain style responds better to modalities than it does to verbal and mathematical stimuli (Gardner, 1999, 2007).

The use of Sheltered Instruction (SI) strategies, as advocated in this chapter and throughout the remainder of the text, ensures that English Language Learners will receive the maximum opportunity to learn English language skills within the content subject areas. The use of SI strategies is very research-based and meets the tenets of No Child Left Behind.

CLASSROOM APPLICATION STRATEGIES

Preplanning

 AUTHOR'S INSIGHT: Teaching that is done well has a natural and fluid look to it, while at the same time masking the true amount of time spent on planning and preparation. In my professional opinion this is also why some teachers quit the profession. They come in expecting an 8 AM to 4 PM job but are overwhelmed by so much behind-the-scenes planning and working on lessons. As you become more dedicated to your students and to your craft, teaching turns from being work into a rewarding, fulfilling, creative, and exciting endeavor that you will truly enjoy doing for your students.

Each day is a "live performance" that will drain you of your energy while at the same time invigorate your spirit. Teachers who do not spend the time necessary to prepare in advance will find themselves becoming dull and lifeless, will always be behind, and will always tell you they wish they had more time to plan exciting lessons.

Figure 4.1 is a checklist and summary of activities involved for use in the preplanning phase. If it's your first time to teach, you're likely to feel unsure of yourself, so take the time necessary to rehearse. Get comfortable with the sequence of

FIGURE 4.1 Planning Lessons for English Language Learners

Use the following checklist to guide your lesson planning.

PREPLANNING PHASE

- Familiarize yourself with these materials:
  - Teacher editions
  - State content standards
  - Teacher colleague materials and suggestions
  - Internet
  - Library/media centers

*What are the **instructional objectives**? (What am I teaching?)*

- District scope and sequence
- State standards
- ESL/TESOL standards (what stage of English language development must you plan for your students?)
- Read the district-adopted textbook—does it align with the state standards and the instructional objectives of the lesson? If so, will the reading level of the student text present problems for any of your English Language Learners?
- Which words or concepts do you anticipate will present challenges for your English Language Learners?

PLANNING PHASE

Planning the Lesson:

Introduction/Anticipatory Set (5–10 minutes)

New **vocabulary** target selection (How will I make this "comprehensible" for my English Language Learners?)

How many days will it take to teach new concepts?

Does this objective connect with the background and experiences of my English Language Learners?

If no, then what must I plan for to make it meaningful to the age level and experience level of my English Language Learners? (**SIOP term; "Building Background"**)

Whole Group Instruction/Direct Teaching (plan for 10–15 minutes)
(Lesson presentation, introduction of new material)

This is how you will deliver the lesson to your students. Rehearse this ahead of time. Ask yourself the following questions: What will students be doing? How will you transition students from desks to groups? Will there be increased noise level in the classroom? If so, how can you control for this while still maintaining order and ensuring that all students are on task? If you anticipate that it will be too chaotic, is there a different way to accomplish the same learning objective?

Can you do any of the following with your lesson:

- Use a different example than the one presented in student text?
- Bring an actual model to class for demonstration and clarification?

- Provide more pictures or illustrations either on a chart or on the computer?
- Demonstrate by doing, using drama, mime?
- How will you introduce new vocabulary words and explain them so that students will understand?
- How will you introduce the lesson concept to pique students' interests and connect with their unique experiences?

Guided Practice/Student Activities (plan for 10–15 minutes)

Students will be working in groups or individually (guided practice—whole group, small group, or individual practice)

- How will students practice or interact with new material?
    Will they work in pairs?
    Will they discover on their own?
    Will they work in groups?
  - Will reading a picture book help?
  - Will it be necessary to gather, buy, or prepare any materials ahead of time?
  - What plan is in place for enrichment and remediation?

Planning for Assessment

- How will students be assessed?

Some assessment tasks to consider using in the classroom:
- Observe students on task by walking around the room.
- Have students perform a task for you.
- Have students write about what they learned.
- Have students complete a practice worksheet.

Teacher Reflection/Self-Evaluation

Ask yourself the following after each lesson or at the end of the day:
- What went well with the lesson?
- What could I have done differently?
- What evidence do you have or will you need to determine to show that the students mastered the objectives of the lesson?
- Which method of assessment will you use to grade students on this lesson objective? (See chapter 8 for more specific assessment strategies.)

steps involved, and get to know the lesson plan . . . and then purposely *overplan*. From my personal experiences and the experiences of teachers I have prepared who are now in the classroom, we strongly warn you of the following: Expect to spend at least twice to three times the length of your lesson in the planning and preparation process when you teach any material for the first time. A general rule of thumb is that for a 30-minute lesson, plan to spend at least 60–90 minutes preplanning and postreflecting on the lesson. The preplanning phase will include reading the appropriate materials, anticipating difficulties students may encounter with the subject and English language content of the lesson, reflecting on how best to present lessons to students, gathering any necessary materials to help make the lesson more comprehensible for students, and so on. This requires time.

Reflection is as equally as important as the preplanning and preparation. Reflection requires you to think and analyze your own teaching so that you can improve your practice and make sure you are meeting the needs of your students (Kronowitz, 2008). Kellough and Kellough (2007) give the following advice to beginning teachers: "Once the school day has begun, there is rarely time for making carefully thought-out judgments. . . . The better your understanding and experience with schools, the curriculum, and the students, and the more time you give for thoughtful reflection, the more likely it will be your decisions will result in students meeting the educational goals" (p. 14).

Gather your curriculum, your state standards, your English language goals; make sure to read the teacher editions and review the textbooks. Do the textbooks support the objectives of the lesson, or do you need to modify the language or rewrite the text to make it an understandable reading level for your English Language Learners?

Are you working with a cooperative team of teachers? Can you divide the planning load? If so, coordinate your activities with other team members. Regular contact with your team will help ensure that others are doing their assigned tasks.

AUTHOR'S INSIGHT: Your first year will be the most difficult. After you've taught the lesson at least once, you'll be more comfortable the next time and you'll be able to better anticipate the needs of your ELL students. Overplan, rehearse, know the sequence of steps, and post them on note cards for reference in the classroom, if needed. Gather books and materials yourself; do not rely on students to bring in materials for science experiments, for example. If you do, make sure materials are collected at least a week ahead of when the lesson is to take place. Overplanning leads to a high degree of self-confidence in the classroom, but always have a backup contingency plan in mind.

Where to Find Inexpensive Ideas and Materials?

Check with your school (or the district) for a media center and see if it has leveled reading books.

AUTHOR'S INSIGHT: Many of my alternatively certified, first-year teachers fail to ask how to use these materials, or even how to find them. Most of all, don't be afraid to ask a mentor, team leader, or another teacher with ELL students how to best use these materials with your students.

There are many useful first-year teaching Web sites listed at the end of this chapter. Check them for ideas about "free stuff" as well as additional tips and suggestions for surviving your first few years in a classroom.

Connecting to Multiple Modalities and Learning Styles of Students

Figure 4.2 provides a breakdown of the multiple intelligences (Gardner, 1999, 2007) and samples of activities that engage multiple modalities and

FIGURE 4.2   Planning for Multiple Intelligences/Learning Styles/Modalities

Try to incorporate any of these in your lesson planning for meaningful lessons that will help connect with the backgrounds of your students.

Intelligence/Modality	What it looks like in the classroom: Student is . . .
Auditory	Actively listening; teacher talking
Visual	Actively listening with supportive visual for language cues
Kinesthetic	Actively moving, dancing, tapping, clapping, making rhythms
Musical	Actively singing, chanting, making songs, making jingles
Interpersonal	Working in pairs or in a group on a collective task or just asking for help
Intrapersonal	Working alone and in quiet reflection; writing or reflecting on own
Mathematical	Working with numbers; working with timelines
Naturalistic	Working with nature; working outdoors

learning styles of students for possible inclusion in the planning process. Check your lesson plan and think about how your ELL students can have the following:

◇ The opportunity to work in a group
◇ The opportunity to manipulate materials during guided practice
◇ The opportunity to see real examples
◇ The opportunity to have the lesson made into a game

Paper and pencil tasks and drill and skill worksheets do not always meet the multiple modalities and learning styles of English Language Learners. Learning must be interactive and it must involve conversation. English Language Learners need to constantly practice their newly acquired vocabulary and language.

Writing Lesson Plans

You must always follow the format required by your district and school, but as a beginning teacher, until you are comfortable with what you're doing, it's always wise to draft notes for yourself that include the whole lesson cycle. Writing out your lesson plan will accomplish two primary tasks. First, it will help you to better remember the lesson plan; and second, it will cause you to consider the *objectives* you want to cover with your students, and how to assess the results. Rarely will it be necessary to write out every single procedure, but if you know you are going to be absent, include all the detail possible, because it will be helpful for your substitute teacher.

Well-thought-out classroom procedures are important because they provide guidelines for exactly what the ELL students will be doing, and just how they will be actively interacting with the planning objectives.

During lesson planning remember to include the opportunity for students to work in pairs, to work in small groups, and to interact with the entire class as a group. Ask yourself, "How can my students have independent practice?" and, "How do I plan for evaluation?" Don't forget to plan for gathering materials and resources; to plan for demonstrating these materials and resources; and to set up one central area where students can rotate in and out if necessary.

 AUTHOR'S INSIGHT: Interaction can be as simple as working with paper and scissors. You should avoid teaching directly from the textbook and instead use an overhead projector or a PowerPoint presentation. *Always* use a visual aid. *Never*, ever, walk around the room with the book on your hip and conduct an auditory lesson. This does not work with English Language Learners or any student, for that matter. Instead there must be direct interaction between the teacher and the students and heavy reliance on nonverbal communication, linguistic cues, visuals, props, pictures, pointing, and so on.

As a beginning teacher your pacing and progress will come slowly and with time. Initially you can expect to get through lessons more slowly than anticipated, and you won't know what is most important for you to focus on. You should focus on the main objectives and focus on the depth of the lesson rather than its breadth, that is, ask yourself, "What is the essential vocabulary and concepts that my English Language Learners need to have to be able to follow along rather than trying to learn each and every vocabulary word?"

Figure 4.3 provides a sample lesson plan format, which might be helpful for beginning teachers. This lesson plan format can be adapted for use in any grade.

Making Content Understandable for English Language Learners

Use the Figure 4.1 checklist when doing your preplanning in order to create your own individualized checklist that is unique to your own teaching situation. It should always be your goal to read and carefully analyze the subject content and then decide how to make it comprehensible at a level that your English Language Learners will understand. Be sure to include *realia*, *demonstrations*, and *hands-on materials*, all of which will provide the support that English Language Learners need to understand and comprehend the regular lesson in English. (More of this will be demonstrated and discussed in later chapters.)

Planning for Active Learning

The effective use of visual aids, modeling, demonstrations, graphic organizers, vocabulary previews, predictions, adapted texts, cooperative learning, peer tutoring,

FIGURE 4.3 Lesson Plan Guide for Sheltered Instruction (Teaching English Through Content)

 AUTHOR'S INSIGHT: There are many variations in planning a lesson plan, but essentially all must have an objective focus (what am I teaching?). All must address how you are going to present this to students, and how they are going to practice and interact with the new concept material. Finally, a lesson plan should include an assessment component.

Lesson plans around the country tend to use different terminology. I have tried to include as many as possible in this example. However, it is best to check with your particular school and district for the specific format and terminology required.

Lesson: Math, science, reading, social studies

Grade level: K–12

Duration:

Objectives:

Student learning objectives (academic content):

English language objectives (vocabulary needed for students to understand and learn content):

Material and resources (needed to teach the lesson):

Support materials: (visuals, manipulatives, books, charts, video, questions to ask, etc.):

Consider all the following aspects when planning your lesson.

 AUTHOR'S INSIGHT: Your lesson plans that you will be required to keep for your own records generally will need to include objectives, student activity, and assessment. The lesson cycle procedure is how you will deliver the instruction in class. It is not necessary to write this out in detail. However, it is essential to have the lesson cycle planned and mapped out in your head beforehand to ensure smooth delivery. It is also not necessary to list all resources and materials in your lesson but it is important to have them ready and with you on the day of the lesson. The lesson planning process will become more automatic with time and practice.

Lesson Cycle Procedures	Teacher Action	English Language Learner Support Strategies to Plan
1. Introduction (5–10 minutes)	Asking question; asking what students already know about topic; using a K-W-L chart; teacher is eliciting background knowledge from students; reviewing the preceding lesson.	New vocabulary on flashcards; provide pronunciation practice; vocabulary available with illustrations; use of picture books; use of actual objects to pique students' interest in lesson; with young children use a puppet, a song, a story to generate interest; with older students use a news clip, Internet to pique their interest.

(*Continued*)

FIGURE 4.3 Continued

Lesson Cycle Procedures	Teacher Action	English Language Learner Support Strategies to Plan
2. Formal Presentation of Content Material Whole group instruction/direct teaching and presentation of learning objectives (10–15 minutes)	Teacher is talking, animated, questioning, and enthusiastic; teacher is using visuals, doing an example step by step; teacher is thinking aloud and modeling learning process for students.	Use blackboard; use illustration; point; speak slowly; check for understanding; use another example; gauge faces of students for puzzlement or frustration; stop and ask questions frequently to check for understanding; get students to rephrase what you just said or retell what they just learned.
3. Guided Practice/less teacher directed/small group/teacher is monitoring and walking around room (10–15 minutes)	Teacher is no longer directly teaching but walking around the classroom; students are working in pairs, divided into groups; students are practicing what was just demonstrated by teacher; teacher is monitoring and walking around the room, helping and assisting.	Student should interact with other students in pairs or groups; encourage students to speak and ask lots of questions during this time.
Extension (occurs during guided practice or small group)	Challenging activity specifically for those students who already know the material.	
Remedial (occurs during guided practice or small group)	Reteaching students who need extra practice. *Note:* Teacher should reteach using different materials and examples than the one given in whole group instruction.	
4. Assessment individualized or group (5–10 minutes)	Oral questioning; group assignment; teacher monitors students by walking around room and observing progress; assessment can occur the next day or at end of week (test, quiz, game, etc.).	For immediate and oral assessment have students work in pairs or groups to answer questions; ensure time for practice and mastery before testing and grading.
5. Closing	Remind students what they just learned; have students tell class what they learned; homework assignment; tell students what they will be learning next day.	

picture books, student engagement, hands-on techniques, and consideration of students' affective needs, will all help create an environment in which the English Language Learner is more likely to take risks. Understanding multiple intelligences theory (Gardner, 2007), using multiple means of assessments, using supplementary materials to support academic books, graphs, visuals, illustrations, audiovisuals, tapes, computers, and adapted texts, during your preplanning will assist ELL students with mixed proficiency levels in attaining English language variations in the classroom.

Sheltered Instruction (SI) recommends focusing on one set of indicators at a time (the best one being "comprehensible input"), along with using the various support and scaffolding techniques available. You should be using these tools and techniques during planning in order to make your lesson more comprehensible to your English Language Learners.

Figure 4.3 can be adapted as a planning guide for creating a Sheltered Instruction lesson. The components of the lesson cycle provided have been derived from many sources, which include but are not limited to Borich (2007), Hunter (1982), and Specially Designed Academic Instruction in English methodology (SDAIE). The lesson plan format highlighted in Figure 4.3 includes the components that you should plan for, while at the same time incorporating Sheltered Instruction for English Language Learners.

Planning should include the following:

Content objectives: Those established by your state, not by textbooks. Textbooks only supplement and support the district's curriculum, both formal and informal.

Language objectives: Those which take into consideration the age of your ELL students; their level of reading comprehension, vocabulary, inference, meaning, new words, and their ability to explain meaning.

Content concepts: Those relating to previous knowledge, what they already know, while connecting with the background and experiences of students.

Materials: Include hands-on manipulatives, realia, pictures, visuals, multimedia, demonstrations, related literature, and adapted text.

Adaptation of content: Use of a graphic organizer with key words, outlines, leveled study guide, highlighted text, taped text, adapted text, jigsaw text reading, marginal notes, and native language texts.

Preplanning: Begin with state standards and take caution in knowing textbooks should never drive the curriculum. Textbooks are only meant to supplement and support the efficient planning done by a teacher.

Use of textbooks: In many cases the textbooks you must use are written at a language level that is different from that of the native speakers. This makes learning more difficult and emphasizes the need for "linguistic lightening." See Chapter 6 for more on linguistic lightening.

Evaluating the Planning Process

When evaluating the planning process you must not only evaluate how well your students progressed, but you must perform a *self-evaluation* on yourself to properly evaluate the effectiveness of your lesson.

What went well? How did your students respond? What part of the lesson plan did you have to modify for your English Language Learners? How comfortable were you with your own progress? Did you do enough planning? These are all questions that must be asked to evaluate the lesson. The ultimate test of how well you planned is answered by the question, "Did my students increase their level of understanding and in the end actually comprehend the concepts being taught?"

Teacher Self-Management

From the most experienced to the beginner, teachers all agree that *careful planning is the key* to success in the classroom. Having your materials ready ahead of time and carefully thought-out preplanning can only occur after school, during evenings, and on weekends. Even though we are allotted planning time by the school, in most cases this time is absorbed by parent-teacher conferences, committee meetings, ongoing training, and staff development. The need for effective *time management* is critical for all teachers, but especially for beginning teachers. Time management leads to a more confident teacher and one who is better able to anticipate difficulties that may arise in the classroom.

 AUTHOR'S INSIGHT: Consider allocating one evening a week to stay late after school to plan for the following week, rather than staying late every evening and doing it over weekends. Make it a routine and a habit, and you will find that you will soon become more efficient and faster and will need less time. This will enable you to achieve more balance in your personal and professional life.

CHAPTER SUMMARY

The focus of this chapter was on lesson planning and preparation as a vital key component of successful teaching. A beginning teacher will have to learn to become adept at personal time management. Lesson planning requires extensive time at the beginning of teaching and may impinge on a beginning teacher's personal time outside the classroom.

Teaching to various academic levels of students and the incorporation of Sheltered Instructional (SI) teaching strategies were highlighted in this chapter. Because English Language Learners are now expected to learn English within subject content areas, it has become necessary for all teachers to use research-based teaching strategies like SI.

The classroom application section provided practical examples for preplanning lessons, gathering resources and materials, as well as strategies to plan lessons connecting to multiple modalities and learning styles of students. The chapter explained how to write a lesson plan incorporating SI strategies.

REFLECTIVE CHAPTER QUESTIONS

1. Why are planning and preparation the keys to successful teaching?
2. How is it possible to teach to various academic levels of students using Sheltered Instruction?
3. What time management considerations are necessary for beginning teachers when planning lessons for students? Did this chapter change your views about planning?
4. Using Figure 4.3, discuss the components of a lesson and how each benefits the learner.

SUGGESTED FIELD-BASED ACTIVITES FOR PRE-SERVICE AND IN-SERVICE TEACHERS

1. Observe a lesson cycle being conducted by a teacher. Develop your own blank template with the information provided in Figure 4.3, record and check what you observed. How well did they do?
2. Download some sample lesson plans. Based on what you've learned so far, critique and evaluate them for their overall effectiveness with English Language Learners. What modifications, if any, would you make to the lessons to meet the comprehensible academic needs of English Language Learners?
3. Refer to Figure 4.2 for planning and incorporating learning style preferences, and multiple modalities and intelligences. Plan a lesson incorporating all the intelligences. If you have an opportunity, teach the lesson, and then evaluate how well you did.

REFERENCES

Banks, J. (2006). *Cultural diversity and education: Foundations, curriculum, and teaching* (5th ed). Boston: Allyn & Bacon.

Borich, G. D. (2007). *Effective teaching methods: Research-based* (6th ed.). Upper Saddle River, NJ: Pearson Merrill Prentice Hall.

Curtin, E. M. (2002). *Students' and teachers' perceptions of culturally responsive teaching: Urban middle school case study*. Dissertation: University of North Texas. Electronic dissertation available at http://www.unt.edu/library.htm.

Curtin, E. M. (2006). *Overcoming the learning curve: The classroom perceptions of beginning teachers during their induction year*. Poster presentation for American Educational Research Association Annual Meeting. San Francisco.

Echevarria, J., Vogt, M., & Short, D. J. (2004). *Making content comprehensible for English language learners: The SIOP model* (2nd ed.). Needham Heights, MA: Pearson Education.

Gardner, H. (1999). *Frames of mind: The theory of multiple intelligences.* Boston, MA: Harvard Business School Press.

Gardner, H. (2007). *Multiple intelligences: New horizons.* Boston, MA: Harvard Business School Press.

Gay, G. (2000). *Culturally responsive teaching: Theory, research, and practice.* New York: Teachers College Press.

Grant, C. A., & Sleeter, C. E. (2007). *Turning on learning: Five approaches for multicultural teaching plans for race, class, gender and disability* (4th ed.). San Francisco: Wiley–Jossey-Bass Education.

Hunter, M. (1982). *Mastery teaching.* El Segundo, CA: Instructional Dynamics.

Kellough, R. D., & Kellough, N. G. (2007). *Secondary school teaching: A guide to methods and resources* (3rd ed.). Upper Saddle River, NJ: Pearson Merrill Prentice Hall.

Kronowitz, E. L. (2008). *The teacher's guide to success.* Boston, MA: Pearson Allyn & Bacon.

Marzano, R. J. (2004). *Classroom instruction that works: Research-based strategies for increasing student achievement.* Upper Saddle River, NJ: Prentice Hall.

Nieto, S. (2001). *Language, culture, and teaching: Critical perspectives for a new century.* Mahwah, NJ: Lawrence Erlbaum Associates.

Nieto, S., & Bode, P. (2007). *Affirming diversity: the sociopolitical context of multicultural education* (5th ed.). Boston, MA: Allyn & Bacon.

Ramirez, D., Yuen, S., & Ramey, D. (1991). *Final report: Longitudinal study of structured English immersion strategy, early-exit, and late-exit transitional bilingual education programs for language minority children.* Washington, DC: Office of Bilingual Education.

Sleeter, C. E. (2005). *Un-standardizing curriculum: Multicultural teaching in the standards-based classroom.* J. A. Banks (Ed.), Multicultural Education series. New York: Teachers College Press.

HELPFUL RESOURCES FOR TEACHERS

Free Stuff

http://www.edpubs.org/webstore/Content/search.asp
Offers free publications.

http://www.free.ed.gov/index.cfm
Offers free resources for all subjects.

http://www.edu4kids.com/index.php?page=11
Offers free "drill and practice" games for students.

http://freeworksheets.com/
Offers free worksheets for teachers and students.

http://freecycle.org/
A site where you can request items for your classroom and also get rid of things you no longer need.

Tips and Advice for Beginning Teachers

http://www.nea.org
This site for teachers provides educational statistics, research articles, and links for a myriad of classroom ideas.

http://www.free.ed.gov/
This site offers tips and advice about surviving your first year of teaching.

For Middle and High School Teachers

http://www.middleweb.com/

http://www.teachersfirst.com/index.cfm
These sites offer advice about discipline, dealing with parents, planning for the first day and first year, as so on.

CHAPTER 5

Interactive Teaching Strategies for English Language Learners

INTRODUCTION

This textbook emphasizes the fact that passive learning is not in the best interest of English Language Learners or any learner and this chapter will be no different. Often teachers teach the way they themselves were taught or they rely on passive learning for ELL students because they fear losing control over the entire classroom.

This chapter will explore cooperative learning, learning centers, and hands-on strategies used within the classroom application context. These are strategies that can be easily implemented with thoughtful planning and preparation on the part of the teacher. Most important, these strategies are research based, classroom proven, and worthwhile interactive teaching strategies for any K–12th grade class.

Although similar in nature, these strategies should be implemented differently for each grade level being taught. Grade-level implementation can be easily modified to suit the emotional and psychological age levels of all your students, not just ELL students. Students at the high school level will respond differently than will elementary children, so your strategy needs to be modified according to your students' ages.

FOCUS QUESTIONS

- ◈ How does a teacher ensure that English Language Learners are involved in and interacting with a lesson?
- ◈ Which teaching strategies are more congruent with the learning needs of English Language Learners?

CLASSROOM SCENARIO

The following classroom scenario demonstrates the teacher's use of interactive teaching (Banks, 2006). Research based on culturally responsive teaching supports the use of interactive teaching strategies. Observe how the teacher uses interactive teaching strategies and how the English Language Learners interact with the teaching strategies.

Interactive Teaching

The students file into Ms. Matthews' fourth period sixth-grade classroom. The desks are organized in groups of four. Ms. Matthews likes order in her classroom and her students know to enter silently, sit at their assigned seats, and copy down the lesson objective for the day, as well as writing their homework assignment in their agenda books. When that is completed the students know to take out their homework. Ms. Matthews always follows this same *predictable routine* at the beginning of every class. When students do not have assigned homework, they know that they should be writing in their journals or reading independently.

All the students take out their homework along with their red marking pens. Ms. Matthews asks students to turn to their partner and to compare their homework answers. She tells them that after they have compared responses with their assigned partners, to check their answers with the other two students in their group. Antonio is having difficulty with this assignment and finds pronouns confusing, so he openly discusses it with his partner. To his dismay, Antonio realizes he's completed the wrong page in his assignment book.

Ms. Matthews is *circulating* about the room when she overhears Antonio telling the other students in his group about doing the wrong assignment. Ms. Matthews looks over the work he's completed and tells Antonio that she appreciates his effort and that he can redo his assignment and turn it in tomorrow. She then asks him to read one of the sentences he copied from his book, and asks him if it contains a pronoun. She talks with him for a moment to make sure he does understand what a pronoun is. Ms. Matthews goes on to tell Antonio that at the end of the lesson he may check out a review folder on pronouns in the writing center, if he feels he needs more practice. Antonio smiles politely and says, "Thank you, Ms. Matthews."

Ms. Matthews continues *walking around* her classroom and glancing at students' papers to make sure they are on task and checking their answers. Students know that they have permission to amend their answers since this homework assignment is one that is never graded.

After another five minutes, Ms. Matthews quickly *flips the lights* off, then on again. The students know this is their signal to settle down and to pay attention to their teacher. Ms. Matthews then asks the class: "Using either the *thumbs-up or thumbs-down* sign, let me know how well you think you did on your homework last night."

She glances around the room and observes that Antonio is giving her a thumbs-down signal while at the same time noticing that four to six other students have also given her a thumbs-down.

Ms. Matthews asks the group leaders for the week to collect the homework assignments and bring them to her desk. "Group leaders," she reminds, "make sure that everyone in your group has actually put a title on their paper as well as their name."

In a *positive* fashion Ms. Matthews *praises* her class for the hard work they've done on their homework assignments. She reminds them that "practice makes perfect," and that even though the homework they completed will not be graded, it is helping them prepare for their formal test on Friday, which will be recorded in her grade book.

Ms. Matthews writes the word *adjective* on the overhead projector and asks the group to *discuss it among themselves* and to come up with a definition. If they do not know the answer, she tells them, the definition is provided in the book on page 48. Although Antonio does not always understand everything Ms. Matthews says, he knows he can ask one of the other students in his group for help without getting into trouble for talking. Antonio does not know what the word "adjective" means.

In the meantime, the other three students in his group have been talking together and turn to Antonio to find out if he knows the definition, to which he responds, "No sure."

"I bet you know," says Patrick. Patrick was carefully selected by Ms. Matthews to be Antonio's cooperative group partner because he is a native English speaker and because he is a patient and sensitive student.

"What are you wearing today?" Patrick asks Antonio.

"I . . . wear a T-shirt . . ." says Patrick haltingly and slowly as he carefully picks his words.

"What color is your T-shirt?" Patrick asks.

" . . . *Blanco* . . . ah, white," says Antonio.

"Very good," says Patrick with a smile. "White is an adjective because it tell us something else about your shirt."

"Ah . . ." says Antonio, slowly starting to understand.

Ms. Matthews tells the class, "Now, groups, remember everyone has a job. Who is the *recorder*, who is the *time-keeper*, who is the *speaker*, and who is the *helper* in your groups? The person who is the recorder, please write down the definition that your group is to discuss."

Knowing he is the recorder this week, Antonio gets a piece of paper, and the group slowly dictates the following: "An adjective is a word that tells us more about something. For example, Antonio is wearing a white shirt."

Antonio likes his group. They spell the word *adjective* for him, and he likes doing the writing. Ms. Matthews sets a timer, and they know they have less than 3 minutes to complete this task. When time is up, Ms. Matthews asks the speaker in each group to read their group response. Antonio is not the speaker this time, but he is very proud that he wrote it down for his group and that he understands what is going on in the lesson.

For their next task Ms. Matthews asks each group to write two sentences. She takes out a picture of a lady walking in the woods and tapes it to the black-board. She asks the class to work in pairs, and to write two sentences about what they think might be happening in the picture. The students work in their groups, discuss the task in pairs, and then write down some sentences on a dry erase board that each of the pairs share. One student dictates, the other one writes, and vice versa.

Antonio has created the sentence: "Lady walking in trees."

Ms. Matthews is walking around the room looking at the sentences her students have created. She stops beside Antonio and says, "Do you like trees?"

"Yes," says Antonio, "we have trees in park and I play."

"Do you know what we call a lot of trees together?" she asks.

"No," he replies.

"Woods," she tells Antonio with a smile.

She then spells the word "woods" for Antonio. He repeats the word and writes it in the notebook he keeps for all the new vocabulary words he learns. He knows he can refer to this notebook at any time and he finds it very helpful when writing.

 AUTHOR'S INSIGHT: Ms. Matthews is aware that Antonio's sentence structure is not grammatically correct, but she accepts the error, knowing the importance of not overcorrecting an English Language Learner's language at this stage of his language development.

"You may use it in another sentence if you like," Ms. Matthews tells him. Antonio smiles at her and writes another sentence: "I like to play in Woods in my home country."

In the background is the sound of a timer going off. The class stops what they're doing while Ms. Matthews spins the spinner on a number board, which stops on the number 3. Each student has an assigned number, and they know if the *spinner* stops on their number they must represent their group for this exercise.

Antonio's number is 3, and he quickly realizes that he must now read the four sentences his group has been working on. He also knows Ms. Matthews will give each group a minute or so to practice their sentences before their representative must read them in front of the class. Knowing it's Antonio's turn to speak in front of the class, the others in his group help him with his pronunciation and reassure him that he will be great.

After the reading, Ms. Matthews praises Antonio and his group on their work and she does likewise with the other six groups. It does not take long for each group to complete this task.

After all groups have finished, she asks the class to put down their dry erase boards and look at Antonio's dry erase board. She explains, using Antonio's sentence, that each group is to pick out all the nouns and to underline them in their sentences. She tells the students each group must *put their heads together* and agree on each sentence. Antonio likes the idea because he is not sure he understood completely, so he listens intently to his classmates and realizes that in his sentences "lady" and "wood" must be nouns because they are names of a person, place, or thing. He knows he is permitted to double-check his work with his group, so he does it a lot. After a few more minutes, Ms. Matthews spins the spinner again. This time it stops on number 1. Everyone in class knows the person assigned the number 1 in each group must now call out the nouns for their group, while Ms. Matthews writes them on the blackboard.

After reviewing with her class why their list of words are in fact nouns, Ms. Matthews then chooses the following sentence written by Antonio's group to write on the blackboard: "The wood has lots of trees." Then she proceeds by asking the class a number of questions including the following:

◇ "What kind of trees do you think they are?"
◇ "What color are the trees?"
◇ "Tell me more about what the lady looks like."
◇ "What other colors do you see in the picture?"

Ms. Matthews takes a piece of chart paper. As the students *brainstorm* out loud, she writes the words on the chart. The chart is now filled with words like: *oak, cherry, green, cloudy, bluebells, white, mysterious,* and so on.

Next Ms. Matthews writes the word *adjective* on the blackboard and explains that many of the words the class just gave her are words that describe what they see happening in the picture. She then writes the following sentence written by one of her students: "The <u>lady</u> is walking in the <u>woods</u>."

Ms. Matthews has underlined the words "lady" and "woods" and explains how words added to the sentence that describe the lady and the woods are adjectives. She asks all students to examine the sentences they've created on the dry erase board and to add adjectives for a more in-depth description.

The students once again come together in their groups to *discuss* what they have written and to come up with alternative descriptive words. Once they've decided as a group which of these additional words to use, they proceed with the task of revising their sentences to include their new adjectives.

The students share their sentences as Ms. Matthews walks around the room. When the allotted time is up she asks them as a group to choose their favorite sentence and then share it with the other groups. The lesson continues like this until there is only 10 minutes of class time remaining. She then asks the students to open their textbook to page 48 and to choose any five sentences on the page, find the noun and the adjective in each, and then compose five sentences of their own using each set of nouns and adjectives they've found. This will be their *homework assignment*. She tells the class that if they finish the assignment before the period ends they may go to the writing center, take out their folders, and continue working on their *writing drafts* for the week.

Quietly taking her three English Language Learners aside, Ms. Matthews lets them know that if they need more help with their adjectives homework, a practice folder is available in the writing center to help them.

Antonio decides to do his homework in the writing center first, knowing his parents won't be able to help him at home since they don't speak any English. He also knows that Ms. Matthews will be available to help him now with any additional questions he might have before the period ends, because she will be walking around the room *checking on the students' progress*. Antonio smiles, knowing he is making progress in his new class. He feels proud because he's learning a lot. Even though it is hard for him to talk in front of the class, Ms. Matthews makes him feel safe and won't allow anyone to make fun of his accent or his pronunciation. He is speaking more in class and feeling more confident every day. He is able to do most of the same work in English as all the other students in sixth grade.

Antonio quietly goes to the end of the room where the *writing center* is located and pulls out the adjective folder.

Guiding Discussion Questions

- ◇ List and discuss all the teacher strategies that Ms. Matthews used to develop and elicit student interaction and involvement (these are italicized in the scenario to help guide you).
- ◇ How did the teaching strategies support the language development of the ELL?

Author's Insight

The teacher is this scenario demonstrated *interactive* teaching by incorporating *cooperative learning* and *learning centers*, and using *hands-on strategies* that greatly enhanced learning for all students, which reduced the anxiety for the English Language Learner (Gay, 2000). Antonio had numerous opportunities to use English language skills, to ask questions of group members, and to speak with his teacher as she walked through the room to check the progress of each group. Most importantly, Antonio was able to practice and use his language and work on academic tasks in a comfortable, risk-free environment. Consequently, his anxiety level was low and he was able to comprehend more of his lessons.

WHAT RESEARCH TELLS US

Interactive Teaching

It is a widely researched and documented fact that *an interactive teaching classroom is preferable for all students, not just for English Language Learners* (Grant & Sleeter, 2007). Interactive teaching can be effectively used with any grade level. For years, elementary classroom teachers have relied on interactive teaching strategies, and now educational researchers support the use of interactive techniques for middle school and high school students as well.

Interactive teaching strategies ensure that English Language Learners have the opportunity to interact in the classroom, work comfortably in groups, and use their newly acquired English language skills with their classmates and with other native speakers (Curtin, 2006a). An interactive classroom ensures that English Language Learners will use the language, experiment with it, and gain confidence in their ability to communicate as time progresses.

Optimal conditions for *second language acquisition* entail a classroom that creates a *low level of anxiety* for students (Krashen, 1985, 2004). Effective teaching for English Language Learners should provide sufficient amounts of *comprehensible input* (Krashen, 1985, 2004). Comprehensible input ensures that English Language Learners understand what is going on in the classroom because the teacher uses verbal and nonverbal communication, visual cues, while providing hands-on teaching opportunities for the student to practice the lesson objectives (Krashen, 2004).

Other classroom conditions that promote and support language acquisition for second language learners must include direct communication opportunities for the students, and the opportunity to use *language in context*. The teacher must be patient and empathetic enough so the English Language Learner understands that *errors may be made without reprisal* (Cummins, 2001).

On the other hand, a didactic/passive classroom is dominated by the teacher talking and is usually silent while students work independently, rarely given the opportunity to interact with one another. Passive classrooms can negatively impact the English Language Learners because of the lack of contextual language being used. Passive classrooms can also negatively affect the English Language Learners by creating a high level of anxiety for them and causing them to feel isolated and alone (Krashen, 1985, 2004; Curtin, 2006b).

Matching Teaching Style to Learning Style of Students

Researchers support the importance of matching the teaching style to the learning style of students (Nieto, 2001). English Language Learners respond most effectively to the teacher who uses interactive teaching strategies (Nieto &

Bode, 2007; Curtin, 2006a). Use of these strategies will consistently ensure an optimal environment for language learning and academic content learning for all students, while at the same time meeting the linguistic needs of English Language Learners at all grade levels.

CLASSROOM APPLICATION STRATEGIES

Cooperative Learning

Cooperative learning was first devised by Johnson and Johnson (1984). It consists of many strategies that enable students to interact together, usually in groups of four, to accomplish academic tasks. Cooperative learning can be used with all grade levels with age-appropriate modifications. Cooperative learning is very beneficial for English Language Learners because it allows a greater degree of verbal interaction than does the traditional classroom setting of rows of desks and lectures. Kagan (1997) and others like Marzano (2004) developed many strategies that are still relevant and useful today.

Use of cooperative learning helps English Language Learners by lowering their anxiety, increasing their level of communication with other students and with the teacher, and by increasing comprehension levels, which enable the student to process the content of the lesson while acquiring English language skills at the same time. Use of cooperative learning for the English Language Learner helps them to develop both communicative and academic content skills. An English Language Learner may have limited English language skills but can still participate and interact with the content of a lesson in a way that is more comprehensible than individualized and passive in-seat work. The scenario at the beginning of this chapter demonstrates the dramatic difference in student interaction when the didactic method is set aside in favor of an interactive style of teaching.

In cooperative learning the teacher carefully organizes students into heterogeneous groups, dividing the class into groups that are varied in terms of gender, English language skills, and academic abilities. Here are some general guidelines for teachers to observe when using cooperative teaching strategies with English Language Learners.

1. It is best for language acquisition purposes that ELL students interact in groups with native speakers of English. English Language Learners will also benefit from seeking help and assistance from others in their own native languages for some or part of the day.
2. When planning groups that include English Language Learners, it is important to consider grouping students with varying academic strengths. This will help ensure that students can get help from one another.
3. Rotate ELL students between different groups so they have the opportunity to interact with all students in the class on a regular basis. Heterogeneous groupings help to ensure a more harmonious atmosphere and to create a positive classroom community. A positive classroom atmosphere helps ensure an emotionally safe learning environment for English Language Learners and

helps to discourage the formation of cliques, which is often a common developmental trait among middle school and high school students.

Benefits of Cooperative Learning for the English Language Learner

There are many benefits to using cooperative learning methods with the English Language Learner. Some of the primary benefits supported by research are the following:

1. Cooperative learning lowers the English Language Learner's anxiety level, because the ELL student is permitted to work with a partner or in groups. The student can ask for help and have many opportunities to speak using English. Working in a group is more relaxing for the student and increases English language learning and comprehension (Kagan, 1997).
2. Cooperative learning permits the English Language Learner more opportunities for language use and interaction in a classroom setting than he or she would have in a traditional classroom with desks set in rows, where silence is required, and seat work predominates (Curtin, 2006b).
3. Cooperative learning provides more opportunity for the teacher to use manipulative materials, realia (real objects), as the students can be grouped and allowed to share materials. Grouping permits easier dissemination of materials in a lesson as well as easier collection; this contributes to more organization and improved classroom management (Kagan, 1997).
4. Cooperative learning has been shown to be more congruent with the learning styles of many immigrant and second language learners who value group work. English Language Learners reveal in studies that they prefer working in groups, particularly with students who originate from group- and family-oriented cultures (Nieto & Bode, 2007).
5. Cooperative learning provides socialization opportunities for every student, regardless of age. This socialization is particularly beneficial to English Language Learners because most are immigrants and new to the United States. Socialization to a new culture and way of life while being in a new environment and school is important for English Language Learners. Many English Language Learners can experience feelings of isolation and loneliness, which can be offset by having a partner or belonging to a group. This can be easily facilitated in a classroom where cooperative learning is the instructional norm (Grant & Sleeter, 2007).
6. Cooperative learning helps develop positive interdependence among students. Students must learn to rely on each other for assistance, which helps to improve relationships among students, fosters team building, and creates a positive classroom environment. This is beneficial for English Language Learners. They are forced to interact with other native speakers, use their English language skills, and get over their inhibitions quickly as they integrate into the classroom (Curtin, 2005).

7. Cooperative learning encourages teachers to plan lessons and instruction that is more student-centered. Teachers planning cooperative lessons are encouraged to examine their lessons from the perspective of the students (Grant & Sleeter, 2007).

8. Cooperative learning propels the teacher toward interacting more with students and to circulate about the classroom more often. This enables English Language Learners to gain more access to the teacher and more access to help, as needed, from group members (Curtin, 2005).

9. Cooperative learning contributes to a less stressful learning environment for the English Language Learner. English Language Learners know they can ask for help without getting in trouble for talking or having to wait for the teacher's assistance (Curtin, 2005).

10. Cooperative learning is a lot of fun for teachers and students alike. It is a great way to practice repetitive drill and skills in a way that is exciting, interesting, and motivating for all learners, particularly those in middle school and high school. Preparing students for standardized tests can be more engaging for the student when cooperative techniques and group work are used to provide a welcome respite from the routine of drill and practice worksheets (Grant & Sleeter, 2007).

Organizing Groups

Organizing groups helps to develop positive interdependence because students, through repeated practice, have the opportunity to learn the teacher's procedural roles as they rotate on a daily or weekly basis (Marzano, 2004).

Effective procedural roles can be incorporated into the organization of cooperative groups by assigning each student in the group a specific role or task during each set of activities. Some suggested roles include:

Recorder: This student is in charge of writing for the group.

Reporter: This student is responsible for orally reporting on behalf of the group.

Time-Keeper: This student is in charge of time management and ensuring the group's time on task is maintained efficiently.

Gaffer: This student is responsible for getting those items, books, or materials that will be needed for the group to accomplish its assigned task, or if necessary getting assistance from the teacher.

Group Leader: This student is responsible for ensuring that everyone is on task and equally involved in their assignments.

AUTHOR'S INSIGHT:

◇ Make sure that ELL students have one of the above roles, even if their English language skills are limited.

◇ Clearly define the requirement for each duty or role within the group and your expectations. Teacher and students alike must have a clear understanding of what is expected for each role.

◇ Rotate the group roles on a daily or weekly basis. If you're teaching in a self-contained classroom, consider rotating group roles on a subject by subject basis.

◇ If roles do not seem to be working at first, you must be patient. It takes time for students to adapt and learn your expectations, so don't be tempted to abandon this approach and return to the traditional way of teaching. Expect it to take several weeks before things are running smoothly.

◇ It's not necessary to use cooperative groups for the entire lesson or for every lesson, every day. A cooperative activity may be used at the beginning, middle, or end of a planned lesson with whole group instruction in between.

◇ Very young students who are emergent readers and writers usually require more oral-based roles or pictorial cues.

◇ When the opportunity permits, observe a Master Teacher using cooperative learning. Otherwise, attend a cooperative learning workshop offered by your school district or the regional service center.

Teaching Components of Cooperative Learning.

The components of cooperative learning are very fluid, can be monitored, and can be adjusted for use in any grade level or subject. Figure 5.1 provides a brief overview of some major components of cooperative learning that can be adapted for any K–12 classroom. A detailed explanation of each component follows as well as practical application suggestions for teaching English Language Learners.

(1) **Brainstorming**: During brainstorming the teacher elicits responses from students and writes words or phrases on a chart or blackboard. Brainstorming helps stimulate thoughts and ideas while at the same time providing a visual model for students to use. If your classes rotate and you are a middle school or high school teacher, save your work and reuse it again. Print out enough copies for use with your ELL students the next day. Many teachers give English Language Learners a printed copy, enabling them to focus on the language used in class rather than having to write and listen at the same time. This will reduce the anxiety level for English Language Learners who are attempting to learn how to speak and use the language. This should be optional since not all of your English Language Learners will require this level of assistance (Kagan, 1997).

(2) **Think-Pair-Share**: Pair two students together, whenever students need more time developing an answer. This method helps to enhance the wait time, which is important for English Language Learners who need more time to process thoughts, first in their native language, and then to translate it into English. This process helps by lowering anxiety levels and increasing the classroom involvement of English Language Learners (Kagan, 1997).

FIGURE 5.1   Components of Cooperative Learning

All these components can be used at any grade level but are most appropriate for content subject areas in the middle school and high school.

Cooperative Learning Component	Brief Description of Component	Strategies for Use with ELL	Language Support Benefits for ELL	Content Learning Support Benefits for ELL
Brainstorming	Eliciting lists and responses from students. Students can work with a partner or the group. Responses are recorded on construction paper or chart paper. Results can be used for display and classroom discussion. Content elicited from brain-storming can be analyzed for themes or patterns.	ELL should be grouped or paired with native speakers. If in sheltered ESL, make sure that English language levels are interspersed. Allow ELL time to respond or look at references or dictionary as needed. Ensure that ELL contributes. Teacher may have to interpret or give English words to ELL as needed.	Vocabulary development; social interaction. ELL has op-portunity to use language in a contextual setting. ELL can make a contribution if given time to prepare and use reference materials ahead of time.	Brainstorming helps develop vocabulary. Can also activate prior knowledge and learning. Benefits ELL in any academic subject requiring writing or creative development of ideas, such as language arts, social studies, creative writing, projects, etc.
Think-Pair-Share	Students are in pairs and share and compare answers; interview each other. Shared reading—take turns reading to each other. Shared writing—share writing samples, edit each other's work for grammar, punctuation, and content.	Make sure ELL is paired with a native speaker. Extend wait time so that students can check each other's answers before the teacher calls on the class; teacher can then use a "thumbs-up/down" to verify answers.	Vocabulary development. Allows ELL the opportunity to think longer when a question is posed by the teacher. Reduces anxiety level of ELLs as they have the opportunity to check answer before being called on by teacher. Less threatening way for teacher to assess if ELL is understanding.	Can be used in all subjects. Students can check homework, compare results in math, etc. Preparation for standardized tests.

(Continued)

FIGURE 5.1   Continued

Cooperative Learning Component	Brief Description of Component	Strategies for Use with ELL	Language Support Benefits for ELL	Content Learning Support Benefits for ELL
Numbered Heads	Assign each student in each group a number from 1 to 4. Teacher then regroups all the number 1 students, number 2, etc. to form larger groups. An organizational strategy that groups students into larger groups when needed.	ELL can interact with the same number in other groups. Allows interaction with larger group.	Vocabulary development. Interaction with more students.	All subjects. Teacher may use any time you want to have students rotate or move to larger and different groups.
Round-Robin	Each student is called on to read or respond in a large group setting. Students are each assigned a number and teacher calls on each student in class.	ELL has to respond and all students must respond; it is done in a predictable sequence. Allow all students the opportunity to practice their response or reading first before calling on them in class.	All students are included, particularly ELL. It is a predictable sequence and ELLs know they will have a turn to participate.	Can be used with reading selections; answers to math problems; brainstorming ideas; definitions or vocabulary development. Can be used for review; for tests; review of facts and details.
Jigsaw	Dividing up large chunks of information; each group reads a section and becomes an expert group. Groups reform with one member from each expert group and take turns sharing information with new group.	ELL may need to have a partner. Students should take notes or create graphics. Teacher can have questions prepared ahead of time that students need to answer.	Reading and language. Works great with older grade levels that have a lot of reading material that needs to be disseminated very quickly. Difficult academic content can be reduced to the main and pertinent ideas for all students. Students are in control of their own learning.	Used with subjects that have a lot of reading content— social studies; research; science; world news and events; any nonfictional reading materials.

Cooperative Learning Component	Brief Description of Component	Strategies for Use with ELL	Language Support Benefits for ELL	Content Learning Support Benefits for ELL
Number Wheel	A device used to randomly choose a number (a wheel made with numbers 1–4) and used to assign roles randomly or call on a student to respond for each group.	Because the numbers are chosen randomly, it ensures that all students are prepared. All students must think and develop own answer. Element of surprise makes students more involved and attentive in classroom activities. Students never know if they are going to be called on to answer.	ELL must actively participate and be prepared to answer. Students are apt to pay more attention and stay engaged in lesson as they may be called on to respond for group.	Use with lesson requiring a lot of fact and detail that requires review for tests; social studies; math; vocabulary words; definitions; any situation where teacher questions for factual responses that are either right or wrong, but can be also used for reaction to reading materials, novels, poems, etc.
Response Boards	Dry erase board for each student or each pair; a visual way for teacher to see from any angle in classroom the responses of students without students calling out answers. Teacher can assess the skill level of students and respond immediately to students having difficulty; eliminates vocal responses.	Ensure that ELL have enough wait time to respond.	Self–paced for all students. Students come up with own answer without having to compete with students who are very vocal and always seem to answer before any others have an opportunity.	Use with standardized test practice, where students respond a, b, c, d. Assessment is immediate for teacher. Teacher can tell at a glance how class is doing and if students need to spend more time on a particular concept. Very useful for mathematical responses and logical and critical thinking where there is only one correct response.

(3) **Numbered Heads**: Students in each group are assigned a specific number that corresponds with a task or process that must be performed when called on. All groups are numbered the same. When and as necessary, the teacher can put similarly numbered students from each group together to compare

responses or help them strategize a response. This strategy ensures that English Language Learners are actively involved in the lesson, and it's not always the same students who respond all the time (Kagan, 1997).

(4) Round-Robin: Every student is called on in turn. Teachers can devise a system of writting each student's name on a lollipop stick, a clothespin, or a flashcard. Be sure to highlight names of English Language Learners for easy identification. By using this kind of system each student will be given the opportunity to respond. Many teachers are inclined to prefer one side of the classroom or another or will call on eager students, who have a tendency to overshadow those who are shyer and more reticent. Many teachers don't realize they are calling on the same students over and over again (Kagan, 1997).

This system ensures that English Language Learners know (and understand) they will be called on and will not be ignored. Teachers should resist the temptation to pass over or not call on English Language Learners for fear of embarrassing them. Research studies show that English Language Learners have a strong desire to be called on in class and to use their English language skills (Curtin, 2002). Teachers can provide flashcards with responses, and students can point to correct answers, or even nod to indicate a response. The sooner English Language Learners begin talking and getting involved in the classroom, the more they feel they're being included and the better for their language development.

AUTHOR'S INSIGHT: Never embarrass students or show impatience, even if their responses are incorrect. Instead, thank students for trying and encourage them to try again. "Saving face" is very important to middle school and high school students of all cultures, not just English Language Learners.

---

(5) Jigsaw: Also known as "expert groups," jigsaw is an excellent means of disseminating large amounts of reading material. Students form a "home group" of three to four students, with each student assigned a number within the group. Each member is responsible for mastering a particular section of the assignment. Students then move to an "expert group" based on all like-numbered students from the other groups (i.e., all students assigned number 2 in their original group), where they discuss their task assignments and provide their own input and interpretation. After students then move back to their original group, they should be able to teach material or concepts to the other home group members. Depending on the language level of English Language Learners, the teacher might pair them with another student who can assist in this process (Kagan, 1997).

AUTHOR'S INSIGHT: In this instance the ELL student is not individually assigned a position in the expert group but is instead paired with another student to work on the task together.

Further, teachers of middle school and high school students should consider giving the English Language Learners a separate copy of the material that has been highlighted or modified to help them better understand the task. This way they can participate more easily in the process without the other students being aware of the extra assistance the teacher has provided them.

(6) Number Wheel: Teacher makes a round cardboard wheel with tagboard and a round-head brass fastener. (These can also be purchased at any teacher's store) (Kagan, 1997).

The wheel should be numbered (1, 2, 3, 4) or lettered (a, b, c, d) to correspond with answers for multiple-choice questions. Instead of students working individually to answer assigned questions, they work in pairs, which provides immediate responses and lets the teacher know who got the correct answer. Teachers also have the option to let students work in pairs or in groups of four and come to a consensus before answering. The wheel can also be used to choose a number of the student from each group who will be required to provide a response for the class.

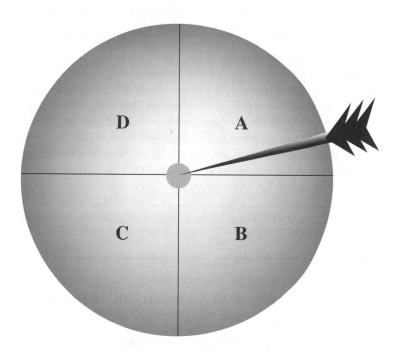

(7) Response Boards: A chalkboard or dry erase board, approximately 12″ X 8″ in size, can be purchased for about a dollar each or a larger board can be easily cut to size at a full-service hardware store. Using a dry erase marker, students can work out mathematical problems step by step, or create sentences using new vocabulary words being practiced in class. This is an excellent tool because it allows students to hold up their boards so the teacher can easily assess their work while walking around and checking on the progress being made by the groups. While students are active in their own learning process the teacher can monitor and adjust the lesson for learning difficulties or move forward with the lesson if all students have mastered the concepts. This is an excellent means of vocabulary and sentence development during language arts and may be used at any grade level, but works very well with middle school and high school students. For English Language Learners it ensures they don't have to compete vocally with students who are better equipped to answer and respond quickly. It also ensures all students are able to respond to questions while giving the teacher more time to think and consider acceptable answers.

 AUTHOR'S INSIGHT: Make ditto/worksheets more interactive and meaningful for all students. Instead of having each student individually complete a worksheet containing multiple questions or problems, assign only a section of the work you want them to complete (i.e., choose odd or even numbers). Students can work in pairs and take turns completing questions/problems (each student completes a different question or problem).

Lessening the linguistic load without compromising the content for English Language Learners can be done easily and discreetly in the aforementioned manner. Paying attention to the frustration levels of English Language Learners should be always the concern of the classroom teacher. This ensures that students are not overwhelmed by vocabulary but instead provided an opportunity to participate at their own pace and language level while still working with grade-level subject content. Having all students complete fewer problems but with better mastery is far more preferable and meaningful in the long run than voluminous "busy work."

 AUTHOR'S INSIGHT: Students of all ages can detect the difference!

Cooperative Learning and Assessment for English Language Learners

With cooperative learning and group work, student assessment is continuous and occurs naturally throughout the lesson, as you saw demonstrated in the interactive teaching scenario. Any ongoing assessment that occurs in the classroom is preferable for the English Language Learner because it is immediate and instant. This is very important for language acquisition (Grant & Sleeter, 2007).

With cooperative learning, assessment is authentic, multidimensional, and includes multiple indicators. Multiple indicators ensure the teacher is not just looking for a correct a, b, c, or d response but is also listening to how the student is arriving at a given response, as well as watching for verbal and nonverbal cues. All are indicators for the teacher to assess both comprehension and understanding. The teacher is not at the blackboard but instead is walking around the classroom and watching for those cues that indicate frustration, progress, or mastery of content (Curtin, 2002). Research studies indicate many English Language Learners feel ignored and after a while may stop raising their hands in class, because they feel they will not be called on to respond (Curtin, 2006a).

In this era of accountability and testing and NCLB, teachers in many states now must prepare students to take state standardized tests. Classroom time devoted to preparation for these tests has become quite extensive. Many states and school districts now give district-designed benchmarking tests every six weeks beginning in third grade. Districts use these benchmarking tests to monitor student progress and to provide necessary diagnostic information for teachers to use. The end result is that students are spending more time in the classroom preparing for these benchmark tests than ever before. The resulting danger that usually occurs because of the additional time spent on drills and practice is that the teaching required is more didactic than interactive. Standardized tests require students to choose a, b, c, or d as an answer, but they do not necessarily test students on how they reach that answer (Kohn, 1992, 2000).

However, in the classroom teachers should always provide an opportunity for students to demonstrate how they reached their answers. For now, standardized testing can't be avoided, but teachers who are creative in their planning can make drill and practice of skills more authentic for students by using many of the interactive and cooperative strategies that have been discussed in this chapter.

Hands-On Teaching Strategies

The term "hands-on" is part of educational jargon that is bantered around in the teaching profession. It literally means the students are touching or manipulating things while learning and are not just passively listening to the teacher. With a little thought and careful planning, hands-on learning activities can be incorporated into any subject at any grade level. What follows are some examples of hands-on learning techniques that can be integrated into any lesson or grade level from elementary to high school:

- ◇ Using manipulative materials, counters, and games to solve mathematical problems
- ◇ Conducting actual science experiments
- ◇ Writing, creating original poems or stories, and writing and making books for other classmates to read
- ◇ Using realia (real objects) to describe, manipulate, or touch, in order to enhance understanding and comprehensible input for the English Language Learner

◇ Listening to books on tape, having students create their own books on tape, having students create presentations for the class

◇ Inviting guest speakers or people who are experts in certain fields to address the class

◇ Taking field trips

◇ Going on nature walks to observe and write about nature in the field

◇ Creating a subject table for science class so students can manipulate or observe lesson items

◇ Using songs, rhymes, and music to help students with reciting multiplication tables, or facts and figures

◇ Using newspapers for scavenger hunts (finding grammar points, subject matter, creating math problems, project ideas, certain inferences, types of advertisements, etc.)

◇ Creating your own trivia games; your own card games to match vocabulary words (definitions, synonyms, etc.), to match pictures to words or sights

---

 AUTHOR'S INSIGHT: When planning lessons with English Language Learners, try to incorporate a picture, an example, a real object, or a video clip that explains the concept you are trying to teach. The Internet gives us access to vast sums of information, news links, graphics files, factual data, and streaming video, which can greatly enhance any social studies and science lesson for elementary and high school students. When using video files or a clip from the Internet you should have questions prepared ahead of time to establish why the class is listening to it; and you should have the ability to stop the tape every few minutes to check on the class's understanding of the subject matter and for students to ask questions.

A good rule is to: (1) always try to make the lesson come as close to real life as possible; (2) if that fails or is too difficult, then use pictures or a video clip; and (3) always replicate or approximate in class by using examples. For example, if the class is doing a unit on tornadoes, it is impossible to actually see the real thing, but it can be shown with a teacher-provided videotape. If a videotape is unavailable, consider demonstrating with a simple experiment that uses two 2-liter bottles taped together at the openings. One is filled about two-thirds of the way with water and the other is empty. When the bottles are shaken and turned over (empty container down) one can demonstrate the swirling motion of a tornado. This experiment can be replicated in class to create a visual example of the scientific concepts underlying tornadoes. Using such a replication or model will generate more talk and vocabulary development for all students including the English Language Learners. Relying solely on information from the textbook is never recommended as the only teaching strategy for any learner and certainly not for English Language Learners.

For writing and grammar development, using strips of paper, dry erase boards, and teacher-made games can help prepare students for standardized tests. These are considered to be "hands-on" as students are experiencing the content in a modality that is more visual and concrete. Many teacher editions of textbooks can provide numerous examples, ideas, and samples, many of which can be modified to meet the interests and cultural needs of students.

Search online for interesting Web sites with teacher-endorsed activities that can be used across all grade levels. While collecting these ideas be sure to create a resource folder for reference and to guide you back to the site in the future. Try ideas by practicing them at home to ensure they work properly and to help you anticipate any difficulties. Many of the ideas available usually require some form of modification by the teacher, either in terms of availability of materials or the level of challenge to students.

Learning Centers

Learning centers are a great teacher tool for all grade levels. Learning centers are often perceived as the domain of elementary education, but this is a misconception. Instead, learning centers should be used at the middle and high school whenever feasible (Kellough & Kellough, 2007). The learning center is a way for all students (advanced, average, or below average) to be challenged by providing more extension and remediation. Figure 5.2 provides some suggestions for using centers in elementary, middle, and high school.

When planning learning centers consider the following:

1. A learning center should be an area that provides additional resources and materials for students needing additional challenges or additional reteaching.
2. A learning center is preplanned by the teacher and should be set up as an area for students to be self-directed at their own learning level.
3. In a learning center teachers can provide opportunities for students to have access, if needed, to additional resources or materials to guide their own learning.
4. Learning centers should be accessible to all students, should be self-explanatory, and should encourage independent research and practice. Students should know it is an area openly available to them when and as needed; however, the teacher must set up guidelines for use and the appropriate activities that occur there.
5. Learning centers provide additional learning support for all learners and not just English Language Learners. Teachers should not use learning centers for some of the students while the rest of the class is participating in group instruction.
6. It is inappropriate to use a learning center exclusively for some students while excluding those same students from the main lesson. Although teachers in the United States are now actively encouraged to include all students in a lesson, this practice has been abused in the past, when many English Language Learners were left isolated in the back of the room, cutting pictures from magazines and listening through headsets to phonetic drill tapes (Curtin, 2002). These practices are no longer considered appropriate because they exclude and isolate the English Language Learner from

FIGURE 5.2 Incorporating Learning Centers in the Content Areas

Learning Centers	Language Arts	Social Studies	Math	Science
Computers	Reading programs; books on CD; publishing written works that have been edited by students; spell check and grammar check; e-mailing to students in other countries; class Web page; newsletter and research projects.	Research, Web sites to related content; publishing and writing research projects.	Research, teacher-created Web sites that offer practice with skills; graphing; surveys; CD with computational and additional math skills practice; research application of math in real-world.	Research; experiments; posting long-term research; results of surveys.
Writing Center	Publishing; writing process (research, rough draft, editing, publishing, peer review).	Publishing finished projects.	Writing about math in real-world application.	Publishing experiment; publishing research results.
Listening Center	Phonics; pronunciation; reading; comprehension; leveled reading programs; books on tape/DVD; student-created recordings.	Listening to recorded chapters on DVD.	Word problems recorded to assist beginning or struggling readers.	Science content condensed and prerecorded to assist beginning or struggling readers.
Word Wall	New vocabulary words introduced; provide a visual; word families; synonyms; new phrases or particularly idiomatic phrases; content-specific words; grammar; definitions.	New vocabulary words specific to content in social studies.	New vocabulary words specific to content in math.	New vocabulary words specific to content in science.

Learning Centers	Language Arts	Social Studies	Math	Science
Library, Reading Center	Content books, fiction and nonfiction; phonic drills and practice; individualized reading tasks that are controlled and monitored for level of reader.	Content books; magazines, newspapers; current affairs.	Concept books relating math to real life; magazines; lives of great mathematicians.	Concept books; periodicals; science magazines; journals.
Early Elementary	Dramatic play; books; listening to books on tape; arts and crafts; puppets; language and speech development, games.	Arts and crafts; people in community; civics; awareness of child in world; language and speech development; vocabulary development.	Sand; water; blocks; measuring; weighing and estimating; exploring math in world around young child; math language and speech development; vocabulary development in math.	Blocks; sand; water; observation table; exploring scientific world around child; scientific language and speech development; vocabulary development.
Special Projects Center	Publishing and writing class poems; stories; Web page; newsletters.	Holidays around the world; customs around the world.	Solving mathematical problems.	Observation of scientific phenomena; observation table; telescope; maintaining a garden; planting seeds; proving a hypothesis; experiments.

the main lesson, which includes appropriate grade-level content skills and concepts.

7. Always involve English Language Learners in the main lesson and provide as much comprehensible input as possible (Krashen, 1985, 2004), including visual aids, hands-on materials, paraphrasing, and so on. During independent practice or at the end of the lesson the learning center can become an additional resource for the English Language Learner needing more practice or more individualized teacher instruction.

Configuration of the Classroom for Learning Centers

Teachers should consider the configuration (layout of furniture and space, etc.) of the classroom to be sure areas are included that enable students to leave their desks and work in a separate area of the classroom, either independently or with a partner.

When students complete tasks early they can go to these centers and find something of interest to work on without being bored or while waiting for other students to finish. A teacher can simply have a box or a folder for each student (particularly the English Language Learner) that focuses on developing language skills as it relates to the academic subject content. These folders can include specifically shortened or modified assignments with a "lightened linguistic load," which we will explore in more detail in Chapters 6 and 7.

Each center should be clearly labeled and its purpose rehearsed often with students so they have a clear understanding of the procedures and protocol used for accessing a center.

Tips for Elementary Teachers

Establish clear rules for taking turns, or for the number of students allowed in each center at any given time. These rules will vary with the age level of the students. Older students can be more autonomous. Younger students need more specific rotational cues (i.e., timer, keeping a chart of rotations, number in each center, etc.)

◇ With younger children, especially kindergarteners, teachers should include the following multiple centers in their classroom configuration: play, blocks, sand, water, art, listening, computer, science, math, reading, and writing.

◇ With elementary children, it is necessary to plan the location of each center depending on the activity levels of students as well as the noise levels. The library center should be located in a quieter area of the classroom, while the art center should be located in relation to a sink and preferably on a noncarpeted surface.

◇ With younger children, it is also necessary to consider the safety of the routes to and from learning centers, while at the same time ensuring that every child in each center is visible to the teacher at all times.

◇ Label all centers and write out the name of the center in English. Be sure to provide a visual (picture or graphic) that indicates the purpose of the center. This will be very helpful for younger children who are emergent readers as well as older English Language Learners who are acquiring the language.

◇ Centers should be a predictable part of each day for the younger children. The predictability part of the process helps provide psychological support and structure for younger students so they know they'll have a turn working in each center and the work to be performed will be fun.

◇ From the perspective of the untrained or uninformed, the learning centers look like play centers, but they are an excellent way of providing hands-on learning for students. Student are not playing; they are in fact applying real-life learning skills in a more authentic setting.

◇ Materials in learning centers should be changed no less often than every two weeks, and in many cases should be changed weekly, to integrate them with the selected lesson themes or with objectives to be used during that particular instructional week.

◇ Materials should be inviting and appealing to the age group being taught, and they should also reflect the cultural diversity of today's world. Make sure books in reading centers are current and do not encourage stereotypical gender roles or perpetuate cultural stereotypes.

◇ Activities in the learning centers should be independently completed by all students. Activities that require substantial teacher assistance are best accomplished in small group instruction and are generally not well suited for learning centers as they can confuse and frustrate all learners. This frustration and confusion can lead to chaos and create classroom management issues.

◇ If classroom space is limited, consider storing learning center materials in boxes that are accessible to students and easily transported and set up in a designated area of the classroom.

Tips for Middle School and High School Teachers

◇ Learning centers for older students are more academic in their focus but can still incorporate a listening center, computers, writing, reading, science, math, and so on, depending on both grade level and focus.

◇ Careful consideration must be given to location within the classroom, frequency of use, and rules for accessing and exiting each center.

◇ Materials must be rotated often and provide adequate reference for students if lesson concepts need to be enhanced or reviewed or more enrichment is needed.

◇ Materials can be categorized in folders that will provide extra practice or more independent research and enrichment.

◇ Reading excerpts can be prerecorded to assist struggling readers, as well as to provide reading material that is leveled (i.e., categorized by reading levels). This ensures that English Language Learners with academic gaps in the education they received in their home countries can read the same lesson content as the rest of the class but at a more simplified level.

◇ Writing centers developed with older students in mind should entail the development of class projects such as a class book of poetry, stories, newsletters, newspapers, sports magazines, and so on. These class projects can provide English Language Learners opportunities to participate and be included regardless of their language proficiency levels. Opportunities for before and after school involvement can be enhanced for all students by being involved in such projects.

◇ Computers are a commonly available resource in most classrooms today. The use of pre-explored, preapproved Web sites and specially selected tutorial programs can greatly assist all English Language Learners with research and independent practice.

◇ Teachers should plan new extension and remedial activities as needed for inclusion in such learning centers. Using such activities enables the middle and high school teacher to individualize more for students who might need extra practice or who may not be on grade level. These activities should be planned appropriately and discreetly so as to enable adolescent learners to "save face" and not feel "dumb" in front of their peers.

AUTHOR'S INSIGHT: Learning centers are a psychologically comforting resource for all learners at any grade level, and if used on a regular basis can provide support for all students to help guide them in their own learning process. If all students work in centers on a regular basis, the teacher will be able to plan more individualized instruction for all students, not just English Language Learners.

Centers provide students with an additional source of engaging and on-task activities that allow the learner who finishes early the ability to relocate to a learning center without having to wait for others to finish. This greatly assists with classroom organization and management at all ages.

Learning centers designed for the high school level can include project work that might take several weeks to complete.

If classroom space is limited, consider storing center materials in boxes that are accessible to students and easily transported to a designated area in the classroom. These materials may also be stored in file folders. Older students should be allowed to transport materials back to their desks.

CHAPTER SUMMARY

This chapter explored three specific interactive teaching strategies: cooperative learning, hands-on learning, and learning centers. Interactive teaching is preferable for all students and not just English Language Learners. A teacher, however, who uses interactive teaching strategies creates optimal conditions for second language acquisition. ELLs can use newly acquired language by interacting with their peers and thus using language in a natural context. The anxiety of learning a second or third language is greatly reduced for students because the tone of the classroom is one of openness and communication among all learners. Interactive teaching benefits all learners in the K–12 grades.

Cooperative learning is an instructional organizational activity that permits students to work collaboratively in small groups to achieve academic and social learning. The chapter discussed the organization of cooperative groups in the classrooms and how to assign each student a specific role and task. Many specific cooperative learning strategies were explored: brainstorming, think-pair-share, numbered heads, round-robin, jigsaw, number wheel, and response boards. The value of cooperative learning as an assessment tool for teachers was also highlighted in this chapter.

Hands-on teaching strategies that enable students to manipulate things while learning was the second teaching strategy addressed. The value of learning centers was the final teaching strategy discussed in this chapter. Learning centers are areas that provide additional resources and materials for all students needing additional challenges or additional reteaching. The configuration of the classroom setting for centers was explained. The chapter ended with specific tips for elementary, middle school, and high school teachers for incorporating interactive teaching strategies.

REFLECTIVE CHAPTER QUESTIONS

1. What are the advantages of using interactive teaching strategies for all students?
2. Why do interactive teaching strategies specifically benefit English Language Learners?
3. How does cooperative learning specifically benefit English Language Learners?
4. What difficulties do you perceive a beginning teacher might encounter with classroom discipline management when organizing and working with students in groups? Reflect on how best to support beginning teachers who are learning new teaching strategies.
5. Discuss the value and importance of hands-on teaching in all classrooms. How would you persuade a traditional teacher who likes students to be silent to use a more hands-on teaching approach in the classroom?

SUGGESTED FIELD-BASED ACTIVITIES FOR PRE-SERVICE AND IN-SERVICE TEACHERS

1. Visit a classroom and observe a teacher who uses a lot of interactive teaching strategies. Document the specific strategies the teacher uses and observe the reactions of the students.
2. Select one cooperative learning component discussed in this chapter. Plan a lesson for a specific grade level and subject content area using one cooperative learning component of your choice. If possible, conduct the lesson and reflect on how you did. Keep practicing the component until you feel comfortable with it. When you have mastered a component, choose another one to incorporate into a chosen lesson or subject area. Reflect daily by keeping a journal or log of your experiences.

REFERENCES

Banks, J. (2006). *Cultural diversity and education: Foundations, curriculum, and teaching* (5th ed.). Boston: Allyn & Bacon.

Cummins, J. (1996). *Negotiating identities: Education for empowerment in a diverse society.* Covina, CA: CABE.

Cummins, J. (2001). *Language, power, and pedagogy: Bilingual children in the crossfire.* Bristol, PA: Multilingual Matters Limited.

Curtin, E. M. (2002). *Students' and teachers' perceptions of culturally responsive teaching: Urban middle school case study.* Dissertation: University of North Texas. Electronic dissertation available at http://www.unt.edu/library.htm.

Curtin, E. M. (2005). Instructional styles used by regular classroom teachers while teaching recently mainstreamed ESL students: Six urban middle school teachers in Texas share their experiences and perceptions. *Multicultural Education, 12*(4), 36–42.

Curtin, E. M. (2006a). *Effective teaching practices from [the perspective of] English language learners.* Paper presentation for American Educational Research Association (AERA), San Francisco.

Curtin, E. M. (2006b). Lessons on effective teaching from middle school ESL students. *Middle School Journal, 37*(3), 38–45.

Gay, G. (2000). *Culturally responsive teaching: Theory, research, and practice.* New York: Teachers College Press.

Grant, C. A., & Sleeter, C. E. (2007). *Turning on learning: Five approaches for multicultural teaching plans for race, class, gender and disability* (4th ed.). Hoboken, NJ: Wiley–Jossey-Bass Education.

Johnson, D., & Johnson, R. (1984). *Circles of learning.* Washington, D.C.: Association for Supervision and Curriculum Development.

Kagan, S. (1997). *Cooperative learning.* San Clemente, CA: Kagan Cooperative Learning.

Kellough, R. D., & Kellough, N. G. (2007). *Secondary school teaching: A guide to methods and resources* (3th ed.). Upper Saddle River, NJ: Pearson Merrill Prentice Hall.

Kohn, A. (1992). *No contest: The case against competition* (rev. ed.). New York: Mariner Books.

Kohn, A. (2000). *The case against standardized testing.* Portsmouth, NH: Heineman.

Krashen, S. (1985). *The input hypothesis: Issues and implications.* London: Longman.

Krashen, S. (2004). *The acquisition of academic English by children in two-way programs: What does the research say?* Paper presented at the National Association of Bilingual Education Conference, February 2004, Albuquerque.

Marzano, R. J. (2004). *Classroom instruction that works: Research-based strategies for increasing student achievement.* Upper Saddle River, NJ: Prentice Hall.

Nieto, S. (2001). *Language, culture, and teaching: Critical perspectives for a new century.* Mahwah, NJ: TF-LEA.

Nieto, S., & Bode, P. (2007). *Affirming diversity: The sociopolitical context of multicultural education* (5th ed.). Boston, MA: Allyn & Bacon.

CHAPTER 6 Teaching Academic Content to English Language Learners

INTRODUCTION

Teaching academic content to English Language Learners is the most challenging aspect of a teacher's job. It is also the most vital part of teaching since it became federally mandated under No Child Left Behind (2001), which requires that all English Language Learners be taught English using grade-level academic content. The teaching strategies presented in this chapter are based on Specially Designed Academic Instruction in English (SDAIE, California State Department of Education, 1994). SDAIE is also referred to as Sheltered Instruction (SI) (Schifini, 1985). Sheltered Instruction is research-based and proven to be effective for teaching English language skills within grade-level content (Echevarria & Graves, 2006). This chapter provides the beginning teacher with an overview of these instructional strategies for English Language Learners. This chapter also includes specific teaching strategies for teaching English Language Learners using the Cognitive Academic Language Learning Approach, commonly referred to by its acronym, CALLA (Chamot & O'Malley, 1994).

The focus of this chapter will be general strategies applicable to all content subject areas. Chapter 7 will address strategies more specific to the four major subject content areas: language arts, math, social studies, and science.

Focus Questions

◇ What is academic content?
◇ What are the requirements for teaching academic content to English Language Learners under No Child Left Behind?
◇ How can English Language Learners be taught academic content at various levels of English proficiency?

Classroom Scenario

Mr. O'Connor is a first-year teacher who successfully completed an alternative certification program. New to teaching, Mr. O'Connor changed professions due to his overwhelming desire to reach the lives of young people and to make a difference. Previously he had been an architect, so he is not new to a working environment.

Mr. O'Connor has an extensive background in math and science, so he's very excited about getting his students motivated to excel in these two fields. He will be teaching fifth grade and will have a high proportion of English Language Learners in his regular classroom.

Mr. O'Connor understands his responsibility to teach *academic content* to his students in addition to reading and language skills. Already, after six weeks of teaching, he knows that many of his students are struggling with reading the science, social studies, and math texts, and he wants to figure out a better approach. He has observed that his students get frustrated easily, and he knows they have a difficult time comprehending what they are reading. The task of trying to explain scientific terms to students is an arduous one, and he struggles to help them understand the intricacies and hidden nuances of the English language.

Mr. O'Connor notices that his ELL students are easily discouraged when attempting to read the assigned science and social studies textbooks, and he doesn't know why. They have a tendency to get off-task, or appear to develop a glossy-eyed look, or moan noticeably when told to take out their science or social studies book. Mr. O'Connor feels he's on the right track because he's using a lot of *hands-on teaching* techniques as well as *cooperative learning* methods, but fears when his ELL students finally take the standardized tests, they will have to read and comprehend passages on their own and will not have the advantage of being able to work in pairs or in groups.

In order for his students to become more independent readers, Mr. O'Connor knows they must develop essential reading skills and comprehension strategies of their own. He also understands he must continue, as best he can, to reach his students and not give up. He knows all too well his responsibility to make the content subject both *comprehensible and understandable* for his students. He is also cognizant of the need to teach fifth-grade academic content even though some students are currently reading below the fifth-grade level.

CLASSROOM SCENARIO 1

Let's observe Mr. O'Connor teaching a science lesson. The subject of his lesson is "mixtures and solutions." The objective of the lesson is for students to understand each of the following:

1. A *mixture* consists of "two or more substances blended together while keeping their own properties and not turning into a new substance" (*McGraw-Hill Science*, 2000, p. 338).
2. Mixtures are created by means of physical combinations (*McGraw-Hill Science*, 2000).
3. Components within mixtures will retain their own unique properties (*McGraw-Hill Science*, 2000).
4. A *solution* "is a mixture in which substances are completely blended so their properties remain the same throughout while the substances remain blended" (*McGraw-Hill Science*, 2000, p. 338).

Mr. O'Connor asks his students to open their *McGraw-Hill Science* books to page 338. On the chalkboard he writes a list of science terms along with their corresponding definitions. As he finishes writing, he clearly pronounces each word, knowing many in his class are new English Language Learners, followed by reading each definition. Using the prompt given in the teacher's edition of the textbook he asks his students, "Why do people call the Mississippi River the Muddy Mississippi? Please look at the picture of the Mississippi River in your textbooks."

Hanh, a fifth-grade student, is in her third year of school in the United States and has been making very good progress. Her English is at an intermediate level, but she has difficulty learning new vocabulary words associated with science. Although she enjoys science itself, she often finds herself overwhelmed by the new vocabulary she is required to learn. She likes the experiments Mr. O'Connor organizes and demonstrates, but she has significant difficulty writing in her science journal because she doesn't comprehend as well as she should.

Hanh is listening to Mr. O'Connor but she has no idea what the Mississippi is, and only after looking at a picture in her book does she realize it must be a river. Now she tries to figure out how it relates to the science lesson for the day.

Without any response from the class to his opening question Mr. O'Connor proceeds by explaining that the spot where the Mississippi River meets the Gulf of Mexico is called the Mississippi Delta. He goes on to explain that the water from the river has been carrying soil and silt, and at this point it drops much of what it is carrying, thus creating the area known as the Mississippi Delta. "Therefore," he continues, "the Mississippi is made up of many things that are mixed together."

First he writes on the board, "A *mixture* is two or more substances mixed together but not chemically combined." Then he asks his students to write this definition in their science journals.

With a puzzled look on her face, Hanh copies the definition from the board and underlines the word "mixture." Upon seeing her expression Mr. O'Connor begins to wonder if his students truly understand the lesson. Determined to find out, he asks the class to give him examples of other mixtures, but gets no response. Mr. O'Connor begins to feel frustrated. He is doing his best to communicate with his students; he is speaking slowly, writing on the board, and pointing to illustrations in the textbook—but all to no avail.

Guiding Discussion Questions

◇ What is the greatest teaching challenge facing Mr. O'Connor in his fifth-grade classroom?
◇ What academic and language difficulties are the English Language Learners experiencing?

Author's Insight

Realizing that his previous example using the Mississippi River did not help connect his students to the concept of "mixture," Mr. O'Connor must now find a way to do so using the prior experiences of his students. This time he will use a different approach. Luckily for Mr. O'Connor, while planning this lesson the previous week, and using the knowledge he gained in his teacher preparation program about the importance of preplanning (discussed in Chapter 4 of this book), he has a contingency approach available to use!

CLASSROOM SCENARIO 2

Mr. O'Connor's Fifth-Grade Science Lesson Continues

 AUTHOR'S INSIGHT Please note the particular strategies he incorporates and how he tweaks and adjusts the lesson upon reflection to make it more comprehensible to the language level of his students.

Mr. O'Connor erases the board. He writes "cake mix" and asks the class if they have ever seen these words before.

Hanh proudly raises her hand and states, "Sir, I see my mom make a cake from stuff in a box."

"What is in the box?" asks Mr. O'Connor.

Smiling, Hanh raises her hand again and says, "Many things together mixed up."

"Very good," says Mr. O'Connor. "Now think about the things that your mom might add to a cake mix so she can bake you a cake, then talk about it with your classroom partner."

Hanh and her partner, Giang, talk in Vietnamese about how their mothers make a cake, what they add to the cake mixture from the box, and how desserts have more than one ingredient.

After a few moments Mr. O'Connor asks everyone in the class to *brainstorm* and name some of the ingredients needed for making a cake from a cake mix. On chart paper he creates a list using the answers provided by his students, including flour, sugar, milk, eggs, water, butter, and oil. They discuss the difference between the dry and wet ingredients and the possibility of keeping the dry ingredients separate from the wet ingredients once they are together in a bowl. This allows Mr. O'Connor to introduce his students to the word "solution" and to ask his students to predict whether ingredients will or will not dissolve in the milk and oil. Using their predictions Mr. O'Connor creates a *graph* to show the ingredients.

Pleased with how the level of participation has changed, Mr. O'Connor reaches into a grocery bag and puts a variety of items on his desk. He passes one container to each group, containing a mixture of sugar, flour, cake mix, and chocolate chips in each. He also gives each group a set of plastic cups and a flour sifter.

Mr. O'Connor asks the class to separate the ingredients in the mixture as best they can as he walks around the room observing. He writes the word "mixture" on the board and beside it he writes "made up of two or more parts that can be separated and do not change." Now he asks his students to write the word "mixture" in their science journals along with his new, less complex definition that is much easier to understand than the one supplied by the textbook.

 AUTHOR'S INSIGHT: The actual textbook definition is: "A *mixture* consists of two or more substances blended together yet keeping their own properties and not turning into a new substance" (*McGraw-Hill Science*, p. 338).

Mr. O' Connor now asks the students to mix everything back together again and this time add hot water to their mixtures and observe what happens. They watch as the flour changes, the sugar dissolves, and the chocolate chips soften. As they continue to mix the ingredients together he asks, "Is this now a mixture? Can you separate the parts? Can you go back and separate each part back into the cups you had at the beginning?"

"Don't answer now," he says, "but instead discuss this with your group and come up with some answers."

The students spend time discussing the assignment and sharing their answers. They agree that the mixture now in their bowl cannot be separated back into its original ingredients.

"Does anyone know a word we could use to describe something that melts or dissolves into something else?" Mr. O'Connor asks the class.

Although he doesn't get the response he is looking for, his students have come up with words like "liquid" and "dissolved." He is pleased that they are thinking and verbalizing their thoughts even though they didn't come up with the correct word.

Writing "solution" on the blackboard, Mr. O'Connor says, "In science we call this a *solution*, because the flour and the sugar and the chocolate are all blended together and cannot be separated." As the students write "solution" and its definition in their science journals, he asks them to come up with examples of solutions they eat or drink every day. Again, they brainstorm (out loud) as a class, and Mr. O'Connor writes their answers on a chart.

Mr. O'Connor gives each group an envelope containing pictures of items that are mixtures, pictures of items that are solutions, and some that are neither. Students are asked to talk and discuss the pictures in their groups and to separate the pictures into two categories: solutions or mixtures. Mr. O'Connor walks around the room observing the progress of his students and asking them questions about their selections. Based on his initial observations, Mr. O'Connor assesses that all students are able to demonstrate an understanding of the difference between a mixture and a solution.

Mr. O'Connor writes the word "substance" on the board and explains, "Sugar is a substance." He asks his students for other examples of substances they've worked with and hands shoot up everywhere. His students eagerly tell him, "Salt, pepper, Kool-Aid, flour," and so on.

He then writes the definition of "solution" on the blackboard, once again making the language less complex than the one provided in the text: "Substances that dissolve or blend together make a solution." (The textbook definition is: "A solution is a mixture in which substances are completely blended so that the properties are the same throughout and the substances stay blended," McGraw-Hill Science, p. 338.)

Later that day during his planning time, Mr. O'Connor reflected on this lesson and realized he spent more time than expected explaining mixtures and solutions. He also felt justified for doing so since the students needed additional time to properly connect the scientific concepts to their personal experiences.

Tomorrow he will introduce his students to some new substances, including iron fillings, sand, salt, iron sulfide, and iron disulfide, as well as explore the concept of mixtures and chemical reactions. As a backup plan he plans to use baking and raising agents if his students need another example instead of disulfide. He plans to explain how compounds are produced by chemically combining substances to form a new substance. He's excited about tomorrow's lesson because his students are becoming more responsive to his teaching examples.

Guiding Discussion Questions

◇ What strategies did Mr. O'Connor employ to ensure that students understood the concept of mixtures and solutions?

⬦ Was this strategy more effective than his strategy in scenario 1? Why do you think this is so?

⬦ What academic language seemed to pose the most difficulty for his students?

Author's Insight

Mr. O'Connor is teaching *academic content* to students by *adapting the lesson* to meet their linguistic needs. He is teaching formal speech patterns to help prepare his students for college and success in life. He taught students the required academic vocabulary by relating it to their household experiences so they could grasp it more easily than they could the example given in the textbook. This scenario demonstrates the importance of a teacher recognizing the frustrations his students deal with.

The scenario also demonstrates how to *lighten the linguistic language* so students can still comprehend the concept being taught. Although Mr. O'Connor used different examples than the one offered in the text and used words that were less complex, he still effectively taught fifth-grade scientific concepts. This lesson demonstrated the use of Sheltered Instruction (SI) techniques as follows:

⬦ The English Language Learners acquired new scientific vocabulary words concurrently with new scientific concepts.

⬦ The teacher connected the new concepts to the students' backgrounds by using the cake mix example instead of the Mississippi River example provided in the text.

⬦ The teacher used *realia* (actual objects) and provided *hands-on teaching materials* for the students to manipulate and use in order to explain the concepts of mixtures and solutions.

All the strategies used by the teacher in scenario 2 helped make the scientific concepts more comprehensible for all students.

WHAT RESEARCH TELLS US

What Is Academic Content?

The No Child Left Behind Act (2001) mandates that all English Language Learners learn English through academic content. There are now consequences for schools that do not meet state accountability levels and do not make adequate yearly progress with all students on state standardized tests. Teachers are now challenged to teach *on-grade-level academic content to English Language Learners*. This task is less challenging with younger ELL students because literacy is still in the emergent phase and there is less academic content. However, teaching academic content to older grade levels is more challenging due to the volume of content as well as their age of arrival in the United States. The combination of these factors makes teaching older English Language Learners more critical since they are in danger of falling behind more easily and ultimately dropping out of school (National Center for Education Statistics, 2007).

In the past many English Language Learners spent numerous years in pullout programs, segregated from mainstream classrooms, and missing out on valuable academic content. Fortunately, schools in the United States are moving away from ESL pullout programs and moving toward Sheltered Instruction within the mainstream classroom.

The teaching of academic English requires a teacher to be very familiar with the content and have the ability to present it in a way that is *comprehensible* and relates to the backgrounds and experiences of the students. Teachers must anticipate in advance any vocabulary and phrases that are new or could be problematic for students (Echevarria & Graves, 2006).

Teachers must be able to differentiate between *social language* (BICS) and *academic language* (CALPS). The ability to have a conversation about the weather, likes and dislikes, and everyday social activities is very different from the academic language required for academic subjects in school. Academic language requires the ability to compare, contrast, classify, order, define, infer, summarize, discuss, evaluate, deduce, justify, and synthesize at a more complex level than is required for social language (Cummins & Hornberger, 2001).

Research by Cummins and Hornberger (2001) demonstrates that it takes anywhere from 6 to 8 years to fully develop *CALPS*. This level of cognitive academic language can only be developed though academic content while students progress successfully though school and all their academic subjects. CALPS is a necessary prerequisite for success in college. It is imperative for English Language Learners who come to the United States at the age of 10 and older to learn English and academic content quickly. At the high school level, academic language is in fast development and even presents a challenge for native English speakers. By using Sheltered Instruction (SI) the teacher plays a vital role in the academic success of English Language Learners (SDAIE, 1994).

Why Teach English Through Content?

The answer is quite simple: It is now federal law. Under No Child Left Behind, teachers must provide the same curriculum for all English Language Learners. The teacher must make curriculum requirements *comprehensible* to the English Language Learner by using research-based instructional strategies like Sheltered ESL and scaffolding techniques. English Language Learners must be exposed to academic content while learning English in order to ensure they do not fall behind academically. Students who do not fall behind academically are more likely to be successful and stay in school (No Child Left Behind Act, 2001).

Another reason for teaching English through academic content is that modern research proves teaching English via content is more effective than teaching grammar and vocabulary in isolation. There is sufficient proven educational research to demonstrate that English Language Learners don't have to wait until they've acquired basic English skills to acquire content (Chamot & O'Malley, 1994; Cummins & Hornberger, 2001; Echevarria & Graves, 2006). It is also possible to teach English while teaching math, science, reading and social studies. Teaching English through academic content provides a context for learning that is more meaningful for students. Thus science vocabulary taught within the context of a science class and math vocabulary taught within the context of mathematical problem solving are easier to understand. English taught through content ensures the language is being taught within its naturally occurring context (Brown, 2006).

It is possible to teach English through content provided that the teacher uses Sheltered Instruction strategies as highlighted in this textbook. It is possible for students to get the "gist" of what is going on in a lesson and still comprehend at their own level of language (Chamot & O'Malley, 1994). Using Sheltered Instruction strategies ensures that English Language Learners will not fall behind academically and will be able to stay current with grade-level content. Teaching English through academic content also ensures ELL students a better opportunity to pass state standardized tests.

How to Teach Academic Content to English Language Learners

It is important for teachers to understand that English Language Learners' *expressive language* and *rates of production* are going to appear latent for a while (Cummins, 1977, 1979). During this latent phase the teacher must recognize that students are still capable of comprehending and understanding the concepts being taught if they are presented in a manner that is at their language level and is comprehensible to them (SDAIE, 1994). This is why the use of Specially Designed Academic Instruction in English—sheltered language instruction—is vital if students are to acquire English language skills while understanding new academic concepts at the same time (SDAIE, 1994).

There are many terms used in academic literature such as "scaffolding models," "sheltered instruction," and "specially designed academic instruction in English" (SDAIE), and they are all synonymous in their instructional purpose: to teach English through academic content. There is no one particular strategy for teaching English through content, but rather a whole variety of strategies. The teacher can pick and choose in this range of strategies the ones that work best within the context of subject matter, age level of students, and English language levels (Echevarria, Vogt, & Short, 2004). *Interactive teaching* is a necessary component for the teaching of English Language Learners, and it should be an integral part of every lesson (Curtin,

2006). English Language Learners should be supported linguistically by a caring and patient teacher and should be provided multiple speaking opportunities daily in class. Students who are encouraged to speak and interact with their classes will develop their academic language faster by using and practicing their English. Furthermore, teachers need to understand the importance of allowing language errors, which will encourage rather than discourage the English Language Learners to continue using speech by trial and error. *Error acceptance* helps create a safe and psychologically supportive classroom environment for English Language Learners (Krashen & Terrell, 1983).

Figure 6.1 provides a summary of Sheltered Instruction practices that may be used by teachers. Figure 6.2 provides a summary of general strategies that are research based and used to teach English Language Learners across all subject areas. These strategies are explained in the Classroom Application section.

The use of one or more of the strategies detailed in Figure 6.2 will add a vital component to teaching content-area subjects. Content-area subjects rely heavily on academic language. Academic language also relies on the assumptions that students have the ability to read, process, and comprehend information independently. Additionally, the use of academic language requires the ELL student to use higher level oral language skills and to understand explanations and directions given in class. The positive news is that it's possible to develop academic language in English Language Learners (Chamot, Barnhardt, Beard El-Dinary, & Robbins, 1999).

FIGURE 6.1   Summary of Key Teaching Strategies for English through Content

- Students should learn **English** always in conjunction with **content** and never in isolation.
- English should be used in its naturally occurring **context,** i.e., students should be learning science words in science, math words in math, etc.
- Even when language production is difficult for students, they should be encouraged to **use language in class** by providing them with cues and words if necessary. Get students to talk about their projects, support students by having them work with a partner, and always accept their language errors. Focus on content and not language errors.
- Try to teach and use acquired **reading skills across grade levels.** Consider using excerpts from science and social studies to teach reading skills like sequence, main ideas, etc. Use these subjects as a means of teaching vital reading and standardized testing skills. Reading skills are an integral part of all subjects, a required prerequisite for academic success.
- **New vocabulary** should be **introduced** and practiced, in all subjects **daily.** Devote the beginning part of each lesson to specific vocabulary and language development.
- Consider themes that **connect with cultural backgrounds and experiences of students.** For example, consider changing lesson examples provided in students' text to ones that better connect with their experiences and backgrounds.

FIGURE 6.2 Research-Based Sheltered Instruction Strategies for Teaching English Language Learners in Content Areas

Specially Designed Academic Instruction in English (**SDAIE**) is also referred to as Sheltered Instruction (**SI**) in research literature. **SI** encourages the teacher to provide instruction in English with lots of cues and scaffolding to make the content understandable for English Language Learners.

Sheltered Instruction (SI) Strategies:

1. **MODIFYING TEXTS:** Teacher rewrites texts **without diluting the content**. Teacher makes English language less complex without altering content or meaning (Short, 1991). Teacher may eliminate extra words in a text, use graphs or graphics to organize information in a simpler manner. Teacher can find comparable texts, with similar content written at a lower reading level.

2. **LIGHTENING LINGUISTIC LOAD:** Teacher is careful with use of language in both oral and written form. Teacher adheres to **more active rather than passive voice** when speaking. Teacher avoids the use of synonyms and pronouns.

3. **TOTAL PHYSICAL RESPONSE (TPR):** Teacher gives tasks and directions to students. Students complete tasks or actions without using language, e.g., open your book to page 18, stand up and go to the door, etc. Teachers can use TPR during student's silent phase.

4. **TEACHER SCAFFOLDING TECHNIQUES:** Anything teacher does to make content more understandable. Some examples include using visuals, realia, hands-on, drama, examples, finished models, repetition, error acceptance, tape recording, signals or cues, outlining materials, graphic organizers, rubrics, templates, vocabulary in bold face, KWL charts.

5. **USING THEMES:** The teacher uses a theme that is interesting to students (e.g., my family, my pets, around the world, etc.) to connect with their backgrounds. The theme should connect as much as possible to all content subject areas. Themes may last 1–2 weeks in younger grades and as long as 4–6 weeks in older grades.

6. **COGNITIVE ACADEMIC LANGUAGE LEARNING APPROACH (CALLA):** Teacher teaches **self-study strategies.** Students who have more developed self-study and self-learning strategies achieve more academic success (Chamot & O' Malley, 1994). Teacher models and teaches students to do the following for themselves: scan and summarize reading passages by Generating Interaction between Schemata and Text (GIST); rehearsal strategies for acquiring new vocabulary and concepts; using graphs to organize and synthesize information; graphic organizers; semantic feature analysis; KWL charts; list and leave, etc.

7. **DIFFERENTIATED INSTRUCTION:** Teacher plans lesson for various learning modalities; visual, auditory, kinesthetic. Teacher provides information in a variety of ways.

CLASSROOM APPLICATION STRATEGIES

Developing Academic Language, Formal and Informal Speech Registers

We all use *informal speech registers* when we communicate with our families and loved ones. We use more *formal speech registers* in situations like job interviews, making a presentation to a group, or giving a speech. Teachers must help students understand the differences between the two registers and the importance of the formal register for their future academic success.

Examples of informal speech registers include:

◇ "You're wrong."
◇ "I don't agree with you."
◇ "Where's she at?"
◇ "I'm fixin' to . . ."

Examples of formal speech registers include:

◇ "I disagree with you for this reason . . ."
◇ "I tend to disagree with you for the following reasons . . ."
◇ "I do not concur with your assessment of the situation."
◇ "My perspective differs from yours in the following respects . . ."
◇ "Where is she at this time?"
◇ "I am about to embark upon . . ."

Implementing Sheltered Instruction (SI)/Specially Designed Academic Instruction in English (SDAIE)

See Figure 6.2 for an outline and brief summary.

Implementing SI/SDAIE is not about one single teaching approach but instead is a *collection of many strategies*. Using some, any, or all of the strategies that will be explained in the next section constitutes using the best known research-based instructional strategies for English Language Learners.

Sheltered Instruction strategies require teachers to plan all lessons carefully in advance. Teachers of all grade levels must collect resources and materials for each lesson that involve the use of visuals, pictures, and realia. They must choose literature, examples, and experiences that connect with the unique cultural backgrounds of students. Consideration should also be given to planning backup and "plan B" options as Mr. O'Connor did in classroom scenario 2 at the beginning of this chapter.

SDAIE originates from the term "sheltered instruction" used by Schifini (1985). The SDAIE goal for the teacher is delivery of grade-level content instruction in a manner that is understandable and comprehensible for English Language Learners regardless of their level of English.

The main components teachers must be aware of when designing and implementing Specially Designed Academic Instruction in English (SDAIE) for ELL students are:

1. The teacher uses *standards* and objectives that are on grade level.
2. The teacher uses *cooperative grouping* and provides opportunities for students to discuss, brainstorm, collaborate, and use language skills.
3. The teacher uses instruction that is highly scaffolded (i.e., *visually and contextually supported lessons*) with the English Language Learner in mind. Vocabulary and difficult concepts must be identified at the beginning of the lesson for students so they have an opportunity to use and understand them.
4. The teacher must use *realia* (real objects) to support and explain the concepts of the lesson.
5. The teacher must provide *hands-on opportunities for students* in order for them to explore new concepts and language structures.
6. The teacher must ensure that *language and texts are simplified without minimizing the content* or the objectives of the lesson.
7. The teacher must use *a multidimensional form of assessment*, more specifically, a combination of multiple-choice questions, true-false questions, essay questions, performance, and authentic tests (see Chapter 8 for more detail on multidimensional assessment).
8. The teacher must use *multiple sources of data* to assess the knowledge and comprehension levels of ELL students.

Sheltered Instruction Teaching Strategies

Modifying Texts

Short (1991) and other researchers have developed numerous strategies and techniques that teachers can use to modify the language of textbooks. Upon close inspection of any grade-level textbook used by a school or school district today, one will discover a level of English language that is not easily comprehensible for students, and most especially for those learning English. As a result it has become necessary for teachers like Mr. O'Connor in the classroom scenario to modify definitions in such textbooks for the benefit of their English Language Learner students. It is also possible for teachers to find texts with similar content written at a simpler linguistic level for English Language Learners.

Figure 6.3 provides suggestions for modifying language without diluting content. Although modifying text is a very time-consuming task for most teachers, it is a necessary component if one is to successfully teach academic content to English Language Learners.

FIGURE 6.3   Modifying Texts

Here are **guidelines for teachers** for rewriting texts (Short, 1991):
- Provide similar vocabulary and use same definition repeatedly.
- Find topic sentence and modify and list the supporting details.
- Look at vocabulary words being used and provide simpler synonyms.
- Make sentences shorter (10 words or less).
- Keep the same key words and avoid using synonyms.
- Look at the use of adjectives. Do they add to meaning or are they there for more expressive ornamentation?
- Use simple verb tenses, e.g., past, present, and future and avoid the use of all others.
- Use the imperative form of the verb.
- Use active and not passive voice.
- Avoid words like "there, it, and that" at beginning of sentences.
- Avoid relative clauses like "who, whom, which" in sentences, instead consider breaking into two shorter sentences.
- Use "not" carefully and avoid using "no longer, hardly, and almost never."
- Avoid using idiomatic phrases.
- Have a planned sequence of introducing transition words like "although, however" and priority words like "important, best of all, the least likely." Gradually introduce sequence words like "first, second" carefully.

AUTHOR'S INSIGHT: Textbook adaptations are only meant to support state curriculum and should not constitute classroom curriculum. Textbooks are an instructional resource used to support the state curriculum. In many cases certain text, including vocabulary definitions, may require modification in terms of length and language in order to teach content at a more language-appropriate level for English Language Learners. Use the suggestions provided in Figure 6.3 as a checklist. Use them to help modify your language while teaching, and to modify language written in too complex an academic manner. This strategy will reduce the frustration level of your English Language Learners, will make you more conscious of your spoken language, and will ensure that ELL students are able to comprehend without being overwhelmed by intricate language.

Lightening the Linguistic Load

Use of the strategies listed in Figure 6.3 should help enhance a teacher's ability to verbally communicate with ELL students. Those strategies plus those that follow will help support the language comprehension levels of the English Language Learners in the classroom. **Teachers must:**

◇ *Speak slowly* and carefully enunciate all words.
◇ *Limit the use of contractions* like "that isn't so," or confusing statements like "that is not so."
◇ Be sure to avoid using the same vocabulary word for different purposes and *avoid using synonyms* whenever possible. English is a very complex

language with one word having many different meanings, depending on the context and how it's used. For example, "service" can be used in conjunction with food, automobiles, military, government, and tennis. In other languages, words may have only one meaning regardless of context.

◇ *Limit pronouns* and use the whole word or the name of the objects, people, or things each time you use it.

◇ Use *active voice* rather than passive voice. Instead of "John was beaten by Paul in the race," say, "Paul won the race," or "Paul beat John."

◇ Purposely try to *make sentences short* and succinct.

◇ Stop and regularly check to see if students understand during a lesson. *Look for non-verbal clues* (making faces, shaking their head, shrugging their shoulders).

◇ *Ask students to restate* in their own words, using mime, showing, or pointing, whatever is appropriate.

◇ *Do not accept a nod as acknowledgement they understand.* Over time, English Language Learners become very good at doing this with the hope a teacher will assume it means the student comprehends.

◇ If possible try to *have a model, picture, graphic, or actual object (realia)* you can point to or refer to.

◇ When possible *mime or act out* what you are saying.

◇ *Draw or write* while talking at the same time.

All the strategies listed above provide extra cues for comprehension that can assist English Language Learners in the classroom. Remember that English Language Learners must focus their attention and concentration on listening to what's being said and then comprehending it, which takes more time. Because this level of comprehension can be an arduous task, it is quite common for the ELL students to tune out the teacher while they attempt to figure out what's being said. If the teacher proceeds too quickly or doesn't stop occasionally to ask if everyone understands, the students fall behind, get frustrated, and tire of the class. The teacher who provides verbal and linguistic cues will help English Language Learners remain focused and motivated in class.

Total Physical Response (TPR) for English Language Learners

TPR or Total Physical Response is attributed to the research of Asher (1972). Asher, a psychologist, discovered people are more likely to learn a second language with less psychological stress if they physically do something while they're listening and learning. Doing while listening and learning is the underlying premise for Total Physical Response.

In the classroom a teacher can give directives like "Stand up" or "Open your book to page 16," and students don't need to verbally respond. They only need to demonstrate their comprehension by actually carrying out the teacher's oral directives. **TPR** is a very valuable teaching strategy for use with English Language Learners, who are normally in the *early silent phase* and the *beginning production language phase.* Use of written directives on cards or a visual are also helpful to use at this stage of students' English language development.

Once students respond to verbal commands, a *picture with the word written below it* can be used. This can be followed by *writing the word* by itself on the board. Once students have mastered simple commands, the teacher can expand sentences into more detailed sentences using additional adjectives and a more extensive vocabulary.

Total Physical Response (TPR) can be used with practically any classroom subject from "How I get up in the morning," to "How I set up the lab area for science," to "How I apply for a job." TPR is a very useful way to teach a second language, and it has proven to be especially successful with English Language Learners. All age levels respond quite well to this teaching method, provided that teachers create a classroom environment that is psychologically comfortable and safe, and one that is conducive to the needs of the students.

Teacher Scaffolding Techniques

The term "scaffolding" is attributed to the work of Lev Vygotsky (1978), a Russian psychologist, who found that learning and cognitive development occur when a student is in what is termed the "zone of proximal development." This zone requires a teacher who supports or scaffolds the learner's move to a higher level of learning. The role of the teacher in scaffolding an English Language Learner is to:

◇ Supply *experiences* and activities as part of the learning process.
◇ *Teach* using active instruction which requires direct interaction with the student.
◇ Provide learning *support* for the students (visuals, hands-on materials, demonstrations, examples, etc.).
◇ Ensure that the English Language Learner will progress to a higher level.

Figure 6.4 provides some examples of scaffolding techniques that effective teachers can use while teaching English Language Learners.

Using Themes to Organize Instruction

Jean Piaget (1969) postulates that students learn best while connecting new ideas to concepts already known to them (existing schemata). New information is better understood and retained if it connects with already existing schema. Mr. O'Connor demonstrated this in classroom scenario 2 when he connected the science lesson about mixtures and solutions to a cooking example that was familiar to his students.

It is always important for the teacher to consider experiences that students may have already experienced and then connect them, when possible, to the subject content.

Student Self-Study and Cognitive Academic Language Learning Approach (CALLA) Strategies

There is much research supporting the notion that many culturally and linguistically diverse students find U.S. schools culturally alienating. Many English

FIGURE 6.4 Teaching Scaffolding Techniques for English Language Learners

Assist/scaffold students in learning new material:
- Use visuals and pictures to point to.
- Use realia.
- Provide hands-on manipulatives for students.
- Incorporate dramatic techniques in lessons.
- Provide a finished model or example for students to see (Curtin, 2006).
- Repeat words.
- Be empathetic, tolerant of error acceptance, tape record lessons, modify tests, modify language of textbooks.
- Signal and provide cues.
- Provide a predictable daily schedule for students.
- Let students know where to ask for help.
- Provide a visual outline for lectures and lessons.
- Provide students with a copy of lecture outline.
- Provide flashcards and pictures for new words.
- Use graphic organizers to introduce new material or concepts.
- Provide opportunities to practice in groups.
- Plan to reteach and plan to provide additional learning support for students in centers.
- Provide the opportunity to follow steps in writing process, i.e., rough drafts, edits, peer edits, and final publication.
- Share grading rubrics with students so they know standards and criteria being used for evaluation (see Chapter 8 for more details on rubrics).
- Introduce and explain new vocabulary words. Provide opportunities for students to practice and rehearse newly acquired words.
- Lighten linguistic load for student by modifying texts and examples in books as needed.
- Use KWL charts.
- Use example congruent with experience level of students.

Language Learners find attending school to be meaningless and cannot connect with the U.S. cultural expectations required of them to be successful in school (Banks, 2006).

Studies by Chamot and O'Malley (1994) demonstrate that English Language Learners who do well academically are learners who possess a lot of *self-study and cognitive learning strategies* to assist them in their own learning. English Language Learners must continue to develop their own strategies not only to acquire academic English but also to acquire the necessary content needed to be successful in school. These students, once taught active learning strategies that they can apply to their own learning, are more likely to stay in school and make academic gains. Students possessing learning strategies are usually more self-reliant and self-motivated in the classroom.

The teacher has a responsibility to teach all students learning strategies they can use for the rest of their lives. Teaching metacognitive strategies like CALLA (Chamot & O'Malley, 1994) helps students to manage their work, monitor their activities, self-motivate themselves, and become independent learners. *Metacognitive* means to think about learning. Students who possess metacognitive strategies can evaluate what they've learned and how they learned it; and students will continue using those learning strategies that work for them. Students have a tendency to learn metacognitive strategies from effective teachers who can actively demonstrate, model, and teach these learning strategies. Then these strategies can be applied to all subject areas.

Teaching Metacognitive Strategies

"Metacognition" is defined as thinking about thinking. The teacher can teach these skills to students so they will become an innate part of the student. Chamot and O'Malley (1994) surveyed students from diverse language backgrounds and asked them to share what they did to learn new information and how they processed difficult information. Their research results proved that students who achieved higher scores academically possessed more strategies than did those students who were less successful academically. Chamot and O'Malley (1994) refer to these combined strategies as the Cognitive Academic Language Learning Approach (CALLA). These strategies are classified under three main areas, (1) metacognitive, (2) cognitive, and (3) social affective. All these strategies can be modeled by the teacher and explicitly taught to students in all subject areas.

Metacognitive strategies are what the student needs in order to *plan* for learning, success, time management, and self-monitoring. The student must learn how to focus, plan for learning, adjust learning, and evaluate the effectiveness of his or her learning. When all students understand that success in learning is within their control and is attributable to their level of effort, then they become more self-efficacious (Bandura, 1986).

Once students are in junior high and high school they have developed more memory skills. With increased memory comes the increased ability to consciously select, describe, analyze, and discuss how they study, how they learn best, and what they need to do. This is a complex process. Students must be able to analyze how to approach a problem, how to adjust their mental performance in order to adapt the new information, and how to monitor their thinking. For example, students may have to learn strategies tailored to their own needs (i.e., first read, then reread, and then underline key words) in order to better comprehend. These metacognitive strategies are very important at the middle school and high school level.

Metacognitive strategies are controlled by the student. The teacher shows students how to organize and plan for the learning process. To be successful students must:

◇ Write down homework assignments and due dates in an organizer or planner.
◇ Plan adequate time for homework.
◇ Divide long-term assignments into shorter, more easily attainable ones.
◇ Set deadlines for completion of work.
◇ Keep a learning log or journal for notes on "what I understood," "what was difficult," and so on.
◇ Use assignment notebooks to file graded work, homework, separate subjects, and so on.

To help students, teachers should:

◇ Provide specific time at the beginning and end of each period for students to write down assignments and organize materials. Teachers should monitor this by walking around the room to ensure that students are doing it. (Note: Some students are more motivated to complete and update daily assignment sheets if given credit.)
◇ Give students verbal reminders.
◇ Develop a timeline for longer assignments or projects and have students submit drafts for review and approval.
◇ Supply a syllabus-type handout specifying the main concepts covered in a chapter, a project, a review for test, and so on.
◇ Provide a storage area in the classroom for review materials and ensure that students have access to such materials during free time in class.
◇ Provide students with organizational checklists for routine activities, materials needed, and steps to be followed.
◇ Have extra copies of materials and not punish any student for being disorganized (be patient). Punishing students for lack of materials only wastes time and creates a negative attitude toward assignments. Students need to know where extra materials are stored, have free (quiet) access to them; and not sit in class doing nothing because they do not have their materials.
◇ Have locker and desk organizational periods in which students can organize materials and file papers. Remember: Practice makes perfect.
◇ Talk with parents to ensure that students have a place to study homework and an agreed-upon, predictable routine for doing so.

Teaching Cognitive Strategies

Cognitive strategies are used by students to actively learn, rehearse, and connect new learning to their existing knowledge base. Cognitive strategies *connect new and old information* and enable the English Language Learner to use certain techniques to increase learning and retention of information, such as:

◇ Memorization techniques
◇ Connecting between their native language and English
◇ Looking for topic sentences
◇ Actively reading and comprehending
◇ Making graphic organizers and flowcharts, and reducing large chunks of information into a manageable size
◇ Creating outlines, notes for a test, using note cards, and categorizing information
◇ Using mnemonic devices, rhymes, songs, tricks for multiplication, formulas, lists, and so on

---

 AUTHOR'S INSIGHT: All these cognitive strategies can be taught to students at any grade level.

SQP2RS: An instructional framework for teaching content with expository texts (Vogt, 2000, 2002). This skill should be explicitly modeled by the teacher. After the teacher models it a few times, the students can practice step by step. Eventually the students should be able to do this on their own each time they have to read and summarize a lot of written materials. This skill can be applied across many content areas that require a lot of reading for research, knowledge, comprehension, evaluation, and synthesis.

Teach the students to:

1. **S**urvey (scanning the text for 1–2 minutes before reading it in detail)
2. **Q**uestion (students generate questions before reading the text)
3. **P**redict (what students think they'll discover)
4. **R**ead (searching for answers to questions— the teacher provides a story map and a list of questions to be answered)
5. **R**espond (finding answers; discussion and analysis of story)
6. **S**ummarize (orally, written, in a map format)

GIST—Generating Interaction between Schemata and Text **(Muth & Alvermann, 1999)**: This is a strategy to help students read long texts with a large volume of new information. The strategy helps students comprehend while reading the text. This skill can be modeled by the teacher and then explicitly taught to students beginning in third grade. It is a strategy for summarizing text.

Teach students to:

1. *Read* the text and *underline* the words or concepts that are most important.
2. Create *one or two sentences* that encompass all of these concepts.
3. *Repeat* the process until the entire passage has been read.
4. Write a *topic sentence* to precede the summary sentences.

Once students have completed the aforementioned steps, they have created a summary.

***Rehearsal Strategies* (Muth and Alvermann, 1999):** Students need the skill of memorization. Mnemonic or memory devices can be explicitly taught to students so they will retain timelines in social studies, scientific data, definitions, and so on.

Teach students to recall verbatim information as needed. Teach students to use flashcards, reduce information to important chunks of data, paraphrase, underline, take notes, and commit information to memory.

***Graphic Organizers*:** A graphic organizer is a visual frame used to represent and organize information and to show how concepts are related (McKenna & Robinson, 1997, 2005).

Teach students to use graphic organizers to properly summarize information. Model for students how to create Venn diagrams, T-charts, timelines, flowcharts, semantic maps, and so on. Teach students to use organizers to analyze and compare information and to maintain sequences of events.

Teach students to:

◇ Talk or write about information presented in a chart.
◇ Actively interact with text by referring, stopping, and self-checking for understanding using a graphic organizer.
◇ Sequence events in story or text.

***Semantic Feature Analysis*:** This strategy helps students understand new vocabulary words and concepts in a text using a grid (McKenna & Robinson, 2005). Students learn to develop word associations and to connect to their own prior knowledge.

Teach students to use a graphic method to list and analyze features, traits, and examples of a particular category or concept. This is useful in science or social studies classes (i.e., list the features and traits of certain animals). Students can set up a table or matrix and then check off the associated traits, use related vocabulary, add to the list of traits, and so on. The skill can also be used for more abstract relationships or for complex concepts such as forms of government, to compare and contrast, and so on.

***Rehearsing*:** Practicing newly acquired information or skills.

Teach students how to review, rehearse, repeat to someone else, reorganize information so it is clear to someone else, repeat orally, paraphrase, write down main points, create a map or table for comparing and contrasting, and so on.

KWL **(Ogle, 1986)**: KWL stands for, "What I know," "What I want to know," and "What I learned." An organizational chart modeled by teachers and used at the beginning of a new unit of study to determine what students know, what they want to know, and what they have learned after completing the unit of study.

Teach older students to use this organizational structure for reading informational texts. This is a useful device for any grade-level student and provides an excellent pre- and postassessment tool for teachers. KWL charts are an excellent teaching tool for connecting with the interests and cultural backgrounds of ELL students in relation to any given topic.

See-Through Study Sheets: Used to reteach concepts that ELL students have been exposed to. This technique provides immediate feedback, takes very little time to implement, can be easily created by the students themselves, and is inexpensive.

Teach students to:

◇ Buy a red college theme binder (acetate type),which effectively blocks out pink and yellow water-base highlighter pens.
◇ Write questions on cards using dark markers and answers in yellow or water-based highlighter markers.
◇ Place cards under the plastic theme cover. Only the problem written in black marker is visible.
◇ Pull out the card to reveal the answer. This provides immediate feedback to students and is an excellent way for them to develop rehearsal and study skills.

Paragraph Study Sheet: Can be used to glean main ideas and details from text and create a summary.

Teach students to find the following information each time they read new text and to find the relevant information. This will assist students to keep details as they are reading and will increase comprehension.

Teach students to find:

Topic sentence

_____

Supporting details

_____

Who?

_____

What?

_____

Where?

_____

When?

Why?

How?

List and Leave: A strategy for teaching students word meanings and context clues. Teach the students to fold a sheet of paper in half lengthwise and use it as a bookmark. When students come to a word they do not know, they list it and the page number on the bookmark. Students look at the context of how the word is used in the sentence, read around the word, and find clues to unlock the meaning of the word. Students then cross out the word when its meaning becomes clear. If students still don't understand the meaning they may leave the word and continue reading. When the reading assignment is finished, students can look up the meaning of any words left on the bookmark.

 AUTHOR'S INSIGHT: Explicitly teach strategies by modeling out loud. Introduce each model, name it, and have students practice it with you, then have students practice it independently for a set period of time. Then discuss how the model helped them, what worked, what did not work well, and so on.

 AUTHOR'S INSIGHT: Provide a visual model of the strategy and post it on a wall in the classroom. Model and teach learning strategies.

More Strategies

Provide students with study sheets and review outlines that can be used independently to guide student learning. Teachers should provide as many of the following as possible during class:

- ◇ List (write out on chart or poster) steps in math processes or lab activity so the student will know exactly what to do.
- ◇ When reading content, ask students to create their own study sheet by listing important people, memorable events, or interesting facts. Then have students list or describe the relationship between the items on their list.
- ◇ Have students write their own study questions after lectures, discussions, or reading assignments.
- ◇ Teach students to recognize key words in lectures and in written material to help guide their self-study.

◇ Provide examples that students can refer to during independent practice or study time.

◇ Teach students to recognize conclusion words such as: e.g., as a result, consequently, in addition, i.e., for instance, and so on.

◇ Provide multiplication or at-a-glance computational sheets during math practice, and study guides for tests.

◇ Consider using your classroom as a study hall before or after school for students who don't have a place to study at home, might have to work in the evening, or may not have the time for study at night. This also provides an opportunity for the teacher to tutor or work individually with students.

Social Affective Strategies

Social affective strategies provide students with the opportunity to work in groups, learn from others, and initiate contact with other sources and resources to better understand and learn. Social affective strategies develop *positive interdependence* for students by allowing them to interact with other students and use their language skills. Language is improved and developed by social interactions with groups and individuals. Asking questions for clarification and feedback are important strategies for teaching English Language Learners. Students who have developed social affective strategies reduce their own learning anxieties by knowing where help is available after school, by using individualized and group tutoring opportunities provided in school, and by learning to form their own study groups (Chamot & O'Malley, 1994).

Differentiated Instruction

Not all students are alike, think alike, or learn in similar fashion. The precept underlying differentiated instruction is that one method of teaching will not meet the needs of all students. Instead, a teacher who differentiates instruction structures teaching and learning so that students have multiple options for acquiring information, that is, the teacher provides choice in assignments, activities, and assessment. The teacher varies instructional approaches in each lesson to meet the variety of learning preferences in the classroom (Tomlinson, 2000).

Use the following techniques to accommodate for various different learning modalities:

Visual Learners

◇ Seat students who are known visual learners in close proximity to the teacher; ensure that visual aids can be easily seen.

◇ Always demonstrate and give examples.

◇ Model the skill being taught.

◇ Allow students to use a visual approach to reading. Be sure to include whole words, configurations, word families, and experience charts in the strategy.

◇ Obtain and use visual clues when lecturing.

◇ Let students use aids like a word list, a dictionary, outlines, lists, flashcards, rebus stories, charts, graphs, and tables.

◇ Teach students to take notes.

Auditory Learners

◇ Provide students both verbal and written directions (some English Language Learners prefer to hear directions rather than read them.)

◇ Record important reading material for students to listen to as they read a particular passage.

◇ Record directions for assignments so students can replay them when and as needed.

◇ Give oral tests rather than written ones.

◇ Record drills with your students so they can play them back on a recorder when needed.

◇ Have students read or drill by themselves, or have them read or drill one-on-one, or read to others.

Kinesthetic Learners

◇ Use classroom demonstrations whenever possible.

◇ Let students build a model instead of writing a report.

◇ Use role play or simulations.

◇ Teach students how to take notes.

◇ Allow students to draw or doodle.

◇ Allow students to move around while listening, (within reason) in the classroom.

◇ Use timelines and number lines.

◇ Use manipulatives.

◇ Use demonstrations. Model the subject for the students, walk through the steps, and use role play if possible.

 AUTHOR'S INSIGHT: English Language Learners are very adept and can express to you how they learn best. Ask them what you can do to teach them better, and they will tell you (Curtin, 2006).

CHAPTER SUMMARY

This chapter provided the theoretical rationale and research-based evidence supporting the reason why it is possible to teach ELL students English through regular academic subject content. Using Sheltered Instruction (SI) teaching strategies ensures that English Language Learners will understand and comprehend what is going in the regular classroom. Sheltered Instruction strategies are effective teaching strategies for all learners. All the teaching strategies presented in this chapter are applicable for all grade levels, but especially grades 3–12 and across all subject content areas.

The classroom application section explained how to teach academic language through content. Seven specific instructional sets of strategies were presented for practical classroom application purposes: (1) modifying texts, (2) lightening linguistic load, (3) Total Physical Response, (4) teacher scaffolding techniques, (5) using thematic instruction, (6) Cognitive Academic Language Learning Approach, and (7) differentiated instruction.

REFLECTIVE CHAPTER QUESTIONS

1. Using the research evidence cited in this chapter as well as what you know about No Child Left Behind (2001), discuss why English Language Learners should learn English via academic content.

2. Explain the difference between social and academic language. What is the role of the teacher in ensuring that all students acquire social language? What is the importance of social language for the academic futures of all learners?

3. How do SDAIE and SI make it possible for English Language Learners to acquire English and academic content concurrently?

4. What are the main components of SDAIE? Explain the significance of each for the learner.

SUGGESTED FIELD-BASED ACTIVITIES FOR PRE-SERVICE AND IN-SERVICE TEACHERS

1. Choose a science or social studies lesson from a state-adopted text (third grade and higher). Using **Figure 6.3** as a guide, modify a lesson from the text without diluting the content.

2. Using the seven Sheltered Instruction strategies presented in this chapter, choose *one per week* to try in your classroom. Keep a journal of your experience with the strategies. Discuss with other teachers their experiences with the strategies. Do some further reading on your chosen strategy for the week, and share some additional information you acquired relating to the strategy.

3. Using the criteria that pertain to SDAIE, cited on pp. 124–125, develop a matrix or checklist of anticipated observable teacher behaviors for scaffolding learning for all students. Arrange to observe a master teacher and check off the teaching strategies you observe. What did you learn from observing this teacher?

REFERENCES

Asher, J. (1972). Children's first language as a model for second language learning. *Modern Language Journal, 56,* 133–139.

Bandura, A. (1986). *Social foundations of thought and action: Social cognition theory.* Englewood Cliffs, NJ: Prentice Hall.

Banks, J. (2006). *Cultural diversity and education: Foundations, curriculum, and teaching* (5th ed). Boston: Allyn & Bacon.

Brown, H. D. (2006). *Principles of language learning and teaching* (5th ed.). Upper Saddle River, NJ: Pearson Longman ESL.

Chamot, A. U., Barnhardt, S., Beard El-Dinary, P., & Robbins, J. (1999). *Learning strategies handbook.* Upper Saddle River, NJ: Pearson ESL.

Chamot, A. U., & O'Malley, J. M. (1994). *The CALLA handbook: Implementing the Cognitive Academic Language Learning Approach.* Addison-Wesley.

Cummins, J. (1977). Cognitive factors associated with the attainment of intermediate levels of bilingual skills. *Modern Language Journal, 61,* 3–12.

Cummins, J. (1979) Cognitive/academic language proficiency, linguistic interdependence, the optimum age question and some other matters. *Working Papers on Bilingualism,* no. 19, 121–129.

Cummins, J., & Hornberger, N. (2001). *An introductory reader to the writings of Jim Cummins,* C. Baker & N. H. Hornberger, Ed. Clevedon, UK: Multilingual Matters Limited.

Curtin E. M. (2006). Lessons on effective practices from middle school ESL students. *Middle School Journal, 37* (3), 38–48.

Echevarria, J., & Graves, A. (2006). *Sheltered content instruction: Teaching English language learners with diverse abilities* (3rd ed.). Boston, MA: Allyn & Bacon.

Echevarria, J., Vogt, M., & Short, D. J. (2004). *Making content comprehensible for English language learners: The SIOP model* (2nd ed.). Needham Heights, MA: Pearson Education.

Krashen, S. D., & Terrell, T. (1983). *The natural approach: Language acquisition in the classroom.* Oxford: Pergamon.

McGraw-Hill Science: Teacher's Multimedia Edition (Vol. 2). (2000). New York: McGraw-Hill School Division.

McKenna, M. C., & Robinson, R. D. (1997). *Teaching through text: A content literacy approach to content area reading* (2nd ed.). New York: Longman.

McKenna, M. C., & Robinson, R. D. (2005). *Teaching through text: Reading and writing in the content areas* (4th ed.). Boston, MA: Allyn & Bacon.

Muth, K., & Alvermann, D. (1999). *Teaching and learning in the middle grades.* Needham Heights, MA: Allyn & Bacon.

National Center for Education Statistics. (2007). Available online at http://www.whitehouse.gov/fsbr/education.html.

Ogle, D. (1986). A teaching model that develops active reading of expository test. *The Reading Teacher, 39,* 564–570.

Piaget, J., & Inhelder, B. (1969). *The psychology of the child.* New York: Basic Books.

Schifini, A. (1985). *Sheltered English instruction.* Los Angeles, CA: Los Angeles County Office of Education.

SDAIE. (1994). California State Department of Education.

Short, D. (1991). *How to integrate language and content instruction: A training manual*. Washington, DC: Center for Applied Linguistics.

Tomlinson, C. A. (2000). *How to differentiate instruction in mixed-ability classrooms* (2nd ed.). Alexandria, VA: Association for Supervision and Curriculum Development.

Vogt, M. E. (2000). Content learning for students needing modifications: An issue of access. In M. McLaughlin & M. E. Vogt (Eds.), *Creativity and innovation in content area teaching: A resource for intermediate, middle, and high school teachers*. Norwood, MA: Christopher Gordon.

Vogt, M. E. (2002). SQP2RS: *Increasing student understandings of expository text through cognitive and metacognitive strategy application*. Paper presented at the 52nd Annual Meeting of the National Reading Conference.

Vygotsky, L. S. (1978). *Mind in society: The development of psychological processes*. Cambridge, MA: Harvard University Press.

CHAPTER 7 Teaching English Language Learners in the Content Areas: Language Arts, Social Studies, Math, and Science

INTRODUCTION

The focus of this chapter is on the integration of Sheltered Instruction strategies discussed in the last chapter into specific subject content areas. It is hoped that by now the reader understands that these strategies are *not* "remedial" in nature and do *not* "dilute" or "water down" instruction.

Traditionally, hands-on teaching methods were considered the exclusive domain of elementary students. Book-based learning with a heavy emphasis on oral language and abstraction was generally the trend in middle and high school. Nowadays, educational researchers prove that using instructional scaffolding for all students provides a context for all learners. All students (from child to adult) benefit from this kind of instruction. Teachers should incorporate these teaching strategies as much as possible with all learners *regardless of whether they have English Language Learners present or not.* A teacher who incorporates these strategies consistently will have to make few adjustments for English Language Learners. Teachers who tend to rely heavily on oral teaching without providing contextualized support often mistakenly think that they are incorporating these Sheltered Instruction strategies only for the benefit of English Language Learners. *This is a misconception. Teachers should be using these strategies with all students.*

This chapter focuses on reading strategies. The importance of reading can never be overstated as it is a vital skill that is a necessary prerequisite for all subject areas. Teaching academic proficiency at varying degrees of oral language proficiency will be addressed in some detail. Specific tips for teaching social studies, math, and science also will be included in the chapter.

The following terms will be used interchangeably throughout the chapter: "scaffolding support" and "contextualized instruction." These terms refer to mean instructional techniques that teachers implement to make the learning understandable for students. These are also Sheltered Instruction techniques for English Language Learners who may be learning English in the context of a particular content subject area.

FOCUS QUESTIONS

- ◇ How is it best to teach English Language Learners?
- ◇ What is the role of national and state standards?
- ◇ How does Sheltered Instruction assist English Language Learners in the subject content areas?

CLASSROOM SCENARIO

High School Scenario

Mr. Baker is a high school English teacher. This is Mr. Baker's first year teaching and it is already the beginning of the second grading period. He finds teaching challenging as he teaches for six periods a day and has different grade levels. His most challenging class, for many reasons, is definitely his last period tenth-grade English class. Not only is it after lunch, and at the end of the day, but in the past few weeks five English Language Learners were mainstreamed into his classroom from the ESL center.

The district has been providing a lot of staff development and training for teachers. The district wants all teachers prepared to teach on-grade-level academic content to all students including English Language Learners.

Mr. Baker is now aware of the importance of academic language at the high school level as the district is trying to decrease its student dropout rates. He is very committed to Sheltered Instruction techniques and incorporates them in every lesson during every period.

Observe how he uses a guided reading approach to structure this lesson for his tenth-grade students.

Poetry Lesson

Mr. Baker is introducing his students to a poetry unit on Alfred Lord Tennyson, and his featured poem for the day is "The Eagle." Observe how Mr. Baker uses strategies to meet the social and emotional needs and interests of high school students.

Mr. Baker begins by standing at the door and greeting all his students by name as they enter his classroom. The students know that when they enter his classroom, they are to write down the learning objective for the day in their assignment journals, as well as their homework assignment in their assignment notebook. During this time, students work silently while Mr. Baker takes roll and makes provisions for any student who is absent or talks with students who were absent and gives them their missed assignments.

1. **Setting the Scene:**   Mr. Baker begins the lesson by displaying a picture of an eagle standing majestically on a rock overlooking the ocean. He asks the students to take out a piece of paper and to list all the adjectives they can ascribe to the scene in the picture. Mr. Baker has been utilizing techniques of cooperative learning and his students immediately know how to get into groups. Each group has a recorder, scribe, time keeper, and task keeper. In less than a minute, groups are formed and the brainstorming has begun.

After a few minutes the timer goes off and Mr. Baker asks for the groups to share. Mr. Baker ensured that his language learners were assigned to heterogeneous groups. He had given the scribe in each group flashcards on which to write the words.

Mr. Baker chooses one person from each group and in turn they come up to the chalkboard to read and stick their adjectives onto the board. The class comes up with many words including "big, bold, blue, high, choppy, and wavy." Mr. Baker discusses each word and the class determines why it is an adjective. Mr. Baker asks them to use the adjective in a sentence that describes the picture display.

Mr. Baker is pleased that they understand adjectives, but in anticipation of the challenging words in the poem he wants them to focus on more literary adjectives that a poet might write.

Mr. Baker now writes the following on the board:

___Sea
___World
___Hands
___Lands

like a ____ he falls

Mr. Baker explains to the class that they are going to be reading a poem today that has a lot of interesting words. He explains to the class he would like them to brainstorm again and see if they can come up with interesting words to describe the nouns above and fill in the blanks. The students brainstorm again in groups for a few minutes and then share their words with the class. This time Mr. Baker asked them to use their thesaurus and to come up with many words of similar meaning (synonyms).

The class comes up with interesting words that might describe what the eagle is doing in the picture. He asks them to discuss what they know about eagles, and many students share what they were learning last week in science.

2. Introduce New and Difficult Words: Mr. Baker continues by writing the following words on the board: *clasps, crooked, azure, wrinkled,* and *thunderbolt.* He asks the students to come up with a sentence for each word explaining its meaning. The students may use their dictionary if they need to. After 5–10 minutes students share their sentences. Mr. Baker questions students and uses drawings and mime to ensure that all the words are meaningful to students.

3. Scan the Text: Mr. Baker asks the students to open their poetry anthology to the poem entitled "The Eagle" by Alfred Lord Tennyson. He asks the students to follow along with him while he reads it aloud. Mr. Baker loves poetry and reads it powerfully to convey the majesty and glory of the eagle. He asks them to listen to it again but this time to fill in the following summary map:

> **Who is the poem about?** (On a clear day a man looks up at a mountain
>   peak and sees an eagle)
> **What happens?** (The eagle looks down and plunges to catch its prey)
> **When?** (One day)
> **Where?** (Near the mountains and ocean)

The students then discuss the poem orally. Mr. Baker questions the class to make sure they understand what the premise of the poem is.

4. Reread Text Using a Graphic Organizer: Now Mr. Baker wants the students to focus on the literary elements of the poem, that is, use of metaphors, simile, imagery, sound, personification. Mr. Baker reviews these elements, which the class studied last week. These elements with their definitions and examples are clearly posted on the wall. He passes out a copy of the poem for students to mark with letters: M for metaphor, O for sound effects (onomatopoeia), P for personification, S for simile, I for image. Students work in groups and discuss the literary elements found in the poem. The students come up with many examples.

5. Orally Discuss Text with Class and Focus on Meaning, Details, Character, Setting, and Author's Purpose: Each student example is written on the board and discussed as a class. The students spend the rest of the class focusing on the meaning of the poem and the intent of the poet and what he was trying to say.

6. Students Evaluate Text: The students discuss their feelings about the poem, what it evoked in their imaginations and feelings. Mr. Baker provides the students with some interesting facts about the life of Lord Tennyson

(1809–1892) to help them evaluate the poem in the time period when it was written. Mr. Baker had a PowerPoint presentation prepared that included the following: pictures from Victorian times, impact of the industrial revolution, stigma of mental illness, a picture of the poet, and Tennyson's blindness.

7. Miscue Analysis: Mr. Baker asks the class to read the poem chorally with him with meaning and expression. He asks the students to find a reading buddy and to practice reading it aloud to each other. Mr. Baker works with a small group of students and listens to them read. He listens for mispronounced or mis-deciphered words. He stops and ask questions about word meaning to ensure that all student are understanding and comprehending what they are reading.

For homework he gives the following choices to students: They can memorize the poem and be prepared to say it with poise and drama in the class the next day; research more about the life of Lord Tennyson and write a summary of his life; write an original poem using any three of the literary elements discussed in class; find another poem written by Tennyson and read and analyze it for purpose and meaning as well as literary content.

Guiding Discussion Questions

◇ Outline the seven steps used by Mr. Baker in this lesson. What was the significance of each step for ensuring that all students were able to comprehend and understand the lesson?

◇ What are the unique challenges for English Language Learners with respect to English poetry and literature?

◇ What did Mr. Baker do to ensure that he connected the poem to the experience level and interests of his students?

Author's Insight

The strategies discussed in this chapter are applicable to all grade levels. It is the strategy or the process of teaching that remains the same and only the context (grade level and subject content) that is different. I wish to emphasize that the majority of strategies discussed in this chapter can be utilized with minimal adaptations for elementary, middle school, and high school students.

The teacher demonstrated the components of effective teaching for all students. The teacher connected to the students' background and set the stage for learning. The lesson demonstrated lots of interactions between students and between students and teacher.

The students were permitted to work in groups, which lowers anxiety levels for English Language Learners. The teacher provided visuals and presented new and difficult words for students ahead of time. The students got the opportunity to practice new vocabulary in a meaningful context by creating their own sentences.

Homework was assigned. Students who do homework consistently develop good study skills and habits, and have more opportunity to rehearse and commit to long-term memory newly acquired skills. Students with well-developed self-study skills become autonomous and life-long learners.

What Research Tells Us

It Is Now Federal Law

Under No Child Left Behind, teachers *must provide the same curriculum* for all English Language Learners. The teacher must make curriculum requirements *comprehensible* to the English Language Learner by using research-based instructional strategies like Sheltered ESL and scaffolding techniques. Teachers must expose English Language Learners to academic content while they learn English to ensure they do not fall behind academically. Students who do not fall behind academically are more likely to be successful and stay in school (No Child Left Behind Act, 2001).

Researchers Prove How English Is Best Taught

Many researchers today prove teaching English via content is more effective than teaching it in the isolation of a pullout ESL program. There is sufficient proven educational research to demonstrate that English Language Learners don't have to wait until they've acquired basic English skills to acquire content (Chamot & O'Malley, 1994). It is possible to teach English while teaching math, science, reading, social studies, and all other content areas. *Teaching English through academic content provides a context for learning that is more meaningful for students.* For example, science vocabulary taught in the context of a science class or math vocabulary taught in the context of mathematical problem solving are easier to understand. Thus English taught through content ensures the language is being taught within its naturally occurring context (Brown, 2006).

Teaching English Language Learners Is Now the Responsibility of All Teachers

In the past English Language Learners tended to be isolated in pullout programs whose purpose was intensive English instruction. There was little if any on-grade-level academic instruction provided for the students in these programs. Many English Language Learners spent years in pullout programs learning enough English before they could participate in the regular mainstream classroom. The misguided assumption was that proficiency in English was a necessary prerequisite for mainstream classroom participation. A review of the educational literature during the past 20 years reveals that many of these ESL programs failed to provide the students with sufficient English to succeed in regular mainstream classrooms.

This pullout method actually exacerbated the students' academic deficiencies because they missed out on content instruction in regular classrooms. Many English Language Learners were forced to repeat grades (Webb, Metha, & Jordan, 1995). This unfortunately resulted in what the literature terms "ESL Lifers"—many students never exited these ESL pullout programs and remained segregated from the academic content in the mainstream classroom (Gamoran, 1990; Oakes, 1990, 1992; Oakes, Wells, Yonezawa, & Ray, 1997).

Research in the past 10 years now proves that it is possible to teach English through the subject content areas of math, science, social studies, and so on provided that the teacher uses Sheltered Instruction strategies (Ovando, 2006). Such a teacher scaffolds and supports the academic learning of students and provides a meaningful context for learning to occur (Faltis & Coulter, 2008). It is now becoming acceptable practice to mainstream English Language Learners sooner so they can gain valuable grade-level academic content. The student is not immersed in a "sink or swim" situation as was common prior to *Lau v. Nichols* (1974), when no educational provisions were made for immigrant and non-English-speaking students entering schools in the United States.

 AUTHOR'S INSIGHT: Prior to the famous *Lau v. Nichols* court case students received no academic support for their lack of English language skills but were expected to perform on an equal basis as native English-speaking students. The Supreme Court found this practice unconstitutional and in violation of the rights of these children. As a result of the Supreme Court decision school districts now provide educational assistance and programs to help student learn English. This marked the beginnings of ESL and bilingual educational programs.

Nowadays the ELL student is immersed in the regular classroom setting with teachers who are better trained and prepared in providing scaffolded instruction and Sheltered Instruction for all learners. This ensures that the English Language Learner can comprehend as much as possible while improving English language skills (Echevarria, Vogt, & Short, 2004).

What Are Content Areas?

The content areas are set by curriculum standards that determine (1) what (Content) students should know and (2) what students should be able to do (process and performance) (Kellough, 2007, p. 141). The Goals 2000 Act, passed in 1994 by the U.S. Congress and amended in 1996 with an Appropriations Act, encouraged all states to set curriculum standards. There are currently both national and state standards governing what teachers teach in schools.

National Standards

The national standards provide guidelines concerning the essential knowledge and information that should be taught to students in each subject and each grade level. These standards are not mandatory and are meant to provide guidance to states for setting their own standards. Standards for the following content subject areas delineate what students should be learning in grades K–12: technology, science, physical education, mathematics, history/civics/social studies, geography, foreign language, English/language arts/reading, economics, business, and arts (visual and performing). Standards are also available from the Bureau of Indian Affairs for Native American students (Kellough, 2007).

State Standards

Nearly all states have developed or are in the process of developing their own standards for each of the content subject areas. These standards are generally available online at the state Board of Education's Web site. The standards are implemented by local school districts. These standards, updated and amended on a regular basis, also guide publishers in the choice of content for student textbooks and teacher support manuals and materials.

 AUTHOR'S INSIGHT: You can access these standards by going to the state Board of Education Web site for your state. Many states have developed their own acronyms for their standards, for example, Texas Essential Knowledge and Skills (TEKS). Many states have also developed standardized tests that measure how well schools are teaching to these standards in the schools, such as the Texas Assessment of Knowledge and Skills (TAKS) in Texas, Standardized Testing And Reporting (STAR) in California, New York Regents Exam in New York, and Minnesota Comprehensive Assessments–Series II (MCA–IIs) in Minnesota.

Caution about Content for English Language Learners: Academic Gaps

Content-area subjects rely heavily on academic language, particularly as students progress from second grade though school. Academic language also relies on the assumptions that students have the ability to read, process, and comprehend information independently. Additionally, the use of academic language requires the ELL student to use higher level oral language skills and to understand explanations and directions given in class. The positive news is that it's possible to develop academic language in English Language Learners (Chamot & O'Malley, 1994).

Many immigrant students enter schools in the United States being literate (read and write) in their own native language and with a vast amount of academic knowledge from their formal schooling experiences in their native country. These students "have attended formal schooling up to the grade level at which they enter U.S. schools." This is referred to as "parallel formal schooling" (Faltis & Coulter, 2008, p. 51). The parents of these students may be well educated and in many cases the student may have received some degree of formal instruction in English while attending school in his or her native country. These students have an advantage when transitioning to schools in the United States.

Conversely, there are many immigrant students who have received what is termed "nonparallel formal schooling" (Faltis & Coulter, 2008). Some of these students may not even be literate (cannot read and write) in their native languages and may have received no formal schooling or very little. A newly arrived 12-year-old immigrant entering sixth or seventh grade in the United States may have a second- or third-grade educational level by U.S. standards. These students often come from poorer socioeconomic backgrounds (Faltis & Coulter, 2008).

These academic differences and literacy gaps that immigrant students bring with them to U.S. schools unquestionably impact their educational achievement levels, especially for students entering middle and high school. The older the students, and the greater the academic gaps in their home country, the more challenging it may be for those students to achieve. It is a dilemma that is being discussed more in education circles today in light of increasing dropout rates and decreasing high school graduation rates (Orfield, 2004). This is all the more reason why the teacher plays a significant role in ensuring that all students and particularly the English Language Learners have an equal educational opportunity (NCLB, 2001). If we want immigrants to make a viable contribution to our society, it is imperative that they be provided the best education possible and not be permitted to drop out of school. The future prosperity and growth of our nation depends on raising education levels for all and not just for some. After all, this was the goal of our founding fathers and the impetus for the vision of Horace Mann (1796–1859), to whom we attribute the title, "Father of American public school education."

CLASSROOM APPLICATION STRATEGIES

General Reading Strategies to Use with English Language Learners

Reading is an integral and pivotal part of all content-area subjects. Students who read well and comprehend what they read are more likely to succeed academically. With all the technological advances and modern-day assistive devices, reading is still the most fundamental skill students must acquire to achieve academic success.

The advantage for teachers of younger children is that as English Language Learners they have more time to develop language and literacy skills. Younger native speakers are themselves still in the emergent phase of language and literacy development, so they have fewer academic hurdles to overcome (Diaz-Rico & Weed, 2006).

Older English Language Learners in middle and high School, without properly developed reading skills in their own native language, may encounter a multitude of academic gaps to bridge. If English Language Learners speak a native language that is not based on the Roman alphabet, one can usually assume their learning how to read and write in English will be a more complex process (Peregoy & Boyle, 2005).

What Teachers of English Language Learners Should Know

◇ English Language Learners who arrive in the United States by the third grade may have developed reading strategies in their own native language that may assist with the transfer to reading in English (Faltis & Coulter, 2008).

◇ English Language Learners may not be familiar with the Roman alphabet structure unless their native language is based on a similar alphabet. Sounds of letters in English may be totally new and different for the ELL student (Whelan Ariza, 2006).

◇ Reading fluency in their own native language does not mean an immediate transfer to reading English because the student may be from a country where other coding structures constitute the written communication used in that language (Whelan Ariza, 2006).

◇ Students may have academic gaps from schooling received while in their native country, or for that matter may have had limited or even no schooling whatsoever (Ovando, 2006).

The next portion of Chapter 7 focuses on literacy development for beginning, intermediate, and advanced readers. Figures 7.1–7.5 provide an overview for the teacher to gauge the existing levels of literacy (reading, writing, and spelling) and language development in ELL students. In addition, these figures provide instructional scaffolding suggestions for the teacher to consider at each literacy level.

AUTHOR'S INSIGHT: It is imperative for the teacher to accommodate the reading level of each student within the social context of age and culture. For example, an eighth grader who is at an intermediate reading level might only read at a fourth-grade level. Despite this fact, the reading content should always be at an eighth-grade level to accommodate the student's level of interest. Content at a fourth-grade interest level for an eighth grader would probably make the student feel bored and embarrassed.

Many basic readers have been specifically designed for English Language Learners (Fountas & Pinnell, 2005). It is important for teachers with a large population of ELL students to have these particular reading materials adopted by the district. Some publishing companies provide reading materials that are carefully written at different reading levels while at the same time honoring the age and interest levels of students. Check with your school to see if a set of such reading materials is available. Ask to examine the materials and don't be afraid to ask how to use them correctly with your students. If you are not sure how to use these materials, ask to be trained. Many beginning and alternatively certified teachers don't realize or discover such materials are available until it is too late in the year. Sometimes these materials are stored in another teacher's classroom and their existence goes undetected.

Literacy Development in Primary School: Emergent and Beginning Readers

Figure 7.1 demonstrates observable behaviors and characteristics of emergent readers and lists possible teacher scaffolding strategies during grades K–3.

For English Language Learners, the development of *phonological awareness* is important for language acquisition. Students must discern sounds, differentiate different sound patterns, and then memorize these patterns in order to learn a new language. Oral language must be developed concurrently with reading and writing skills. A highly developed verbal language skill and speech patterns lead to successful reading and writing development.

For successful literacy and language development, certain skills must be learned. Teachers must ensure these skills are developed daily with their emergent and beginning readers (Cummins, 2003).

FIGURE 7.1   Characteristics of Emergent/Beginning Readers

Characteristics of Emergent Reader, Student understands that:	Teaching Strategies to Support Emergent ELL, Teacher provides the following:
Print has meaning, possesses a desire to imitate and pretend to read	Environmental print, using labels, names of students, models reading and writing from left to right (directionality of print), sweeping finger under print
Enjoys books being read aloud	Reading and circle time (3–4 books a day), reading library with variety of books, involves parents, sends books home, provides reading buddies with other grade levels, provides silent reading time daily to encourage student's enjoyment of books
Learning alphabet—understands the alphabetic principles, decoding, and phonological awareness	Systematic and daily phonetic instruction, letter of day, letter blends, onset, rime, rhyming words, word families, sequence cards, flashcards with sight words
Beginning to write and understands that written words have meaning	Daily writing, stages of writing development, teacher models writing
Systematically developing vocabulary and reading sight words	Word walls, matching objects and pictures, print posted throughout classroom
Comprehension is developing—student can retell a story including beginning, middle, and end; sequence of events; student is beginning to infer and make predictions	Models use of story maps, semantic maps, outlines, retelling story in sequence, and GIST

◇ **Phonological Awareness:** The principle that each language is made up of its own discrete sounds. English Language Learners will already be familiar with the sounds in their own native language. To a beginner all English will sound the same, but with time learners will slowly begin to differentiate and learn different sounds, tones, and so on. Initially, students will begin discerning sounds that are similar to those found in their native language. For example, Spanish-speaking children are already familiar with the /M/ sound in Spanish and find that the /M/ sound in English is almost identical. However, other sounds in Spanish, such as /b/ and /v/, may present more of a problem due to their difference in English, and ELL students may need more drill and repetition work with the letters /b/ and /v/ as used in English (Whelan Ariza, 2006).

◇ **Phonemic Awareness:** The principle that words are made up of individual sounds, i.e., the smallest unit of sound (Tompkins, 2007, p. 8).

◇ **Alphabetic Principle:** The principle that each letter of the alphabet corresponds to a different sound (Mandel Morrow, 2001).

Teachers should use all the strategies listed in Figure 7.1 on a *daily* basis to support the growth and development of emergent and beginning readers.

No Child Left Behind (2001) legislates that all children be reading proficiently by third grade. All third-grade students and older should become more independent readers. With readers who are considered fluent, the teacher's emphasis should be more on developing comprehension and teaching these students to monitor and continue developing their own reading abilities (Cognitive Academic Language Learning Approach)—CALLA (Chamot & O' Malley, 1994), which was discussed in Chapter 6. Teachers of fluent students and older readers should focus more on developing those students' higher level of appreciation and analysis of literature.

Literacy Development in Secondary School: Intermediate, Fluent, and Advanced Readers

Figure 7.2 provides a summary of reading behaviors and teacher support strategies for intermediate and advanced readers. These specific strategies will be explained in more detail in the following pages.

Specific strategies that teachers should be using to help develop fluent and advanced readers include:

◇ **Strategic Reading Strategies** should be the teacher's main emphasis with older readers in middle school and high school. This strategy is about actually comprehending what is being read and not just phonologically sounding it out. Students are expected to spend more time reading silently and on their own, and be able to comprehend within their own reading strategies. So teaching students by using active strategies should be the basis of reading instruction with older students.

FIGURE 7.2   Characteristics of Intermediate/Advanced Readers and Suggested Support Strategies

Characteristics of older ELL readers of English:

- **Reading independently** and using self-checking and self-monitoring devices to ensure comprehension
- Reading for enjoyment—Drop Everything And Read **(DEAR)** or Silent Sustained Reading **(SSR)**
- **Read for a purpose**—research, reading to acquire information, reading for other subjects
- Infer
- Comprehend
- Find out word meanings independently without relying on adult by using context clues and dictionary

Teaching strategies to support the older ELL reader:

- Provide **daily reading opportunities**—set purpose for reading; provide research opportunities for students to read independently; provide choice in reading assignments; provide incentives for reading; provide opportunities for student to read in pairs, in groups, or independently as often as possible
- **Set a purpose** for reading by activating students' prior knowledge before they read a selection
- **Model and teach students specific skills that will enable them to become more independent readers:** decode print, find the meaning of an unknown word using context cues; use dictionary to obtain meaning of word; learn elements of print; use graphic organizers, semantic mapping for comprehension purposes; review key words
- Use **Survey Question Read Recite Review (SQ3R)**—look at pictures for context clues; make an estimation or prediction of what the story may be about; scan; answer questions; infer; find main ideas; create a story map; summarize in less than five sentences; create a story sequence; create a story board
- Teach **appreciative literary skills,** e.g., foreshadowing; flashbacks; analysis of a character; motive; plot; mood and themes; pronunciation; rhythm
- Develop **reading aloud skills:** read a paragraph; read in pairs; choral reading; repeated reading; echo reading; repeat after the teacher; use a commercial recording of story; act out story; write/create a different ending and act it out or read it aloud

◇ **Comprehension,** which entails responding to text, formulating questions, evaluating the text, making judgments, making inferences, making predictions (all these skills are measured on standardized tests), and not just merely answering low-level questions. It is important for teachers to understand just how difficult it is for English Language Learners to "read between the lines" and grasp inferences (this too, is a skill measured on state standardized reading tests).

English Language Learners at the beginning reading stages tend to be very literal and must learn idiomatic phrases. English literature and academic English is heavily idiomatic and is full of metaphors and images that cause real frustration for English Language Learners.

English Language Learners must learn that many words in the English vocabulary have more than one meaning, and can mean something completely different when used in a different context.

English Language Learners must differentiate between slang, informal, and formal speech registers, as was discussed in Chapter 6. Developing formal speech registers and academic language is the key to success in school for English Language Learners and is something that should be addressed daily in the classroom (Chamot & O'Malley, 1994).

Teaching Survey, Question, Read, Recite, and Review

Known as SQ3R, the Survey, Question, Read, Recite, and Review strategy that was developed by Robinson in 1961 is still an excellent model that can be explicitly taught to all readers. This reading strategy model can be taught as early as third or fourth grade and should be explicitly taught to students though high school. The steps used in this reading comprehension model and their applications in the classroom are:

STEP 1: *Survey.* What you are about to read—look at titles, headings, charts, illustrations, then read the first and last paragraph (introduction and conclusion) of the reading selection.

STEP 2: *Question.* Turn a title into a question, answer the question, and write down any questions that come to mind during the survey. Turn headings into questions; turn subheadings, illustrations, and graphic aids into more questions; write down unfamiliar vocabulary and try to determine the meaning for each term.

STEP 3: *Read actively.* Read to search for answers to questions and respond to questions; use context clues for unfamiliar words whenever there are unclear passages and confusing terms; then create more questions.

STEP 4: *Recite.* Put the book down and recall what you've read. Recite answers to questions aloud or put them in writing, then reread the text for unanswered questions.

STEP 5: *Review.* Answer the main-purpose questions, look over all answers, separate and reorganize information, summarize the information by creating graphic organizers, using main ideas and details. Write a summary, write an explanation of how the material read has changed your perceptions or applies to your life.

Teaching Comprehension Skills

Teach your students how to:

◇ Identify key words that carry meaning.
◇ Connect their own cultural background to the story and setting (look at illustrations, etc.).
◇ Recognize *context clues*. Have students determine the meaning of a word by reading the sentences around it before looking up the definition in a dictionary.

◇ Recognize the *main idea*. Have students examine topic sentences, headings, introductory and concluding paragraphs.
◇ Recognize the *topic sentence*. Have them use topic sentences as much as possible while writing.
◇ Look for details that support the main ideas.
◇ Use a dictionary to find meanings to unknown words.
◇ Develop strategies that will help them retain new vocabulary words.
◇ Properly sound out words.
◇ Self-correct their own errors.
◇ Reread texts using a highlighter or underlining words or sentences until they are able to increase their level of comprehension (Weaver, 2002).

Teaching Strategies to Develop Reading and Fluency

Students should be given the opportunity to engage in the following activities on a weekly basis:

1. Reading Aloud: Give English Language Learners the opportunity to read aloud to a partner or a small group if a larger group environment is too intimidating. ELL students should be given the opportunity to rehearse assignments by practicing their reading with a partner or in a small group. Regular practice develops intonation, appropriate pausing, and breath control, which are important skills for reading aloud in public.

2. Shared Reading: Use reading selections for younger children that include rhymes, repetition, and predictability. With older middle and high school students consider using a selection from a novel or a poem that lends itself to dramatic vocalization. Always choose texts for ELL students that are familiar and at a lower reading level if necessary. Developing fluency entails practice and repetition with text familiar to students. The teacher should model and read aloud either from a big book (younger children) or from a chapter book for middle and high schoolers with all students following along in their own copy of the text. This can be done with the class as a whole or with small groups of students.

3. Independent Reading: Students should be given the opportunity to read independently at home, during breaks at school, after an assignment is completed, waiting for other students to finish, and so on. Students should have access to a multitude of books from the classroom library or the school library that will meet the needs of their individual reading levels. This practice will increase contact with text, enhance vocabulary development, and improve reading comprehension. It is important for the teacher to have read and become familiar with a variety of books and literature that will appeal to the interest of the students at their age level. The "Century Club" (reading 100 books) or the "Reading Marathon" (reading for long periods of time) can provide incentives for students to keep track of books they've read. Evaluating books, placing books students recommend on a list using a simple scale devised by the teacher, or writing short book reviews for other students are additional motivational ideas.

4.   Scheduling "Silent Sustained Reading" (SSR) or "Drop Everything and Read" (DEAR)   on a daily basis for 20 to 30 minutes helps ELL students develop an interest in reading. This should be a predictable activity to help develop the habit of reading in all students. Students are encouraged to read silently for a sustained period of time daily (elementary school) or for one period every two weeks or as often as the schedule permits for middle and high schoolers (Pilgreen, 2000).

5.   Individual Student Conferencing: Periodically, the teacher should conference individually with each student. This time can be used by the teacher to ask the students about a novel or book they are reading in order to check their levels of comprehension and interest. It can also be used to share reading strategies for comprehension and understanding. Conferencing time can be used to have students read aloud while the teacher conducts an informal reading assessment of the student (Sweet & Snow, 2003).

6.   Reading Workshop: The teacher begins with a mini-lesson, or a brief instructional lesson with the entire class or just a small group. (a) The teacher models the target reading skill (one at a time is preferred). (b) The students practice aloud by themselves or with a partner the skill just modeled by the teacher, while the teacher walks around the room monitoring student progress. (c) The teacher reviews what the students have just practiced and discusses how they can incorporate what they've learned into their own individual reading. (d) Choose another target reading skill for the next day or the next week and repeat the process then (Atwell, 1998).

7.   Text Analysis and Preparation for Standardized Testing: All of the following components of a text must be explicitly taught to ELL students. Each constitutes an element that makes a text more challenging for English Language Learners to negotiate. These components are: genre, structure, content, theme, strategies for making meaning, literal and inferential comprehension, literary features and devices (point of view, dialogue, chronology, flashback, stories within stories, language devices, idioms, active voice, passive voice, metaphors, imagery, etc.), and writing structure (conjunctions, syntactic patterns). The difficulty level of the text can be determined by the quantity of these components that are present in the text. When those component features occur in literature, the teacher should model them, explain them, or target them each time (Tompkins, 2007, p. 218).

Generating Interaction between Schemata and Text (GIST)

Generating Interaction between Schemata and Text or GIST (Cunningham, 1982) is a strategy that enables students to read long, highly academic, and informational text. Subject content in social studies, science, and nonfiction can be read quite effectively when using this strategy. Students can work independently or in a cooperative group.

Students silently read a paragraph. The individual student or the collaborating group then write one sentence that summarizes the "gist" of the paragraph. The students continue in this fashion until the entire text has been read. When finished, they will have a short summary of the entire text. This reading strategy can be taught to intermediate readers, who can use this valuable tool to help them tackle and comprehend the heavy academic content they will be reading on their own.

It is important for the teacher to model and ensure that each student can identify and get to the "gist" of a paragraph in just one sentence. Students can compare their work with the sentences of others which can be done as a whole-class activity, in groups, or individually (Herrell & Jordan, 2008).

Strategies for Vocabulary Development

Developing and expanding student vocabulary requires exposing them to different strategies for practice and rehearsal. Try using one or more of the following strategies in your class:

◇ Write and illustrate words.
◇ Use drama to explain word meanings.
◇ Have students develop their own sentence using vocabulary words in a different context.
◇ Create word walls with high-frequency words.
◇ Act or mime the word (Beck, McKeown, & Kucan, 2002).

Textbook Strategies

Teach students how to use the contents of a textbook for better knowledge and understanding of the subject matter. Students should be taught the meaning and purpose of:

◇ The table of contents and the index
◇ Chapter titles, subtitles, and headings
◇ Chapter summaries
◇ Glossaries
◇ Highlighting key words and phrases
◇ Focusing on boldface words in a text
◇ Scanning and reading graphics
◇ Scanning and reading visuals embedded in text
◇ New usage of familiar words
◇ Use of synonyms (Sweet & Snow, 2003)
◇ Use of idiomatic words and phrases

Developing Writing Strategies for English Language Learners

Writing skills take the longest to develop for English Language Learners (Whelan Ariza, 2006). Figure 7.3 summarizes behavioral expectations and additional supporting scaffolding techniques that teachers need to be aware of to assist the English Language Learner during each phase of writing.

FIGURE 7.3   Behaviors of Emergent Writers and Teacher Scaffolding Techniques

Behaviors of Emergent Writer	Teaching Strategies to Support
Scribbling stage (2 yrs) Child imitates adult and experiments with writing tools; child is beginning to understand that print communicates meaning	Ask children to tell you what they are "writing." Do not attempt to classify what is drawn. Provide lots of paper and writing tools for children to experiment with.
Liner repetitive (2–3 yrs) Child begins scribbling from left to right; aware of directionality of print; child draws successive lines of scribbles	Ask children to communicate what they have written; provide lots of pens and paper and encourage the imitation of writing mechanics.
Random letter (3–4 yrs) Continuation of scribbles but letters that look like "O" and "M" start to appear; child begins to recognize letters used in his/her environment and imitates those letters, e.g., letters used in grocery story or fast-food restaurants	Teach the formation of letters; teach the sounds of letters; read books to students; read poems, rhymes, sing, develop language skills; develop an enjoyment for print and reading by reading aloud to students.
Linear lettering without spacing (3–6 yrs) Child starts stringing letters together without spaces; letters and actual words may be combined	Continue teaching the formation and sounds of letters; continue reading aloud and developing language and vocabulary of students; give students daily opportunities to write.
Early phonetic (4–6 yrs) Child begins to imitate letters and words and begins to communicate in writing; child writes letters upside down or backwards or in mirror image	Continue teaching the formation and sounds of letters; continue reading aloud and developing language and vocabulary of students; give students daily opportunities to write; focus on developing fluency in writing by encouraging students to use phonetic spelling in their rough drafts.
Transitional spelling (6–7 yrs) Child is doing formal letter practice, learning all alphabet letters, learning to write name and simple words; child spells words phonetically	Provide spelling homework daily for students; maintain a word wall in prominent display for new or commonly spelled words; have students maintain a word dictionary; teach students to write a rough draft and edit for spelling and punctuation.

Behaviors of Emergent Writer	Teaching Strategies to Support
Late phonetic (6–8 yrs)	
Student writes more fluently; student acquires rules of syntax, grammar, and spelling; student is aware of spelling conventions and requires assistance with this	Encourage students to write daily (simple sentences); give daily opportunities to learn spelling and new vocabulary words to use in writing; students should be learning beginning grammar structures—naming word (noun) and action word (verb).
Conventional spelling (6–8 yrs)	
Student has acquired all the mechanics of writing and is developing fluency and style in writing; student is acquiring the beginning of formal writing structure—syntax, grammar, paragraph construction, audience, purpose of writing, etc.	Students should have mastered the conventions of writing; students are acquiring the beginning of more complex adult writing; students should be working on longer writing pieces that are developed over a week; beginning of writing process (prewriting, writing (successive drafts), editing, proofing, and final publication).

Source: Adapted from Machado (2007).

Note: The age of child is meant as an approximate guide only. There will be much overlap and differences in ages of skills attained.

Classroom Strategies for Teaching Writing to English Language Learners

Written script is referred to as orthography (Pinnell & Fountas, 1998). Orthography is the relationship between sounds and symbols. Some English Language Learners may speak a native language that has a written script which differs from English. English Language Learners must now learn a new alphabet, a new set of letter-sound relationships, new reference words, new transition words, new punctuation, and new spelling (Pinnell & Fountas, 1998).

The most effective way to teach writing is by modeling it to your students. With young children using flip charts and writing on the chalkboard provides modeling. Younger students learn to write by copying a model. Once students understand they are communicating meaning through print, they need to be supported and encouraged to write every day. A daily journal can be used with younger children so they can draw pictures or write about their experiences (Graves & Kittle, 2005). Students can share what they write with the class in small groups (consider using an author's chair) or share what they've written one-on-one with the teacher. Writer's workshops and mini-lessons (Tompkins, 2007) should be used as needed to teach capitalization, punctuation, editing, the use of adjectives, and so on.

Writing Process

The writing process is usually introduced in the second or third grade. Process steps should be clearly posted in the classroom. By early in the third grade, writing assignments should be completing and published for all to see by the end of each week. Students can develop writing portfolios by using samples of their own work. Students can chart the progress of their writing samples from the prewriting stage through the final draft. Encourage students to be creative and expressive during the early steps of the writing process, and then as they progress into the later stages they should pay more attention to spelling and punctuation. By the final draft stage they should be able to see their progress in the completed work. Students should have the opportunity to share their writing with and interact with other students, classes, and teachers (Graves & Kittle, 2005).

At the secondary school level the writing process should be second nature to students, and their creativity as well as their skill set should be continually challenged and developed. Writing is a process of continuous development even for the most experienced writers (Graves & Kittle, 2005).

The phases of teaching the writing process (Dorn & Soffos, 2001) are:

1. **Prewriting Phase**—Begins with finding a topic to write about, which can be difficult at all age levels. One of the following strategies can help your students decide on a topic to write about:
   Brainstorming
   Show and tell
   Use of oral communication or drama
   Use of poetry
   Literature
   Story starters
   Pictures
   Music
   Creating lists from which to develop ideas
2. **Writing Phase**   (Drafting)
   Outline subject.
   Determine audience.
   What is the purpose?
   Plan the amount of time needed.
   Will work be done in pairs or individually?
   Create immediate and ongoing feedback between student and teacher.
   Develop adjectives and adverbs.
   Include more description.
3. **Revising and Editing:**   The editing process should be taught and modeled to the students. The teacher can help students develop the following skills:
   Rubric for punctuation
   Capitalization
   Use of "The"
   Use of pronouns, etc.
   Peer review
   Use of writing conferences with the teacher
   Proofreading

Topic sentences and supporting details
Making corrections in margins
Avoiding plagiarism

4. **Publication:** "Author's chair" (Graves & Kittle, 2005) involves having the student authors share their work with the class by reading aloud what they've written. Some innovative ideas for publishing student writing could be the creation of:

Accordion books
Circular stories
Three-part books
Wall stories
Story quilts
Rewriting the text of a book to include one's own name or by using different characters
Rewriting the ending to a story

AUTHOR'S INSIGHT: English Language Learners generally enter at the transitional phase of writing if they are in the third grade and higher, and they may have a tendency to spell phonetically. The more similar their first-language or native language is to the basic structure of English, the easier their writing skills will transfer. This is the time when they should begin interactive writing and journaling.

The *intermediate English Language Learner* will have an increased vocabulary and will start using more complex sentences. These students understand the genres of personal and expressive writing, letter writing, note taking, and short essays. English Language Learners at this level generally struggle with subject and verb agreement, vocabulary, and the correct forms of plural nouns, pronouns, and verb tenses. English Language Learners usually make errors when using phrases containing adverbs, adjectives, and clauses; use run-on sentences; and incorrectly use verbs and prepositions.

The *advanced English Language Learner* should be on grade level but almost always needs support and development with spelling, syntax, grammar, and descriptive writing.

Spelling Development

Formal spelling must begin in first grade and by the time they reach third grade students should be cognizant of the need to edit. By third grade, students should be capable of checking their own work for spelling errors (Gentry, 2005).

An overview of the approximate *spelling development* phases along with possible teacher support strategies at each level can be found in Figure 7.4.

Spelling Activities for Drill and Practice

1. Students alphabetize words.
2. Students do a word search.
3. Students put words into sentences.
4. Students write words in foam, sand, or play dough.

FIGURE 7.4 Stages of Spelling Development

Stage	Student Characteristics	Teaching Support Strategies
Emergent/prephonetic spelling	Developing knowledge of alphabet; scribbling; some letters visible	Learning letters; making and forming letters; drawing is considered communication in print
Early phonetic	Letter-sound correspondence (alphabetic principle); understands that print goes left to right (directionality)	Knows each letter has discrete sound; copying sentences; teacher models writing daily; student dictates to teacher, teacher writes and student copies
Phonetic spelling	Misspellings are common and words spelled as they sound	Spelling lists provided for students; practice spelling words correctly in sentences; illustrating words; word wall with high-frequency words; editing writing
Transitional spelling	Learning to spell formally	Continue providing spelling lists for students to master; practice spelling words correctly in sentences; illustrating words; using word wall with high frequency words to monitor and edit own writing
Conventional spelling	Knowledge of word structures like prefixes, suffixes; uses large amount of known words in writing	Spelling lists; editing and development of vocabulary; learning word roots and synonyms; editing own written work

Source: Adapted from Gentry (2005).

5. Students find assigned words in a newspaper.
6. Students play charades using these new words.
7. Teacher holds a spelling bee.
8. Students play Hang Man on the chalkboard.
9. Students play Wheel of Fortune with words and a spinner.
10. Students play Word Bingo.

Teaching Academic Content at Varying Oral Language Proficiency Levels

A brief review of teacher support strategies for teaching academic content to students with varying oral language proficiency can be found in Figure 7.5.

FIGURE 7.5 Stages of Language Development and Teacher Support Strategies

Stage of Language Production— What to Expect from ELL	Teaching Strategies to Support ELL
1. Beginning/silent stage—student can show, point, and nod	Teacher provides extra linguistic cues to convey meaning; teacher can modify speech, choose words carefully, and use simple grammatical structures in speech; teacher can restrict sentences in length, use repletion, intonation (vary a lot, exaggerate), use gestures, use pictures, and actions to clarify meaning; use art, movement to express meaning and understanding; use predictable books, movement, art, chants, songs, and read alouds; tell students to "point to" "find the . . ." "raise your hand," **TPR** (Total Physical Response) and "show me . . .", students demonstrate that they comprehend teacher without producing much speech
2. Beginning (early production)—student can usually answer yes or no or give a one- or two-word answer	Teacher continues to use all the above strategies and elicits "yes" or "no" responses initially and then one- or two-word responses; give students a choice between two answers, e.g., "Is this right or wrong? Is this black or white?"
3. Intermediate stage—student can respond with simple sentences	Teacher continues to use all the above strategies and elicits longer sentences, e.g., "How is the weather today?" Teacher uses active and ongoing questioning; teacher teaches new vocabulary and uses brainstorming to activate prior knowledge and vocabulary of students.
4. Advanced/transitional stage—student can respond to a question like, "What do you think?" and can formulate own opinions	Teachers allows students to work in groups, in pairs; teacher calls on student to respond and participate in class; teacher asks more high-level questions that involve comparison, evaluation, and synthesis, e.g., "What do you think?" Teacher continues to expand vocabulary and develop more complex grammatical structures in both oral and written language

1.   Beginning/Silent Stage: It is important for teachers to understand that the ELL student may be in his or her silent period, a development stage in which comprehension may exceed production. Just because students are not talking or verbally responsive does not mean that they are not cognitively processing what they hear or see. It is equally important for the teacher to understand that the English Language Learner is in fact learning (as an infant does) while in this silent stage.

Teacher Support Strategies

⬦ Modify your own language. Do not use intricate grammatical structures. Always simplify and make your own language as clear and direct as possible. Use short sentences, avoid pronouns, and avoid synonyms.

⬦ Learn to talk, model, point, show, and demonstrate at the same time.

⬦ Activate the ELL student's prior knowledge and experiences by using pictures or by connecting the lesson to examples that are relevant in their lives.

⬦ Plan levels of questions to fit the appropriate level of language (use questions that require yes/no answers or one- or two-word answers).

⬦ Accept errors to encourage students to answer.

⬦ Use *TPR—Total Physical Response* (Asher, 1982)—with your ELL students. When using TPR students respond to directives from the teacher, demonstrating that they are comprehending commands in English. Firmly state, "Stand up," "Sit down," or "Quiet, please." The students will follow your directives once they see their fellow classmates' response. Once the students respond to verbal commands, you can introduce a picture of the command followed by a picture with the written word. In a short time only the actual words designating the command are needed. By then the students have begun to read the written words. Label and introduce all vocabulary words. After students have mastered simple command words, extend sentences to include more detailed vocabulary and sentence structure.

2.   Beginning/Intermediate Stage: At the beginning or intermediate stage the English Language Learner is not only developing language but is developing reading and writing skills as well. At this stage teachers should reduce the linguistic load on their students and dramatically increase the use of scaffolding techniques. By this stage, teachers should notice students interacting with other students and should see that students are totally immersed in the printed word. Teachers should be reading aloud to their students, and by now students should be taking an obvious interest in books and enjoy reading.

3.   Advanced Stage: In the advanced stage the teacher continues to lighten the linguistic load, and the ELL student requires less input and support. However, with older advanced stage students the teacher must keep in mind that substantially more academic content must be covered and students must develop their own self-study techniques for required reading and comprehension. During this stage of language development the Cognitive Academic Language Learning Approach (see Chapter 6) can be introduced to students. It is vital for advanced students to continue developing cognitive academic skills on their own, but they must be explicitly taught to do so prior to or during this stage of language development.

4. Transitional Stage: During the transitional stage, the ELL student is relatively indistinguishable from the other students in the classroom, but he or she may still need more moral and emotional support. Students at this language stage still feel somewhat awkward about their writing abilities and feel a sense of inadequacy when comparing themselves to native speakers and writers of English.

General Tips

When Students Have Difficulty Reading Textbooks (also see Chapter 6)

◇ Find a text on the subject matter written at a lower readability level. There are many "leveled" (Fountas & Pinnell, 2005) texts available that are designed for older readers who need a simpler reading level.
◇ Highlight main points and topic sentences in the text.
◇ Rewrite the text yourself for use by students at a lowered readability level, without diluting the content.
◇ Use sheets with questions to guide reading and ensure comprehension; provide page number indicators, etc.
◇ Use predictive questions to encourage students to read.

When Students Have Difficulty Reading Worksheets or Tests

◇ Use more white space between sections.
◇ Preteach related vocabulary before assigning a study sheet.
◇ Reduce vocabulary level by using less complex words but without diluting content or skill.

When Students Have Difficulty Writing

◇ Allow them to give oral reports instead.
◇ Allow them to create a collage or cartoon strip.
◇ Allow them to draw maps
◇ Allow them to create a diorama (3D re-creation).
◇ Allow them to create an exhibit.
◇ Allow them to dictate their work for someone else to write down.
◇ Allow them to prepare just an outline with main points.

When Students Have Difficulty Spelling

◇ Allow them to dictate the words.
◇ Allow them to rehearse with flashcards and a partner.
◇ Teach peer editing review so they can check each other's work for spelling and grammar before turning it in.

◇ Allow them to use the spell check feature on the computer.
◇ Provide a "word wall" within easy view of all students to use for reference.
◇ Use tactile practice techniques like writing in foam and writing in paint to learn spelling words.

The strategies discussed here in Chapter 7 apply across all disciplines that require reading and writing. While reading, writing, and spelling have been addressed in detail so far, this chapter would not be complete without delving into general strategies needed for teaching social studies, math, and science to English Language Learners.

Teaching Social Studies to English Language Learners

Social studies as a subject can be used to enhance the development of the reading and comprehension skills in all students. Social studies also provide the teacher with an excellent opportunity to build on the interests of older ELL students and to develop increased global and cultural sensitivity (Banks, 2004).

Social studies that provide "comprehensible input" (Krashen & Terrell, 1983) for English Language Learners should promote the use of hands-on group learning activities, computers, simulations, field trips, videos, projects, group work, experiential learning, and discovery learning. Use of living drama and community resources can bring social studies to life and make it relevant to the lives of all students. Because English Language Learners are new to the United States, they need to acquire the nuances, customs, historical background, and a more complete understanding of the country that is new to them. This knowledge is described as "cultural capital" in research (Schug, 2003).

Teacher Support Strategies for Teaching Social Studies

Reading Large Amounts of Text

Teachers should consider using all the following strategies when teaching social studies:

◇ Highlight text and lighten the language load.
◇ Preview the text for the upcoming lesson to seek out the difficult vocabulary used and plan how to introduce these words to students.
◇ Provide examples in action, use pictures, include realia, and whenever possible dramatize historical figures and situations.
◇ When attending to large chunks of data, be sure to use a graphic organizer, mnemonics, and timelines. Preplanning and preparation will make the task easier on the teacher and the students.

Providing "Examples" (Curtin, 2006)

Provide a finished model of your projects so English Language Learners can see, touch, and refer to it in the classroom. Save examples from the previous year. This will provide much needed psychological support for ELL students.

Culturally Validate.   Use social studies as an opportunity to culturally validate your students. Let your English Language Learners give their own perspective from each of their own cultural backgrounds. Beware of historical bias and make sure that it can be overcome from several different perspectives (Banks, 2004).

Stay Current and Up-to-Date.   Be sure to keep up with current events. Keep articles and stories to use as a teaching tool for oral language development, that is, "weave past into current events" (Faltis & Coulter, 2008).

Teaching Math to English Language Learners

It is a common misconception that math is easier for English Language Learners because they only have to manipulate numbers and symbols and do not have to rely as heavily on words. In fact, ELL students require well-developed vocabulary and language skills in order to understand and demonstrate mathematical thinking and reasoning (Whelan Ariza, 2006).

Many English Language Learners may have already learned different ways of solving or computing mathematical problems in their home countries, some of which may not be congruent with how things are taught in the United States. An example of this difference comes from the British Isles. There, children do not go through the process of regrouping during addition, but instead borrow and pay back the 10 through a process of memorization.

The National Council of Teachers of Mathematics (NCTM, 2007) provides very clear guidelines about teaching math. These guidelines are appropriate for teaching English Language Learners. The Council recommends that teachers of grades K–12 include the following processes when teaching mathematics:

- ◇ Using manipulatives and concrete materials to explain math concepts
- ◇ Encouraging students to work in pairs or groups to solve math problems
- ◇ Encouraging students to orally share math solutions with the rest of the class
- ◇ Asking students predictive questions
- ◇ Writing about the mathematical process
- ◇ Integrating content with math (using math in social studies and science whenever possible)
- ◇ Using calculators and technology
- ◇ Using assessment as an ongoing tool to modify and change instruction

Teaching Math Vocabulary to English Language Learners

There are new vocabulary words and terms that the ELL student must become familiar with and understand, such as "predict," "sum of," "carry," and so on. It is critical for teachers to be clear and concise about the correct use of each term and to make their students aware of the many synonyms used for these words that usually show up in standardized tests. Teachers can develop concept families to post on the wall that explain each word or term and list commonly used synonyms. Teachers should strive always to connect mathematics to the real and immediate world. Additionally, mathematics should be presented to students in an integrated fashion connecting reading and literacy and all other content subject areas (Whitin & Whitin, 2000).

It is important for teachers of English Language Learners to be aware that this new math vocabulary may cause difficulty for students when reading their textbooks. Preview all upcoming vocabulary and have realia and pictures in hand, and be ready to demonstrate and explain these new terms to students. Teachers should consider using quizzes for math vocabulary to ensure that students are truly learning and comprehending the new words (Whelan Ariza, 2006).

 AUTHOR'S INSIGHT: Teachers should practice and develop pronunciation with their students in the classroom. Pickreign (2004) stresses the importance of teachers using six exposures to each new word used during a lesson designed for English Language Learners. Students should have at least 30 different exposures to each new word throughout the month following its introduction.

The following example helps to explain the complexity of mathematical terms for English Language Learners. In mathematical terms "simplify" means to make simpler. However, using "simplify" within the mathematical expression "simplifying a radical expression" can generate a cumbersome process resulting in a final answer that appears much less simple. Teachers need to clarify mathematical expressions that may have multiple meanings, such as terms like "reciprocal," "rationalize," "numerator," and "denominator." (Whelan Ariza, 2006, p. 129).

Additional Teacher Support Strategies for Teaching Mathematics

It is important for students to *verbalize the steps* they are taking within each mathematical problem. Using a response board and working in pairs provides students with the opportunity to practice math and use the English language in an emotionally safe classroom environment.

Teachers should *model mathematical solving* and provide completed examples of problems for their ELL students by using appropriate words and language. Have students model with you and provide a choral response when necessary. Have students practice by repeating the words and vocabulary terms with you. Focus on the mathematical understanding of the concept first and always remember to accept language errors (Chamot & O'Malley, 1994).

Modify the language of the math textbook as needed to suit the linguistic level of your English Language Learner (Echevarria et al., 2004).

Use *realia* (e.g., egg cartons for fractions) as much as possible and try to compose word problems based on meaningful situations for your students (Echevarria et al., 2004).

Have students keep a *math journal* so they can write about the subject, and how they solved their math problems (Whitin & Whitin, 2000).

Use *Math centers* for extension and remediation. Use folders for reteaching and review (Whelan Ariza, 2006).

Teaching Science to English Language Learners

Teaching science should be "hands-on" and connected directly to the experiences of students. In addition to using all the strategies already provided in Chapter 6, teachers should make sure the content is understandable for the English Language Learner by doing the following:

◇ *Preview each text* for difficult vocabulary and complex language. Then simplify the text for your students without diluting the content.
◇ Provide for *vocabulary practice* and development in each lesson. Be sure to plan for multiple exposures to each newly introduced word.
◇ *Assess new vocabulary* and assess student retention.
◇ Provide *hands-on* experiments and demonstrations.
◇ Encourage *talk and discussion* to give your English Language Learners the opportunity to use their newly acquired academic words.
◇ *Explain* with words, actions, and actual objects.
◇ Use *realia* (real-life objects and examples).
◇ Provide "multiple-abilities" (Cohen & Lotan, 2004) to learning for all students, that is, each science activity should include opportunities for students to read, write, discuss, calculate, create art, demonstrate, show, and so on (Faltis & Coulter, 2008).

CHAPTER SUMMARY

This chapter demonstrated the use of Sheltered Instruction strategies in the content subject areas of reading, social studies, math, and science. The strategies emphasized are not remedial in nature and do not dilute the curriculum. The strategies are designed to contextualize learning for students by connecting with their backgrounds and experiences. The use of hands-on teaching strategies, once considered the domain of elementary teachers, can be implemented with great success in intermediate and high schools.

Research proves that English is best taught to English Language Learners through academic content. Teaching English through content provides a content that is more meaningful for students. Now, teaching English Language Learners is the responsibility of all teachers. Therefore the importance of the teacher's role is paramount to ensure that English Language Learners learn

English and on-grade-level academic content. The difference between "parallel" and "nonparallel" forms of schooling was explained and the implications for the academic success of students.

The classroom application strategies presented were very specific to reading development. Specific strategies for each of the following were explained in detail: literacy development from emergent reader to intermediate, fluent, and advanced readers; SQ3R; GIST; textbook strategies; and comprehension skills. Developing writing skills as well as teaching academic content at varying oral language proficiency levels were also discussed. Useful tips for teaching social studies, math, and science were also included in this chapter.

REFLECTIVE CHAPTER QUESTIONS

1. What is the purpose and role of state standards?
2. Discuss the statement at the beginning of the chapter about Sheltered Instruction strategies: ". . . these strategies are *not* 'remedial' in nature and do *not* 'dilute' or 'water down' instruction." What is the importance of this statement for all teachers? What is the importance of this statement for English Language Learners?
3. What is meant by the term "contextualize," and what is the significance of this for English Language Learners?
4. What is meant by the terms "parallel" and "nonparallel" forms of schooling for English Language Learners? How do literacy and academic gaps in immigrants' home countries impact their educational progress in the United States?

SUGGESTED FIELD-BASED ACTIVITIES FOR PRE-SERVICE AND IN-SERVICE TEACHERS

1. Research your state's standards and download one grade level. Read the standards. Develop a grid or matrix and create an outline of the learning objectives for students, i.e., a scope and sequence.
2. Find out if your district's home page posts a scope and sequence for parents and teachers to use. If so, download it for one grade level, read it, and present a summary for class. If your district does not have a scope and sequence posted, visit with a local district coordinator, teacher, or principal and ask if they have a developed scope and sequence for each grade level. Ask how the district developed this.
3. Plan to observe a high school teacher and an elementary teacher. Choose one content subject area for both teachers. What were the differences you observed in the two classroom settings? What differences/similarities in teaching strategies were you able to observe?

Helpful Resources for Teachers

Math Sites

http://www.aplusmath.com/
A math site that student can use. Includes flashcards.

http://www.eduplace.com/math/brain/
A site that has weekly brain teasers for students.

http://www.webmath.com/
A site for students/teachers to use to get help for solving math problems in all areas.

http://www.ccs3.lanl.gov/mega-math/
A very stimulating Web site created by Los Alamos National Laboratories.

History

http://historyforkids.org/index.htm
History Web site for kids.

Science

http://kids.yahoo.com/science/
Yahooligans science Web site.

Language Arts/Reading

http://www.funbrain.com/grammar/
Grammar gorillas and other educational games.

Keyboarding Skills

http://www.computerlab.kids.new.net/keyboarding.htm
A site for developing keyboarding skills.

General Information Sites for Students and Teachers

http://www.studystack.com/
A site with study aides and games for content subject areas.

http://www.aea14.k12.ia.us/technology/ScavengerHunt.html
Site for scavenger hunts to use with students.

http://www.busyteacherscafe.com/
A site to help busy teachers.

http://www.internet4classrooms.com/on-line.htm
A tutoring site for teachers to assist with various computer technologies and programs.

References

Asher, J. (1982). *Learning another language through actions: The complete teachers' guidebook*. Los Gatos, CA: Sky Oaks.

Atwell, N. (1998). *In the middle: New understandings about reading and writing with adolescents* (2nd ed.). Upper Montclair, NJ: Boynton/Cook.

Banks, J. (2004). Multicultural education: Historical development, dimensions, and practice. In J. Banks & C. McGee Banks (Eds.), *Handbook of research on multicultural education* (pp. 3–29). San Francisco, CA: Jossey-Bass.

Beck, I. L., McKeown, M. G., & Kucan, L. (2002). *Bringing words to life: Robust vocabulary instruction.* New York: Guilford Press.

Brown, H. D. (2006). Principles of language learning and teaching (5th ed.). Upper Saddle River, NJ: Pearson Longman ESL.

Chamot, A. U., & O'Malley, J. M. (1994). *The CALLA handbook: Implementing the cognitive academic language learning approach.* Reading, MA: Addison-Wesley.

Cohen, E., & Lotan, R. (2004). Equity in heterogeneous classrooms. In J. Banks & C. McGee Banks (Eds.), *Handbook of research on multicultural education* (pp. 736–752). San Francisco, CA: Jossey-Bass.

Cummins, J. (2003). Reading and the bilingual student: Fact and friction. In G. Garcia (Ed.), *English learners reaching the highest level of English literacy* (pp. 2–33). Newark, DE: International Reading Association.

Cunningham, J. (1982). Generating interactions between schemata and text. In A. Herrell, & M. Jordan, *Fifty strategies for teaching English language learners* (3rd ed.). Upper Saddle River, NJ: Pearson Merrill Prentice Hall.

Curtin, E. H. (2006). Lessons on effective practices from middle school ESL students. *Middle School Journal, 37*(3), 38–46.

Diaz-Rico, L., & Weed, K. Z. (2006). *The crosscultural, language, and academic development handbook: A complete K–12 reference guide* (3rd ed). Boston, MA: Pearson Education, Allyn & Bacon.

Dorn, L. J., & Soffos, C. (2001). *Scaffolding young writers: A writer's workshop approach.* New York: Stenhouse.

Echevarria, J., Vogt, M., & Short, D. J. (2004). *Making content comprehensible for English language learners: The SIOP model* (2nd ed). Needham Heights, MA: Pearson Education.

Faltis, C. J., & Coulter, C. A. (2008). *Teaching English learners and immigrant students in secondary schools.* Upper Saddle River, NJ: Pearson Merrill Prentice Hall.

Fountas, I. C., & Pinnell, G. S. (2005). *The Fountas and Pinnell leveled book list, K–8, 2006–2008.* Portsmouth, NH: Heinemann.

Gamoran, A. (1990). How tracking affects achievement: Research and recommendations. *National Center on Effective Secondary Schools Newsletter, 5*(1), 2–6.

Gentry, J. R. (2005). *The science of spelling: The explicit specifics that make great readers and writers (and spellers!).* Portsmouth, NH: Heinemann.

Graves, D. H., & Kittle, P. (2005). *Inside writing: How to teach the details of craft.* Portsmouth, NH: Heinemann.

Herrell, A., & Jordan, M. (2008). *Fifty strategies for teaching English language learners* (3rd ed.). Upper Saddle River, NJ: Pearson Merrill Prentice Hall.

Kellough, R. D. (2007). *A resource guide for teaching K–12* (5th ed.). Upper Saddle River, NJ: Pearson Merrill Prentice Hall.

Krashen, S. & Terrell, T. (1983). The natural approch: Language acquisition in the classroom. Oxford: Pergamon.

Machado, J. (2007). *Early childhood experiences in language arts: Early literacy* (8th ed.). Clifton Park, NY: Thompson Delmar Learning.

Mandel Morrow, L. (2001). *Literacy development in the early years: Helping children read and write* (4th ed.). Boston, MA: Allyn & Bacon.

National Council of Teachers of Mathematics. (2007). Available online: http://www.nctm.org.

Oakes, J. (1990). *Multiplying inequalities.* Santa Monica, CA: RAND.

Oakes, J. (1992). Can tracking inform practice? Technical, normative, and political considerations. *Educational Researcher, 21*(4), 12–21.

Oakes, J., Wells, A. S., Yonezawa, S., & Ray, K. (1997). Equity lessons from detracking schools. In A. Hargreaves (Ed.), *Rethinking educational change with heart and mind* (pp. 43–72). Alexandria, VA: Association for Supervision and Curriculum Development.

Orfield, G. (Ed.). (2004). *Dropouts in America: Confronting the graduation rate crisis.* Cambridge, MA: Harvard Education Press.

Ovando, C. J. (2006). *Bilingual and ESL classrooms: Teaching in multicultural contexts.* New York: McGraw-Hill.

Peregoy, S. F., & Boyle, O. F. (2005). *Reading, writing, and learning in ESL: A resource book for K–12 teachers.* New York: Pearson Allyn & Bacon.

Pickreign, J. (2004). *Field experience guide: Resources for teachers of elementary and middle school mathematics.* Boston: Allyn & Bacon.

Pilgreen, J. L. (2000). *The SSR handbook: How to organize and manage a sustained silent reading program.* Portsmouth, NH: Boynton/Cook-Heinemann.

Pinnell, G. S., & Fountas, I. C. (1998). *Word matters: Teaching phonics and spelling in the reading/writing classroom.* Portsmouth, NH: Heinemann.

Schug, M. (2003). Teacher-centered instruction: The Rodney Dangerfield of social studies. In J. S. Leming, L. Ellington, & K. Porter (Eds.), *Where did social studies go wrong?* (pp. 94–111). Washington, DC: Thomas B. Fordham Foundation.

Sweet, A. P., & Snow, C. E. (2003). Reading for comprehension. In A. P. Sweet & C. E. Snow (Eds.), *Rethinking reading comprehension.* New York: Guilford Press.

Tompkins, G. E. (2007). *Literacy for the 21st century: Teaching reading and writing in prekindergarten through grade 4.* Upper Saddle River, NJ: Pearson Merrill Prentice Hall.

Weaver, C. (2002). *Reading process and practice.* Portsmouth, NH: Heinemann.

Webb, L. D., Metha, A., & Jordan, K. F. (1995). Foundations of American education (2nd ed:). Upper Saddle River, NJ: Prentice Hall. Cited in Curtin, E. M. (2002). *Students' and teachers' perceptions of culturally responsive teaching: An urban middle school case study.* Doctoral dissertation, available online at University of North Texas library collection.

Whelan Ariza, E. N. (2006). *Not for ESOL teachers: What every classroom teacher needs to know about the linguistically, culturally, and ethnically diverse student.* New York: Pearson Allyn & Bacon.

Whitin, P., & Whitin, D. (2000). *Math is language too: Talking and writing in the mathematics classroom.* Urbana, IL: National Council of Teachers of English.

Actively Assessing and Monitoring Academic Progress of English Language Learners in the General Education Classroom

INTRODUCTION

This chapter explores the nature of assessment and its role in determining the academic progress of students. The words *assessment*, *testing*, and *measurement* are used interchangeably in research and in this book. Regardless of which term is used, the role and function of assessment, testing, and measurement is to "collect evidence from students so that educators can make inferences about the status of those students" (Popham, 2007, p. 17).

The majority of testing that occurs in classrooms today are tests devised by teachers themselves that are administered regularly (weekly, monthly) and throughout the year. These tests are generally *multidimensional* in nature and have a variety of forms. Teachers are required to develop their own tests, depending on their subject content area.

The second category of testing addressed in this chapter concerns *externally produced assessment methods*. Standardized achievement tests and standards-based accountability tests are the most commonly used and widely known of the externally produced assessment methods that a pre-service or in-service teacher is most likely to encounter. These tests are generally either norm-referenced or criterion-referenced and are externally produced. Standardized tests are not devised by teachers, though in many instances they are administered by teachers.

Standardized tests have many uses but are generally concerned with measuring students' educational outcomes with other students in different parts of the country and the world. The tests are standardized because they measure students on objective standards and criteria. For this reason these tests are considered *more objective* in nature because teachers do not create them specifically for their own students. Many school districts are now adopting merit pay for teachers whose students demonstrate improvement on state standardized achievement tests. The need for teachers to prepare all students for these tests is paramount.

All teachers must possess the ability to administer, score, and interpret the results of both externally produced and teacher-produced assessment methods (Standard 4 of Standards for Teacher Competence, 2007).

This chapter will give readers an understanding of the variety of assessment measures and their appropriate use in planning instruction not just for English Language Learners but for all students. The role of standardized tests in this era of high-stakes testing will also be explored, and the role and responsibilities of classroom teachers in the preparation of all students for these tests. All the assessment strategies and tips addressed in this chapter are beneficial for all students and not just English Language Learners.

Assessment is a very broad field, beyond the scope of one chapter in this textbook, whose purpose is to serve as a beginning guide to teaching. I have attempted to focus on the most salient points for a beginning teacher to know and understand about assessment.

FOCUS QUESTIONS

- ◇ What is the purpose of assessment?
- ◇ What is high-stakes testing?
- ◇ What is the difference between criterion-referenced and norm-referenced tests?
- ◇ How can I prepare English Language Learners for high-stakes testing?

CLASSROOM SCENARIO

A High School Teacher's Perspective on Assessment

Ms. Josten teaches literature, composition, and grammar at the high school level, and she is frustrated. She carefully plans lessons that are culturally relevant and meaningful for all her students. She is especially aware of the needs of her ELL students who are mainstreamed into her classes. She writes her own tests and modifies them for the varying English language levels of her students. For some students she gives true or false questions, for others she lowers the linguistic content so the test doesn't confound her English Language Learners. She uses *multiple forms of assessment*, which helps to ensure all her students will have the opportunity to demonstrate their knowledge and not be penalized for what they don't know.

Ms. Josten notices that the English Language Learners in her classroom have good conversational English and participate well in classroom discussions. However, during assessments periods some of their struggles with the academic format of multiple choice and writing prompts become evident.

Recently Ms. Josten received the results of a *state standardized practice test*, and she is concerned about the academic progress of some of her students. She knows her students get confused by the state tests, but she also knows they are capable of performing far better in her classroom than what the standardized tests reveal. Ms. Josten is anxious and wonders if she needs to reexamine her teaching methods and reevaluate her testing methods in order to help her students improve their scores on these *high-stakes tests*. Ms. Josten is aware of the importance of these tests for the future of all her students. She is also aware that some of her English Language Learners have only had three years to gain academic proficiency in both written and oral language skills. Yet these students must perform on par with native English speakers. At times, she feels overwhelmed by the responsibility that has been placed on her shoulders, but she knows that she has the support of her colleagues and administration to ensure that she can provide all her students with the skills needed for success.

Ms. Josten believes that "giving up" is not an option. She reflects upon her assessment techniques in the classroom and determines that she needs to additionally *align* her regular classroom assessments more similarly to the standardized tests. Doing this, she reflects, will ensure students become more familiar with the test format and receive more practice in understanding the academic language of tests.

An Administrator's Perspective on Assessment

Mr. Easley, an assistant principal, shares his thoughts about assessment and accountability and reminisces about his experiences as an English Language Learner himself in the 1960s in the United States.

"Many years ago when I was a student in school, there was very little accountability for teachers when it came to growth and progress of English

Language Learner–type students from a state level. I remember watching many of my friends drop out of school, and when I'd see them while playing in the street or playing in their front yards, I'd ask why they were no longer going to school, and the answers were always the same, 'Because I can't speak English,' or 'Because the teachers were too mean.'

"So I guess those of us who were able to survive the system are thankful for the opportunity we were given, and for having such wonderful teachers. Without those teachers we wouldn't have been able to beat the system.

"With respect to the education system that exists today, it is wonderful when compared to what we had when I was in school. Fortunately for the non-English speakers of today, it must now be provided at the district level as a result of state and federal government mandates. When I was growing up there was almost no *accountability*, and now I think there is at least a quantifiable form of accountability.

"I for one am glad and extremely grateful that No Child Left Behind exists because it holds everybody accountable for the teaching of our children and for the progress of the learning of all our children . . . even the ones that don't speak English" (Curtin, 2002).

Guiding Discussion Questions

1. What is the administrator's view on testing and accountability?
2. How does the administrator's view compare to and differ from the teacher's?
3. What are your concerns as a pre-service or in-service teacher concerning testing and assessment?

Author's Insight

Assessments drive accountability, and school administrators see the value of ensuring that we don't exclude any group of students from their educational attainments who may have been excluded in the past. Assessment is a real part of education and it is here to stay.

For the teacher it is the discrepancy between student results on teacher-made tests and on standardized tests that often leaves a teacher wondering, "How can a student be passing in my class and still fail a standardized test?"

The answer lies in the nature of the test. Teacher-created tests and regular tests used in the classroom tend to be *multidimensional* (i.e., the teacher does not rely on any one form of testing to assess the progress of the students). A teacher has multiple opportunities to assess students throughout an academic period and does not rely solely on any one type of test. A teacher will utilize different forms of test, for example, multiple choice, open ended questions, true-false, projects, essays, performance tests, and so on. The students' scores on these different tests are generally averaged or "weighted," and the teacher possesses a lot of autonomy concerning which scores to consider and which to omit. The teacher also controls the time and nature of these tests and may modify tests and tailor them to individual needs of students.

On the other hand, standardized tests are administered at specific times of the year and according to standard rules of confidentiality and administration. The same test is administered to all students, and the teacher must administer it in a standardized format using the script provided. A student may not test well on that particular day due to anxiety, illness, or other factors. If a student does not test well within the parameters of the test on that one day, there is generally no other opportunity to demonstrate knowledge or skill levels after that. How well a student performs on that given day is all that matters. Consequently, the stakes are high for all students and their teachers when taking state, district, or federally mandated standardized tests. Although standardized tests may have many administrative forms, the majority are generally standard multiple-choice tests. The results of these tests are compared against established objective criteria and groups are compared across age levels. So, many standardized tests, because of their nature, are considered *one-dimensional*.

Another reality of testing the English Language Learner is that many of these students in their third year of residency must take tests that require a high level of academic content. Many English Language Learners may lack the language skills but they don't necessarily lack the content skills, a dilemma faced every day by teachers of all grade levels in the classroom.

WHAT RESEARCH TELLS US

What Is Assessment?

Assessment is an integral part of the teaching and learning cycle. Assessments allow the teacher to determine what is already known or mastered by each student. Assessment allows a teacher to determine if a student is ready to move on, if the teacher needs to reteach certain areas, and to determine just what progress students are making in a class. Assessment should be made an integral part of the teaching and planning process.

"Educational assessment, testing, or measurement; all three terms describe a process by which educators use students' responses to specially created or naturally occurring stimuli in order to make inferences about students' knowledge, skills, or affective status" (Popham, 2007, p. 4). Teachers measure students in order to arrive at "inferences" about the academic progress of those students. So a teacher has to measure how well a student is learning material in the classroom. A teacher will devise some form of a test and then make an inference or draw a conclusion about how the student is doing based on the result of that test. A teacher may give 25 multiple-choice questions. If the student gets a total of 20 out of the 25 questions correct, the teacher must assign a meaning to this score. This number may be assessed as a percentage, and then the teacher has to determine what an acceptance mastery score is. This process entails what Popham (2007) refers to as an inference or interpretation that the teacher must make about the students' work.

Purpose of Assessment

The purpose of all assessment should be to *monitor student progress*, and based on that progress to make instructional adjustments and decisions. So assessments are designed to focus on student academic progress, and consequently they focus on student learning (Gronlund, 2006).

Two kinds of inferences or interpretation can be made with test results: *relative, norm referenced-interpretations* and *absolute, criterion-referenced interpretations* (Popham, 2007).

A *norm-referenced interpretation* is used to provide data on where the student is ranked relative to other students of similar grade level. A norm-referenced test is used to compare student outcomes to other groups of students of similar age and ability. Terms like *percentiles* are used in conjunction with norm-referenced tests.

A *criterion-referenced interpretation* can be used to gauge how well a student can perform a specific learning task (Gronlund, 2006). Both of these types of inferences or interpretation often constitute achievement tests and are used widely in our educational system to make academic placements for students. These are high-stakes tests for students because their future academic success depend on these scores.

A *criterion-referenced test* does not compare student scores with those of other students. A criterion-referenced test instead compares student scores to an objective set of criteria, such as how many the student got right out of 100. In this instance the teacher has knowledge of what a student can and cannot do but does not know how the student did in comparison with other students.

Students' scores from both criterion-referenced and norm-referenced tests enable the teacher to monitor the educational progress of all students. This is invaluable information for the teacher as now he or she possesses the necessary data to make instructional adjustments for all students.

Assessment that is ongoing and used during the learning process/period is generally referred to as *formative assessment*. Formative tests determine the student's learning outcomes during a lesson or during a learning unit. The teacher determines if the student is making satisfactory progress or if remediation or reteaching is needed. The purpose is to make necessary instructional modification if needed so that all students can learn. Generally no formal grade is assigned during formative assessment (Gronlund, 2006).

Assessment that occurs at the end of a learning period/cycle is termed *summative assessment*. The purpose of this assessment is to determine if the student has succeeded in mastering the specific learning objectives and if the student is ready to progress to the next unit of instruction. Generally a formal grade is assigned at the end of this instructional period (Gronlund, 2006).

High-Stakes Testing and Accountability

The No Child Left Behind Act (NCLB) is a reauthorization of the 1965 Elementary and Secondary Education Act (ESEA) during the presidency of Lyndon B. Johnson. This federal act, designed to increase federal funding to local schools, made a dramatic difference in how states and schools could operate. These monies were termed Title I funds and were allocated for schools serving low-income and minority students. The schools were obligated to administer standardized tests and to demonstrate that students in Title I schools were making appropriate academic gains (U. S. Department of Education, 2006).

NCLB differs substantially from this ESEA act of 1965 in that now all schools and not just Title I schools are required to test students. Math and reading tests are now administered yearly in grades 3–8, once in grades 10–12, and science tests are administered once in grades 3–5, 6–9, and 10–12. Overall, the level and quantity of testing required under NCLB has more than doubled since ESEA (Popham, 2007).

Case Against Standardized Testing

Recently, standardized and high-stakes testing have been receiving a lot of reaction, both positive and negative. Opponents of standardized testing maintain that such testing has resulted in the creation of a hostile environment in our schools (Kohn, 2000). The outcome of standardized tests are used to rate schools under very specific guidelines established by No Child Left Behind legislation, which now penalizes those schools for failing to show adequate yearly progress. The schools that are most penalized tend to have the poorest children and have the least amount of financial resources to redress the failing scores (Meier, 2002; Meier & Wood, 2004). In many instances the Federal government is unable to provide the necessary financial support for failing schools to redress low student achievement (Darling-Hammond, Noguera, Cobb, & Meier, 2007).

Research indicates the current wave of *standardized testing* places great pressure on teachers of English Language Learners to do well regardless of the English language skills of their students (Batt, Kim, & Sunderman, 2005). They contend that state standards and tests have forced some schools to standardize academic content at the expense of other concerns, which can negatively impact the educational interests of English Language Learners (Abedi, Hofstetter, & Lord, 2004; Bohn & Sleeter, 2000). A xenophobic climate is developing and anti-immigrant sentiments are increasing because English Language Learners as a subgroup could cause a school to fail or get a low or unacceptable rating. Low or underscoring results for English Language Learners could potentially cause a school to lose federal funding, so the pressure is on (Bohn & Sleeter, 2000).

Many factors that are beyond the control of the individual teacher affect educational processes. Factors such as level of community support, state, availability of books, numbers of computers, class size, and socioeconomic backgrounds of students can have an impact on student scores on high-stakes testing (Tucker & Stronge, 2005).

Alfie Kohn (2000), a very strong opponent of standardized tests, believes that all students need to be intrinsically motivated and that traditional education with an emphasis on stars and stickers and grades does not intrinsically motivate students. He encourages teachers to leave traditional and reward systems behind. But in this era of accountability this is not possible, because it is against federal law.

Case for Standardized Testing

The positive aspect of No Child Left Behind is that schools are now accountable for the learning achievements of lower socioeconomic class students, students from diverse groups, and English Language Learners. Student failure is determined to be the result of ineffective instructional practices and not the students' fault (Freeman, Freeman, & Mercuri, 2002). In the past students who were failing were permitted to continue failing, and in many cases they just dropped out of school or became ELL "lifers" (see Chapter 7).

Now each school is held accountable for the progress of each student. Students who are failing are provided with afterschool tutoring or summer school, and parents can now send their children to other schools if the local school is considered "low performing" or "academically failing." The stakes are high for principals and teachers, and not just for students (NCLB, 2001).

Identification and Placement of English Language Learners

By law, English Language Learners are entitled to receive the educational assistance necessary to provide them access to core curriculum and instruction while concurrently providing them access to English language development (NCLB, 2001).

English Language Learners undergo their first assessment upon entering a school district. If the student is of reading age this initial assessment is a test in English designed to determine reading proficiency. The result of this test determines placement in an ELL program based on language ratings the student achieves, usually designated as "beginning," "intermediate," "advanced," or "high." Even if a student's score is at the advanced level, academic language support is still required and the student must be monitored for at least two years. Usually a native language survey is used to determine the language spoken at home.

There are many English proficiency tests available. Some of the most common ones are Language Assessment Scales (LAS), Language Assessment Battery (LAB), and the Stanford English Language Proficiency (SELP). Even though there are a multitude of commercial tests available to choose from, many school districts elect to develop their own identification and placement processes (Faltis & Coulter, 2008). Teachers should be aware of the testing process used in their district and the criteria for placement (discussed in Chapter 1).

Preparing English Language Learners for State Standardized Tests

The fact that English Language Learners are required by law to sit and take state standardized tests at the completion of their third consecutive year in the United

States only serves to emphasize the importance of the testing and the correct placement of each student. School districts must also ensure that English Language Learners are academically ready to take grade-level tests. The burden of this responsibility generally falls on the campus administrators and teachers. The importance of teaching academic content concurrent with English language, and the importance of preparing English Language Learners for the test format are vital aspects of all teachers' jobs today (Batt et al., 2005; Figuerora, 2002).

NCLB (2001) requires that all students be tested in reading or language arts, math, and science. In the case of ELL students, this legislation stipulates that reasonable accommodations shall be made for them, but after three years in the United States these students shall be assessed in English proficiency. To accomplish this, ELL students are tested in areas of listening comprehension, reading, and writing skills.

It is important for all teachers to teach *test-taking strategies* to ELL students so they become familiar with the standardized testing format of the test. It is equally as important for teachers to avoid the danger of teaching solely to these tests, since research demonstrates this is precisely why low-performing schools are stymied in their test scores. The focus for all learners, but especially English Language Learners, should be growth and improvement over time (Faltis & Coulter, 2008). Teachers need to ensure that ELL students have an equal access to curriculum and future educational opportunities.

Assessment *should be ongoing and should be directly in line with instruction.* Teaching to the state standardized test and subjecting children to drill and skill practices is counterproductive for English Language Learners. Teaching to the *learning styles* of all students while concurrently using the interactive, sheltered, and scaffolding strategies discussed in this book is important. Preparing students to take the test should not dominate classroom time; this should be devoted to teaching the competencies, and how to assess in a manner similar to the test (Banks, 2006).

Literature and current thought on what's best for English Language Learners indicates that assessment should be *multidimensional* and more specifically, that the assessment used should incorporate many types of test and not be just one format. Students should be assessed, for example, by using a combination of oral, project based, essay, and multiple-choice questions. Teachers should employ a variety of assessments to properly evaluate the progress of their students. Literature also suggests using such multiple modalities (learning styles) as writing samples, projects, portfolios, and so on (Perogoy & Boyle, 2005).

CLASSROOM APPLICATION STRATEGIES

The Standards for Teacher Competence in Educational Assessment of Students (2007) specifies seven standards that encompass the scope of a teacher's professional role in relation to student assessment. Refer to Figure 8.1 for a list of these seven standards and a brief analysis of standard 1 and its practical application purpose in the K–12 classroom.

FIGURE 8.1 Standards for Teacher Competence in Educational Assessment of Students

Standard 1: Teachers should be skilled in choosing assessment methods appropriate for instructional decisions.

Classroom Application:

- Teacher should have knowledge of a broad *range of assessment alternatives*, i.e., both teacher-produced tests and externally produced tests.

  Assessment Options:
  Text and curriculum-embedded questions and tests
  Standardized criterion-referenced and norm-referenced tests
  Oral tests
  Performance assessments
  Portfolios
  Exhibitions
  Demonstrations
  Rating scales
  Writing samples
  Paper-and-pencil tests
  Seatwork
  Homework
  Peer- and self-assessments
  Student records
  Observations
  Questionnaires
  Interviews
  Projects
  Products, and others' opinions

- Teacher should have knowledge of *strengths and weaknesses of each assessment method.*
- Teacher should be able to *evaluate the appropriate assessment method* to suit instructional plan.
- Teacher should be able to use results from tests to *provide feedback to students*, diagnose group and individual learning needs, plan for individualized educational programs, motivate students, and evaluate instructional procedures.
- Teacher should understand how to use/adapt assessment options that meet the cultural, social, economic, and language backgrounds of students.

Standard 2: Teachers should be skilled in developing assessment methods appropriate for instructional decisions.

Standard 3: Teachers should be skilled in administering, scoring, and interpreting the results of both externally produced and teacher-produced assessment methods.

Standard 4: Teachers should be skilled in using assessment results when making decisions about individual students, planning teaching, developing curriculum, and school improvement.

Standard 5: Teachers should be skilled in developing valid pupil grading procedures which use pupil assessments.

(*Continued*)

FIGURE 8.1   Continued

Standard 6: Teachers should be skilled in communicating assessment results to students, parents, other lay audiences, and other educators.

Standard 7: Teachers should be skilled in recognizing unethical, illegal, and otherwise inappropriate assessment methods and uses of assessment literature.

Source: Standards for Teacher Competence in Educational Assessment of Students (2007), American Federation of Teachers, National Council on Measurement in Education, and National Education Association. http://www.unl.edu/buros/bimm/html/article3.html.

Standard 1 will be the main focus of the assessment methods chosen for this chapter. The depth of information needed to do a thorough analysis of assessment is beyond the scope of one chapter. A description of assessment options in standard 1 will be addressed in this chapter with a brief explanation of their application in the K–12 classroom setting.

All the assessment options in this section are applicable to all grade levels. Tips specific to English Language Learners will be included as necessary and at the end of this chapter. The assessments strategies suggested in this chapter are effective for all learners and not just English Language Learners.

Multidimensional Assessment Options for Use in K–12 Classrooms

Schools should not rely on one single measure to assess English Language Learners. *Single measures of assessment may place English Language Learners at greater risk of failing in the regular mainstream classroom* (Faltis & Coulter, 2008). It is very important to use a variety and a range of the following assessments when assessing all learners. *Using a variety of assessment measures provides a more holistic view of the academic progress of students.*

Norm-Referenced Assessments—Externally Produced Tests

See Figure 8.2 for examples of norm-referenced tests commonly used throughout the country. There are many others and perhaps many additional ones are used in your school district. These tests are generally group administered, and you will be asked to follow the prompts and directions given in the administration section. Generally the school district, counselor, or educational diagnostician will guide you in this regard. *These tests measure and compare your students with those of similar grade level across the country.*

Your role as a teacher will be to:

◇ *Administer the test* according to district guidelines. Read the directions for administration ahead of time and follow all procedures and guidelines outlined in the test.

FIGURE 8.2   Norm-Referenced Assessments—Externally Produced Tests

Administered by teachers or trained personnel (counselor or diagnostician). Results are used to compare students with others of similar age and grade level.

Example of norm-referenced assessment measures (K–12) for the subject content areas of reading, math, language, spelling, science, social studies:

- **ITBS**—Iowa Test of Basic Skills
- **SAT9**—Stanford Achievement Test
- **MAT8**—Metropolitan Achievement Tests
- **CAT/5**—California Achievement Tests
- **CTBS**—Comprehensive Tests of Basic Skills (4th ed.)

Example of norm-referenced assessment measures (2–12) for writing process:

- Writing Process Test
- CTBS Writing Assessment System

Example of norm-referenced assessment measures (K–12) for reading:

- **Gates-MacGinitie** Reading Tests, 3rd ed. (vocabulary and reading comprehension)
- **Gray Oral Reading Test**, 4th ed. (oral reading—rate and accuracy, comprehension, miscue analysis)
- **SDRT**—Stanford Diagnostic Reading Test (1–12—decoding, vocabulary, comprehension, and scanning)

Source: Adapted from Tucker & Stronge (2005).

◇ *Interpret* these results and in many cases explain them to a parent or guardian. (Check with the counselor, principal, or other school personnel first.) Familiarize yourself with the meaning and use of standard scores, stanines, percentiles, averages, normal curve (refer to Popham, 2007 for more detail and classroom application).

◇ Ascertain how the overall achievement of students in your classroom compared with that of other students in other parts of the school and district.

◇ Ascertain how students in your school district compare with national norms or with another district (Tucker & Stronge, 2005).

◇ Use the results from the test as baseline data for making instructional decisions that benefit individual students.

Criterion-Referenced Assessments–Externally Produced Tests

These tests are designed to test how well a student has mastered particular knowledge in a given skill area. What is the student's level of mastery? How many did the student score correctly out of a set number? What are the student's strengths and weakness in a given domain? What changes in performance level are occurring? (Tucker & Stronge, 2005).

See Figure 8.3 for examples of criterion-referenced tests.

FIGURE 8.3   Criterion-Referenced Assessments—Externally Produced Tests

The tests are administered by teachers or trained personnel (counselor or diagnostician). These tests are designed to test how well a student has mastered particular knowledge in a given skill area.

- **State Benchmark Assessment**—in compliance with NCLB. Subjects vary by grade level— reading, writing, math, science, and social studies (3–12)
- **Regents Exam** (New York)
- Tennessee Comprehensive Program (**TCAP**)
- Standards of Learning Tests (**SOL**)—Virginia
- Texas Assessment of Knowledge and Skills (**TAKS**)—Texas
- **SRI**—Standardized Reading Inventory (1–6)
- **Kindergarten Skills Assessment** (reading—letter recognition, phonemic awareness, letter-sound, auditory discrimination)
- **Flynt-Cooter Reading Inventory** (K–12) for the classroom (used to determine instructional reading level)
- **Monroe Standardized Reading Tests** (3–12)
- **DSA**—Developmental Spelling Analysis (K–12)
- **ERB Writing Assessment Program (4–12)**—scored by two readers using 6-point scale

Source: Adapted from Tucker & Stronge (2005).

Assessing Student Knowledge Prior to Testing

For essay style and short-answer tests, the student must know the material, process a large quantity of material, demonstrate good memory skills, demonstrate good organizational skills, read at test vocabulary level, have good writing skills, and have an excellent conversational ability (advanced level of language).

For matching lists tests, students must know the material, process a large quantity of material, demonstrate good memory skills, demonstrate good organizational skills, read at test vocabulary level, and have good writing skills (syntax structure or grammar is not as important in this process).

For fill-in-the-blank tests and computation-style tests, students must know the material, demonstrate good memory, read at test vocabulary level, have good writing skills, and be able to copy answers properly.

For multiple-choice tests, students must know the material, read at test vocabulary level, be able to copy answers properly, and recognize the correct answers.

For true/false tests, students must know the material, read at test vocabulary level, and be able to recognize and copy the answers correctly.

When looking for alternatives to giving a test, consider having students read the story of their choice and then:

◇ Draw a picture to illustrate the story.
◇ Make a mobile to illustrate the story.
◇ Draw a picture of their favorite character in a story.
◇ Write a poem, haiku, or limerick.
◇ Give an oral report.

◇ Rewrite the ending so that the outcome is different.

◇ Select five words from the story and write a definition for each.

When reformatting a test:

◇ Capitalize and underline words such as "always," "never," and "not."

◇ Keep alternatives to multiple-choice answers brief.

◇ Avoid questions stated in the negative, especially when using true/false questions.

◇ Make sure no more than 10 items are included when creating matching lists–style questions.

◇ Provide short-answer alternatives if you want students to spell them correctly on fill-in-the-blank tests.

◇ Avoid trick questions. They only serve to invalidate your test and increase test-taking anxiety.

◇ Use shorter sentences, i.e., questions approximately 10 words in length are about a fourth-grade reading level.

◇ Lower the readability level of the test questions. An example is: "Compare and contrast the personal attributes and characteristics of Huck Finn and Tom Sawyer." Revise it to read: "How are Tom Sawyer and Huck Finn alike? How are they different?"

◇ Use highlighted text. Highlight key words and answers to questions on a test; highlight main ideas and answers from worksheets; highlight important dates, names, vocabulary and picture captions; use different colors to train students for match-up and eye-tracking.

◇ Mark text with an asterisk to point out what is most important.

◇ When teaching students to identify key points and corresponding highlighted detail, use markers to highlight overhead transparencies and use colored chalk to distinguish activities.

◇ Use big books in younger grades (model and provide examples). Lower level students may need numbers or line numbers so they can follow along.

Other Assessment Options—Teacher-Produced Tests

Teachers spend a lot of time developing assessments to measure how well students are doing in the classroom. A teacher should use a variety of testing procedures, as previously discussed. Using a variety of assessment methods provides a greater perspective on student learning. Please refer to Figure 8.4 for a brief overview of teacher-produced assessment options. Each of these assessment options will be discussed in this chapter.

 AUTHOR'S INSIGHT: Assessment can be very overwhelming for a beginning teacher, so it is best to try out a few at a time until you are comfortable and see what works. Remember to *vary your assessment measures* (tests) and use the results to determine the averages and grades of your students for report cards.

FIGURE 8.4   Other Assessment Options

1. Test and curriculum-embedded questions and tests
2. Oral tests
3. Performance assessments
4. Portfolios
5. Rubrics
6. Paper-and pencil tests

1. Test and Curriculum-Embedded Questions and Tests

These are tests and questions that are provided in teacher's manuals and supplemental kits that accompany state-adopted textbooks. These may be practice sheets, quizzes, reteach worksheets, end-of-chapter tests, end-of-chapter reviews, end-of-unit reviews, and so on.

Practical Tips for Teacher

◇ Preview tests ahead of time for language or complexity that may confuse English Language Learners (either rewrite or prepare students for these before test).
◇ Use test-provided guide and be prepared to create your own if necessary.
◇ If test is multiple choice, have students explain on a separate sheet why they choose a particular answer (if they choose the incorrect response but had a valid rationale for doing so, consider assigning some extra points for explanation).
◇ Use one test to test other areas, e.g., if test is short answer based on a content area (science, social studies, math), assign a handwriting grade and a spelling grade as well.

2. Oral Tests

Oral tests can be given whenever students may have difficulty with reading or comprehension. Oral tests may also be used with younger children who are still learning to read.

Administering Oral Tests. Often English Language Learners may truly possess the skills and competencies being tested on a test but they may lack the necessary reading skills or the language skills needed to fully understand the test. To assess true competence, (authentically) it may be necessary to administer the test orally by reading test questions to the students and having them write out the answers. Other ways include:

◇ Give a short oral exam with students responding orally.
◇ Allow students to participate in a skit or role play to emphasize concepts related to test material.

◇ Students can participate in panel discussions covering test material prior to the test being administered.
◇ The test can be divided into two parts with part A given one day and part B another. This way the teacher can provide students feedback on the first part of the test, allow a day between test parts, and then administer the second part.

Practical Tips for Teacher
◇ Use flashcards for word and letter recognition.
◇ Have students indicate the correct answer for multiple-choice tests read aloud by choosing from four cards indicating A, B, C, or D response.
◇ For emergent readers use picture cards for assessing phonemic awareness, sound identification, letter recognition, rhyming sounds, or nonrhyming sounds.

3. Performance Assessments

Performance assessment is used when students must demonstrate what they actually know about concepts or material learned. Performance assessment can take place when students accomplish something that can be videotaped or presented orally. It could be something as simple as reading a selection of text, performing a poem, conducting a science experiment, or a project relating to a social studies research assignment. Its purpose is to test a learning outcome that is immediately observable as opposed to explained and written in a textual format. Exhibitions and demonstrations also fall under this category.

Practical Tips for Teacher
◇ Consider using performance assessment at least once every grading period.
◇ Pick a subject each grading period and consider how students can incorporate some of the following elements in their performance: music, song, drama, arts, research, clay, dance, create posters, exhibitions, displays, PowerPoint presentation, and so on.
◇ Invite parents, administrators, other classes to observe performances.
◇ To save class time, have students conduct performances at home and videotape them.

4. Portfolios

Portfolios are collections of student work gathered at intervals over a period of time by either the student or teacher for the purpose of demonstrating academic growth and progress. Portfolios are commonly used by painters, designers, writers, and many professionals to show what they can do (Borich, 2007). Portfolios serve a similar function in the classroom. Student work can be stored digitally, in a binder, or in a box. Three kinds of portfolios may be used for classroom purposes:

1. **Working portfolio** (Borich, 2007): This is a temporary collection of "work in progress." A student should have easy access to his or her portfolio to retrieve items in progress.

2. **Display/show portfolio** (Borich, 2007): This is a display of the best of the student's work. It can be very motivating for students to observe their own best work. Display portfolios can be shared with parents during conferences and can be used to showcase what students are accomplishing in school.

3. **Assessment portfolio** (Borich, 2007): This is a collection of work completed by the student over a period of time, which is then turned in for a grade.

Practical Tips for Teacher

What to put into portfolio:

◇ Writing samples—narrative, persuasive, expository, and descriptive
◇ Student drawings, diagrams, graphics
◇ Student-selected works
◇ Teacher-selected works
◇ Comments from peers or teachers (Marchesani, 2007)

How to assess a portfolio:

◇ Establish *a specific set of criteria* (rubrics) ahead of time and make sure that all students understand the criteria that will be used to evaluate their portfolio. Possible criteria: organization, neatness of presentation, all items included, mechanics of writing.
◇ Decide how much each criterion is worth in terms of points or percentages. Prioritize the criteria selected in terms of most important to least important and assign the points accordingly.

5. Rubrics

A rubric may be defined as a "scoring guide that provides criteria to describe various requirements or levels of student performance. The use of rubrics helps to score student work more accurately, quickly, fairly, and reliably and can lead to shared standards among faculty about what constitutes quality in a response" (Diaz-Rico, 2004, pp. 79–80).

One of the most effective aspects of using rubrics for all learners, but especially for English Language Learners, is that a rubric provides specific feedback. The most effective strategy is to share a blank rubric with all your students ahead of time. This way, students will understand ahead of time the focus for a particular project or assignment. Developing a rubric means defining in advance the specific observable characteristics that make an assignment exceptional, very good, average, or below expectations when it comes to grading.

Creating a Rubric   See Figure 8.5 for a sample rubric and some guidelines for scoring and using.

6. Paper-and-Pencil Tests

Teacher-constructed tests are specifically designed tests based on a particular lesson and how that lesson was taught. The most commonly used paper-and-pencil tests are true-false, matching items, multiple choice, completion items, essay, short

FIGURE 8.5   Sample Rubric

Steps for creating a rubric for a writing sample:

1. Determine *all* the criteria that must be evidenced all of the time for excellence, i.e., grade A.

Organization of paper

Length (2 pages)	Topic sentence in each paragraph
Introductory paragraph	Concluding paragraph (summarizing)
4 supporting paragraphs	

Mechanics of writing

Punctuation	Spelling
Grammar	Sentence construction

Style of writing

Use of synonyms	Flow of thoughts
Use of adjectives and descriptions	Interesting

2. Determine *most* of the criteria that must be evidenced for an above-average rating, i.e., grade B.

Organization of paper

Length (2 pages)	Topic sentence in each paragraph
Introductory paragraph	Concluding paragraph (summarizing)
3–4 supporting paragraphs	

Mechanics of writing (1–2 errors)

Punctuation	Spelling
Grammar	Sentence construction

Style of writing

Use of synonyms (evident most of the time)	Flow of thoughts
Use of adjectives and descriptions (evident most of the time)	Good

3. Determine *some* of the criteria that must be evidenced for an average rating, i.e., grade C.

Organization of paper

Length (2 pages)	Topic sentence in each paragraph
Introductory paragraph	Concluding paragraph (summarizing)
2–3 supporting paragraphs	

Mechanics of writing (3–4 errors)

Punctuation	Spelling
Grammar	Sentence construction

Style of writing

Use of synonyms (evident some of the time)	Flow of thoughts
Use of adjectives and descriptions (some of the time)	Average

(Continued)

FIGURE 8.5   Continued

4. Determine criteria that is evidenced for a below-average rating, i.e., grade D or less.

Organization of paper

Length (1 page)
Introductory paragraph
2 supporting paragraphs

Topic sentence not evident in each
    paragraph
Concluding paragraph (summarizing)

Mechanics of writing (errors evident)

Punctuation
Grammar

Spelling
Sentence construction

Style of writing (fair)

Use of synonyms
Use of adjectives and descriptions

Flow of thoughts
Fair

Categorize the criteria into a matrix or table for easy at-a-glance grading. Determine the point value of each observable criterion. Determine how many points to deduct in the categories below "excellent." While grading you can check off the appropriate box, tally the points, and determine the final grade.

Excellent	Above Average	Average	Fair/Barely Passing	Unsatisfactory
Criteria *always* evidenced	Criteria *almost always* evidenced	Criteria evidenced *some of the time* (but not all the time)	Criteria evidenced *sporadically but not consistently*	Criteria *never* evidenced
Organization of paper (20%)				
Length (2 pages) (2%)				
Introductory paragraph (4%)				
4 supporting paragraphs (5%)				
Topic sentence in each paragraph (5%)				
Concluding paragraph (4%)				
Mechanics of writing (30%)				
Punctuation (5%)				

Grammar (5%)				
Spelling (5%)				
Sentence construction (15%)				
Style of writing (50%)				
Use of synonyms (10%)				
Use of adjectives and descriptions (15%)				
Flow of thoughts (15%)				
Overall impression (10%)				
Total Points (100%)				
Final Grade				

answer. Following are examples of teacher-constructed tests as well as some general teacher tips and guidelines for writing effective test items.

TRUE-FALSE:

Example:

Read the following question and decide if the statement is true or false. Circle either true or false.

Barcelona is the capital city of Spain.

True   False

MATCHING ITEMS:

Match the items (countries) in column A with the items (capital cities) in column B.

Column A	Column B
Ireland	Paris
Spain	Lisbon

Portugal	Dublin
Norway	Berlin
Germany	Oslo
France	Madrid

MULTIPLE CHOICE:

___ is the capital city of Spain.

a. Seville
b. Lisbon
c. Barcelona
d. Madrid

COMPLETION ITEMS:

World War II began in the year____. The war ended in the year____.

ESSAY:

Extended-Response: A question that requires a higher level of cognitive thinking (analysis, synthesis, and evaluation). This test requires a lot of time to organize thought processes and can be used as an assignment over a number of days or as a take-home test (Borich, 2007, p. 413).

Example:

Compare and contrast the role of the United States as a military power during World War II and in the Vietnam War.

Restricted-Response: The student must answer by including specific criteria included in the question (Borich, 2007).

Example:

Discuss the factors that contributed to the Holocaust during World War II. Include in your answer the role of Adolph Hitler, propaganda, and the economic, social, and political climate at that time.

SHORT-ANSWER TESTS:

Administering Short-Answer Tests: Some students may have good subject matter competence but may not possess the necessary writing skills. When faced with the task of answering long or short essay questions many English Language Learners may feel panic and can become obsessed with their writing mechanics rather than content. To help avoid this, consider using the following strategies:

◇   Provide students with the opportunity to give shorter answers by reducing the concepts that must be covered in a single answer or by breaking a question down into two or three separate, simpler questions.

◇   When essay answers are required, allow the students to answer by listing concepts rather than writing paragraphs.

Tips for Writing Tests for Improved Readability and Comprehension

Improving readability is necessary for all students. To improve the readability of test questions and reading course materials, keep the following factors in mind:

1. *Use of vocabulary.* Do not "water down" the content material; drop less frequently used words and substitute more familiar synonyms; and add an extra phrase or even a paragraph to make a concept clearer. Your task is to rewrite the material without diminishing its content, while using a format that is easier for ELL students to read and understand.
2. *Sentence structure* is critical. Shorter sentences are less complex and easier to understand.
3. *Paragraphs* should always have *a topic sentence* at the beginning followed by supporting detail or topic elaboration.
4. *Physical format* is important. The layout should be attractive and font size should be large enough to be easily read.

AUTHOR'S INSIGHT: If you have access to clip art, use it to add visual clues and hints for students.

---

5. Use the *10×10×2 strategy for modifying readability for learners who are reading below grade level.* Here is a guide for modification to a fourth- to sixth-grade reading level: Use no more than 10 sentences made up of no more than 10 words per sentence, and do not allow more than 2 difficult words (words of 3 or more syllables) per 100 words. Don't count proper nouns, compound words, and words that are three syllables only because they are plural (i.e., "s" or "ed" on the end) as difficult words.

Examples of Original Test Questions Revised for Improved Readability

---

AUTHOR'S INSIGHT: It helps to **boldface** significant or key words.

Original Question 1: Compare and contrast the personal attributes and characteristics of Huck Finn and Tom Sawyer.
Revised Question 1: How are Tom Sawyer and Huck Finn alike? How are they different?
Original Question 2: Describe and discuss the probable effects of wage and price controls during periods of inflation.
Revised Question 2: What might happen if **wage and price controls** were used during **inflation**?

Assessment Options for English Language Learners

Figure 8.6 provides assessment strategies to match oral language proficiency levels of English Language Learners.

Choice in Assessments

Assessments should provide all students the opportunity to demonstrate what they know about a given area. English Language Learners, depending on their level of oral language proficiency, should be given alternatives to extensive writing projects. An English Language Learner who is developing English writing skills could be given the following options:

◇ Time line
◇ Graphic representation
◇ Venn diagram, various map products
◇ Drawings
◇ Visual tapes
◇ Using graphics to express knowledge (Reiss, 2008)
◇ Performance-based assessment
◇ Assessment of content, not English language skills (Reiss, 2008)
◇ Grades for progress and effort (Reiss, 2008)
◇ Extra chances, i.e., allow students to retake tests, hand in a second draft, or do an assignment again (Reiss, 2008)

Additional Tips to Consider for English Language Learners

Students may not perform well on a particular test for many reasons. You should be aware of *cultural bias* problems, which occur when students are

FIGURE 8.6   Assessment Strategies to Match Levels of Oral Language Proficiency

Language Level	Recommended Assessment
Silent period—beginning	SOLOM—Student Oral Language Observation Matrix; observation; TPR; thumbs up, thumbs down; response board; students illustrate understanding; number wheel with pictures; fill in blanks
Intermediate	Fill in blanks short answer; multiple choice; true-false items; demonstrations (performance assessments techniques); portfolio; rubrics; use of simple sentences; write simple paragraphs; matching vocabulary items; develop test items with increased readability
Transitional/advanced	Self-checking strategies; portfolios; rubrics; essay; on-grade-level tests but still teaching following skills: CALLA—study and organizational skills

stumped by the terminology used in a question, not because they did not have adequate knowledge. For example, a writing prompt that discusses a stairwell may create difficulties for a student who is not aware of what a "stairwell" is, because a different term is used in his or her culture. English Language Learners, are also learning the culture of a new country, and unfortunately they can become victims of the cultural bias that appears in reading materials and in tests.

Substantial evidence has been provided by multicultural researchers to demonstrate that schooling and education in the United States has a tendency to present cultural discontinuity for culturally and linguistically diverse students because its origins are based on traditional European, white, middle-class values (Banks, 2006; Gay, 2000).

Diaz-Rico (2004, p. 86) identifies the following biases that teachers should be concerned with in relation to English Language Learners:

◇ **Language-specific bias** exists when a test is developed in one language and then is simply and literally translated into another. When this happens it can be quite confusing for the ELL student, especially when compounded by the failure of the teacher to furnish appropriate on-grade-level vocabulary.

AUTHOR'S INSIGHT: I have personally seen this happen.

◇ **Geographic bias** occurs when test questions feature terms that are only used or commonly known in one particular geographic region of the country, e.g., the use of the term "stairwell" or "basement."

◇ **Dialect bias** occurs when certain expressions or colloquial terms are used, which are only generally known or expressed by a certain cultural group of people. A good example is the terms "y'all" or "fixin' to" commonly used by Texans.

◇ **Cultural bias** can exist in very simple items like food items, sports, music, nursery rhymes, and children's stories, which may not be common knowledge within the culture of certain immigrant groups and/or recently arrived ELL students. As a result, many terms, cultural events, and traditions will be new to the world of the newly arrived English Language Learner.

◇ **Class bias** can exist at several levels in the classroom. For example, in schools that don't have a mandatory uniform policy, classes and subcultures of students can develop based on how students dress or what activities they participate in (i.e., jocks, cheerleaders, rappers, computer geeks, nerds). Other class bias can develop based on where a student lives or what his or her parents do for a living.

Involving Parents

Communication with parents of the ELL student can often make the difference between success and failure for the English Language Learner. Teachers should make every attempt to:

◇ Communicate with parents often about the academic progress of students.
◇ Make sure that parents are aware of failing grades.
◇ Provide students with the opportunity to have tutoring or assistance, if there is no one at home who can help them.
◇ Avoid assigning a grade to homework. It is important for ELL students to have the option of doing their work in the classroom (before or after school or during free periods) where help and assistance in English is always available when they need it. If a student is absent make sure he or she has the opportunity to make up class work (so the student doesn't fall behind).

Grading and the English Language Learner

Teachers are permitted to give a modified grade to English Language Learners during their first three years. Focus should be on course content, and individual progress should be monitored without comparing them to other students. Teachers should select specific grammar that can be easily developed rather than redlining everything. Early learning mistakes should be ignored and the focus should be on constantly reteaching content. Provide criteria and rubrics well ahead of time, allow ELL students to create numerous drafts of their work, and perhaps even allow second chances so students can gain mastery of the content.

Teachers should collect *two formal grades a week* from their students; all other assignments should be considered as practice or rehearsal. *Do not call out student grades in class;* do not allow students to grade each other's work—have them grade their own papers (when this is used the paper should be practice). Do not allow students direct access to your grade book, and do not allow them to record their grades in your grade book.

Other Useful Grading Tips:
1. Give grades for effort, creativity, and improvement.
2. Allow students to select a certain number of questions to answer instead of all of them if the test is long.
3. Give a group grade in lieu of an individual score (this works well on the group review prior to a test).
4. Give partial credit for questions attempted (e.g., total points for the correct answer multiplied by the percent you feel is correct, completed, or mastered. If the question is worth 5 points and you feel the student's response was 60% correct, complete, or mastered, the answer would be worth 3 points).
5. Give multiple grades on the same assignment (i.e., one grade for effort, one grade for content, one grade for form, one grade for properly following directions, etc.).

6. Write positive remarks and comments in the margins of the paper.
7. Highlight or notate good answers so students can see what you like and what you expect of them.
8. Review the grading process. Determine the content from which most of the grade came to determine how to average grades for students.
9. Find alternatives to giving zeros. Learning is not taking place where excessive zeros are given and students will get into a hole that they can't get out of.
10. Specify the grading criteria you will use in your class and post it so students will know what is expected of them.
11. Grade any work by students that will help them be successful in your class.
12. Promptly grade and return any and all material—immediate feedback is important for students.
13. When establishing grading criteria, remember to include "M" for "modification." The M grade given on folders or report cards indicates it is a modified grade.

Preparing for High-Stakes Testing

In many states, like Texas, ELL students in their third year of residence in the country must be prepared to take their grade-level tests. These scores count, and school personnel are held accountable for how well their ELL students do on state tests. Although occasional exceptions are made, under No Child Left Behind (2001) schools are accountable for the academic growth and development of their English Language Learners.

When preparing students to meet state standardized testing, teachers should:

a. Focus on depth rather than on breadth.
b. Familiarize students with the text format.
c. Give students parallel tests.
d. Give two answers to choose from at first, and then add three and finally four as with actual state standardized tests.
e. Teach predictable patterns.
f. Teach phrases students can expect to see on tests.
g. Teach test-taking skills like highlighting, underlining key words and phrases, eliminating wrong answers, and so on.
h. Model this process out loud and have students do the same.
i. Understand how students arrived at a given response.

Test-taking strategies are best done closer to the time the test is administered. Most school districts now provide teachers with scope and sequence, and benchmarks, which provide valuable information to educators about where instructional planning should focus. Specifically, teaching inference and opinion will be helpful, as will reading and underlining, rereading the test, eliminating choices, and so on.

When preparing for state standards teachers should focus on key or core concepts (the gist of things) and not worry about covering everything. Research literature suggests depth rather than breadth (Reiss, 2008).

Format familiarization (usually once a week) or giving your classroom tests in some multiple-choice format (giving students two choices at first, then three, then four); teaching predictable patterns and phrases, and testing accommodations as permitted by most states (Reiss, 2008) are all useful teaching tools. Other useful tools include:

1. **Presentation**—the test can be read aloud; it can be simplified, paraphrased, translated into native language if the state allows, and/or recorded ahead of time by community volunteers. Students should be allowed to request clarification during the actual test.
2. **Response**—providing a dictionary; marking answers in the test book.
3. **Setting**—providing a quiet place.
4. **Timing**—providing extra time.

Final Reminder: The Importance of Using a Variety of Assessment Strategies

Do not rely on just one type of test for your student assessments. Use a variety of strategies so your students can demonstrate their knowledge in various ways. It also helps to remove reading barriers or a language barrier, and at all times consider the language levels of your ELL students.

CHAPTER SUMMARY

This chapter discussed the purpose of assessment as the collection of learning outcomes data used by educators to make inferences about student learning. Two major categories of tests were discussed: *externally produced* assessment methods, and *teacher-produced* assessment methods.

Externally produced assessment methods are either *norm-referenced* (used to compare student outcomes to other groups of students of similar age and ability) or *criterion-referenced* (used to gauge how well a student can perform a specific learning task). Standardized tests are generally either norm or criterion referenced. The case for and against standardized testing was discussed and the reason why a student can be passing in the regular classroom but fail a standardized test. The answer is the nature of standardized tests as one-dimensional and only testing one aspect of the learner. A student may have many reasons for failing a standardized test that are unrelated to abilities. Standardized tests rely on one type of assessment to make an evaluation of student learning.

Teacher-produced tests are more **multidimensional** in nature, and the teacher does not rely on one type of assessment to make an evaluation of student learning. A teacher may use text- and curriculum-embedded questions, oral tests, performance-based tests, portfolios, rubrics, and many paper-and-pencil tests to assess how students are learning. The chapter emphasized that assessment for all learners is best when it is multidimensional, ongoing, and used to guide teacher instruction.

Classroom application strategies in this chapter explained all the afore-mentioned teacher-produced tests as well as many tips for the creation of true-false, matching items, multiple choice, completion items, essay, as well as short-answer tests. Tips for writing tests and improving readability and comprehension for English Language Learners were also discussed. Assessment options for teachers to use with English Language Learners were presented as well as grading tips, and how to prepare all students for high-stakes testing. The chapter ended with the importance of using a variety of assessment for all learners.

RELECTIVE CHAPTER QUESTIONS

1. What is the true nature and purpose of assessment?
2. How has No Child Left Behind changed how student failure is perceived? Discuss the pros and cons of this perception.
3. In the section "What Research Tells Us," one of the impacts of NCLB is that the level and quantity of testing required has more than doubled since ESEA. Why is this so? Is this a positive or negative change for schools? What do you think will be the future implications for schools, teachers, and students?
4. Discuss the differences between each of the following and give an example of each: criterion-referenced and norm-referenced tests; externally produced and teacher-produced tests; formative and summative evaluation; one-dimensional and multidimensional testing.
5. What is the importance of using a variety of assessment practices for all learners?

SUGGESTED FIELD-BASED ACTIVITIES FOR PRE-SERVICE AND IN-SERVICE TEACHERS

1. Interview a teacher (grade level of your choice) about the assessment procedures he or she uses in the classroom. Ask the teacher to explain how he or she maintains grades and averages for reporting purposes; how he or she communicates failing grades to students and teachers; how he or she prepares students for standardized tests.
2. Choose one criterion-referenced and one norm-referenced test mentioned in this chapter. Research as much as you can about these tests in terms of history and development, and purpose and use in schools.
3. Find out what standardized test is used in your state for accountability purposes under NCLB. Find out how this test is administered, scored, and reported in your school district. Try to find the results reported in the past year for your local school district. Try to find out how each school did in your district. What is your local school's rating and the overall district rating?

REFERENCES

Abedi, J., Hofstetter, C. H., & Lord, C. (2004). Assessment accommodations for English language learners: Implications for policy-based empirical research. *Review of Educational Research, 74*(1), 1–28.

Banks, J. (2006). *Cultural diversity and education: Foundations, curriculum, and teaching* (5th ed). Boston: Allyn & Bacon.

Batt, L., Kim, J., & Sunderman, G. (2005). *Limited English proficient students: Increased accountability under NCLB.* Harvard University: Policy Brief from the Civil Rights Project.

Bohn, A. P., & Sleeter, C. (2000). Will multicultural education survive the standards movements? *Phi Delta Kappan, 82,* 156–159.

Borich, G. D. (2007). *Effective teaching methods: Research-based practice* (6th ed.). Upper Saddle River, NJ: Pearson Merrill Prentice Hall.

Curtin, E. M. (2002). *Students' and teachers' perceptions of culturally responsive teaching: Urban middle school case study.* Dissertation: University of North Texas. Electronic dissertation available at http://www.unt.edu/library.htm.

Darling-Hammond, L., Noguera, P., Cobb, V. L., & Meier, D. W. (2007, May 21). Evaluating "No Child Left Behind." *Nation,* 11–21.

Diaz-Rico, L. (2004). *Teaching English learners: Strategies and methods.* Boston, MA: Pearson Allyn & Bacon.

Faltis, C. J., & Coulter, C. A. (2008). *Teaching English language learners and immigrant students in secondary schools.* Upper Saddle River, NJ: Pearson Merrill Prentice Hall.

Figuerora, R. A. (2002). Towards a new model of assessment. In A. J. Artiles & A. A. Ortiz (Eds.), *English language learners with special educational needs.* Washington, DC & McHenry, IL: Center for Applied Linguistics & Delta Systems Co.

Freeman, Y. S., Freeman, D. E., & Mercuri, S. (2002). *Closing the achievement gap: How to reach limited-formal schooling and long-term English learners.* Portsmouth, NH: Heinemann.

Gay, G. (2000). *Culturally responsive teaching: Theory, research, & practice.* New York: Teachers College Press.

Gronlund, N. E. (2006). *Assessment of student achievement* (8th ed.). Upper Saddle River, NJ: Pearson Education.

Kohn, A. (2000). *The case against standardized testing.* Portsmouth, NH: Heinemann.

Marchesani, R. J. (2007). *The field guide to teaching: A handbook for new teachers.* Upper Saddle River, NJ: Pearson Merrill Prentice Hall.

Meier, D. W. (2002). *In schools we trust: Creating communities of learning in an era of testing and standardization.* Boston: Beacon Press.

Meier, D. W., & Wood, G. H. (Eds.). (2004). *Many children left behind: How the No Child Left Behind Act is damaging our children and our schools.* Boston: Beacon Press.

Peregoy, S., & Boyle, O. F. (2005). *Reading, writing and learning in ESL: A resource book for K–12 teachers* (4th ed.). Boston, MA: Allyn & Bacon, Pearson Education.

Popham, W. J. (2007). *Assessment for educational leaders.* Boston, MA: Pearson Allyn & Bacon.

Reiss, J. (2008). *102 content strategies for English language learners: Teaching for academic success in grades 3–12.* Upper Saddle River, NJ: Pearson Merrill Prentice Hall.

Standards for teacher competence in educational assessment of students. (2007). American Federation of Teachers, National Council on Measurement in Education, and National Education Association. Retrieved 7/5/2007: http://www.unl.edu/buros/bimm/html/article3.html.

Tucker, P. D., & Stronge, J. H. (2005). *Linking teacher evaluation and student learning.* Alexandria, VA: Association for Supervision and Curriculum Development.

U.S. Department of Education. (2006). No Child Left Behind: What parents need to know (Rev.). Available online at www.ed.gov/nclb/overview/intro/.

CHAPTER 9
Motivational and Classroom Management Strategies for English Language Learners

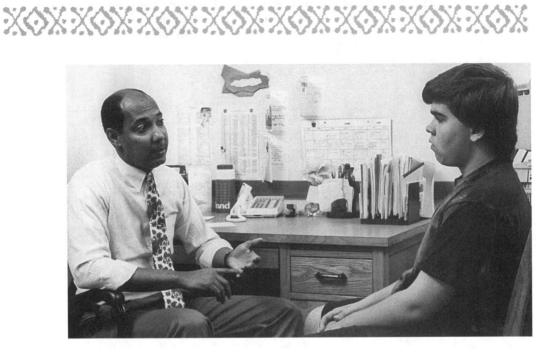

INTRODUCTION

For the teacher, skillful management of student behaviors in a classroom is critical in order for learning to occur. Teaching is more than just crafting great lessons; teaching is about imparting knowledge in a manner that interests our students. Effective teaching is measured by how well students learn. The challenge for a teacher is to simultaneously capture the interest of students, teach them, and maintain order and discipline in the classroom. Learning cannot occur in a classroom that is badly managed, where students are not listening, and where they are talking out of turn.

This chapter addresses practical strategies for the beginning teacher who must deal with classroom management and student discipline issues. Three discipline models are presented in this chapter followed by an analysis of the advantages and the disadvantages of each. The models chosen are all research-based, are the most effective, and are commonly utilized in today's classrooms. Practical tips and strategies are presented that will be helpful for beginning and experienced teachers alike who may be searching for new techniques to try in the classroom. Many of these tips seem oversimplified but are very effective and do work.

It is recommended that beginning teachers choose a discipline model that resonates with his or her general philosophy of teaching and one that integrates with his or her personality and emotional sensitivities. Many experienced teachers will tell you they do not rely exclusively on any one discipline model plan but instead use a little of each and develop their own individualized approach to discipline that fits their unique classroom dynamics. One size fits all rarely works in an actual classroom setting.

Classroom management encompasses far more than this chapter can provide and requires an entire book to cover the depth of research and information on this topic alone. This chapter highlights what beginning teachers should know in order to survive during their first years of teaching. Although this chapter does not provide the panacea for out-of-control and violent behaviors, it does provide substantive and practical advice and strategies for teachers dealing with minor classroom disruptions and off-task behaviors. Additional resources are provided at the end of this chapter for further in-depth reading on this topic.

FOCUS QUESTIONS

⬦ How can beginning teachers anticipate classroom disruptions and the discipline problems that may occur in the classroom?

⬦ How does a teacher decide which discipline model to choose?

⬦ How does a teacher deal with minor student disruptions in class like talking out of turn and off-task behaviors?

CLASSROOM SCENARIO

An excerpt from the Teacher Reflection journal of Ellen, a seventh-grade teacher during her first year teaching:

It's 30 minutes into the class period and Sergio is still fidgeting in his seat, his book is closed, and no paper or pencil are to be seen.

"How can I help you get started, Sergio?" I inquire with a forced politeness. I'm sure my exasperation is evident, although I am taking great pains to hide the frustration that has been growing all day. It is now 7th period, the last period of the day, thank goodness, and I have been dealing with children like Sergio all day.

So far all of my classes had rebelled against the assignment on the board, which states: "Read pages 138–145 on Newton's Laws." My grand plan was to have the class read for about 30 minutes while I spent time with some individual children who needed one-on-one help. Then the class would cover a worksheet that clarified the 3 laws of physics that the class had supposedly just read about. In reality I needed TIME—time to deal with the 21% of my class who were failing. Grades were due to be turned in that night and my goal was to give some last-minute make-up work to this group of irresponsible, pain-in-the-behind students. More than likely, they had their assignments in their folder or crumpled up somewhere in their backpacks.

I thought (I thought, yeah, right!), this is such a simple request. Read 7 pages with lots of pictures mixed in, and while an admittedly boring assignment it was a quite simple task to perform. But instead, as I do every day, I had to be a policewoman in the classroom. Not 15 seconds could pass without someone in the class talking when they weren't supposed to.

"Reading is individual work!" I would squawk at my students each and every period. "You can't talk and focus on your reading at the same time." Time and again I ask myself, "Will they ever learn?"

Then after about the 5th time shushing them I began my lecture on how they needed to learn the correct way to read and search for information; and that someday they would realize this effort was really a GOOD THING and something to be thankful for, for the rest of their lives. The look of contempt on their faces equated with flipping me off, in mass. ("Ungrateful brats," I retorted silently to myself.)

I have come to learn that the first thing out of a 7th grader's mouth, when a teacher explains that he/she has four missing papers, is, "I turned that in!" They say it with absolute disdain and assuredness, and in the past I used to fall for it. In fact, that's one of the reasons why I got into teaching. I remember as a seventh grader not being respected or listened to by my teachers. Even as early as the fifth grade, when I was 11 years old, I had promised myself I would NEVER forget just how smart and aware I was at this young age. I promised myself that I would never treat MY kids like they didn't count.

I became a teacher because I wanted to help kids rise to their highest potential, to confront their minds with puzzlements if for nothing more than the adrenaline rush of being challenged. I envisioned kids on the edge of seats, hands held high, "Me! Me!" I envisioned science experiments, with groups of learners trying to explain to each other why something happened. I envisioned being one of those cool teachers who could smile as she entered the room and pleasantly ask for everyone to be seated and quiet now because the bell has rung. I envisioned my students to be similar to what I was in 7th grade because I had told myself that I would never forget just how smart and aware a 10-year-old really is.

Yet my heart feels broken most days. I bark like a drill sergeant, and when I do allow a smile to escape me, my students take this as a false signal to do as they please with even more fervor than they were already doing it. My lessons are ill-thought-out and unengaging, partly because I have no experience, but mostly because I spend my evenings calling parents and serving detentions instead of putting together materials for great lessons. Moreover, I am fearful of being my normal animated self, one of my greatest assets to teaching, and I do not trust my students to perform experiments without ruining or stealing all of my equipment and supplies.

The vicious circle of the new teacher and her misbehaved class:

1. The students refuse to follow simple instructions like reading the textbook because it does not seem to apply to their lives.
2. Rather, they need something hands-on and engaging to motivate them.
3. However, hands-on activities require students to exhibit responsible behavior and the ability to follow simple instructions.
4. Back to #1.

I've had to grow up this year and abandon my selectively idealistic 10-year-old perspective. When I look back a little more honestly, I can remember that I certainly was not so pure; I was out to get what I wanted, just like the kids I teach. No sooner than the teacher was turned I was talking, or passing notes, or cheating off someone else's paper.

On the other hand, there are some things that I will never be able to make a personal connection with, such as screaming threats across the room, or yelling at a teacher, "I didn't do it!" I will never be able to relate to my students who choose to be suspended for 3 days because they are duty-bound to fight somebody who just said something about their momma. I will never be able to relate to my students who choose to leave answers blank rather than apply a tiny bit of effort toward critical thinking.

The best I can do is to accept each kid, warts and all. I have no control over how they come to me, and besides, they're just making a short pit stop with me on the racetrack of life. My goal is to survive my first year of teaching without blowing the vein that runs through the middle of my forehead. It's a daily rededication, because daily I have thoughts of just walking out and going back to mowing lawns rather than take this kind of pounding.

"Hi, Ms. O'Leary!" I look up from my computer to see Dorothy Pritchard; she's just been allowed back to school after being suspended for her third fight in 12 weeks, two of them in my class. "Hey sweetheart; I've missed you. Are you back?" Dorothy is one of my favorites, and I instinctively extend my arm out for her to come over and give me a hug. "Yeah, they let me come back today. Hey, is there any work I'm missing, or extra credit? I wanna do good in your class." My heart is breaking again, but for joy this time, because I see such potential in this young lady who may very well wind up in an alternative school before the year is out, who wears the same dirty little white shirt every day, whose mother arrived at my door during 7th period one day, affronting me with the smell of gin. "You're doing great in my class," I reply. I turn to look at her squarely in the eyes: "I am so impressed with your tenacity." Dorothy smiles to herself and looks down, but then looks up inquisitively: "What's tenacity?" . . .

So, there the conversation goes. The teacher and the learner, but which is which? Dorothy reminds me that something is being taught, even if it is not science. I need her to come see me every day to remind me that diamonds can indeed be found from within the ashes of a disastrous day . . . or a disastrous life (Curtin, 2006b).

Guiding Discussion Questions

◇ What are the frustrations experienced by the teacher?
◇ What are the problematic behaviors being exhibited by her students?
◇ If you are an in-service teacher, what are your current experiences with classroom management and discipline? If you are a pre-service teacher, what are your future concerns about classroom management and discipline?

Author's Insight

Teachers must try to understand the motivation behind the behavior. Many students use avoidance tactics to get out of doing something or to get the teacher's attention. Many students have experienced failure at home and at school as a normal part of their lives, and avoidance tactics are the only form of success they know. These students succeed at failure and at avoiding how to learn. Teachers must reach all students and discover the true motivation behind such behavior. Students will only learn when they are disciplined and self-motivated.

WHAT RESEARCH TELLS US

Motivation and Learning

Motivation and learning are linked and very closely related because in order to continue learning one must be motivated. When a person is successful at the learning process, then there is motivation to continue learning. When students experience self-efficacy (Bandura, 1985), which is a feeling of satisfaction and a sense of being responsible for their accomplishments, then they are more likely to try a task again rather than just giving up.

Learning English as a second language requires a lot of internal drive and motivation; it is at times an overwhelming and daunting endeavor for students of all ages. The importance of success at each stage of language development, from the silent period to the beginning language phase, to the intermediate phase, to the advanced phase is paramount for the English Language Learner. Although teacher support and scaffolding is important in the classroom, the English Language Learners must acquire lifelong skills for those periods that go well beyond the scope of the classroom (Brown, 2006).

The term "self-efficacy" describes the student's perception of success and failure as it directly impacts academic motivation (Stipek, 2001). Students may attribute ability, effort, task difficulty, luck, and other people as factors contributing to their success or failure (Schunk, Pintrich, & Meese, 2007).

When students possess high self-efficacy, they are more likely to believe they have the potential within themselves to be successful. Self-efficacious students will not blame their academic failure on someone else. It is important for

English Language Learners to possess *high self-efficacy* because students with low self-efficacy are more likely to give up too easily and will not equate their own personal efforts with a successful outcome in the classroom. Students with low self-efficacy tend to blame teachers and the system, and they are more likely to act out in class and become a behavioral problem (Bandura, 1985).

Good and Brophy (2007) suggest that teachers who motivate students in the classroom should:

◇ Provide a supportive classroom environment.
◇ Provide structured activities with appropriate levels of challenge for the students, but that are not too difficult.
◇ Teach and connect learning objectives that have personal meaning and relevance.
◇ Teach students to set personal learning goals and perform self-appraisals.

Students who are taught learning strategies become *independent* and *autonomous* learners. Students who possess their own set of learning strategies understand their academic success can be controlled by their own individual efforts, planning, and preparation. Personal efforts on the part of students not only increase academic success but also improve self-esteem and self-confidence (Chamot & O'Malley, 1994).

Self-Fulfilling Prophecy

The famous study "Pygmalion in the Classroom" is attributed to Rosenthal (1987). Pygmalion was a mythical sculptor who carved a statue and then brought it to life by his own desires and wishes. Essentially the Pygmalion theory suggests that what we think can become real, if we think about it enough and believe in it. In the classroom, the perception teachers have of students (positive, negative, or both) can result in the students actually becoming these perceptions. This phenomenon is also known as the "self-fulfilling prophecy" (Woolfolk, 1999). Students have a tendency to live up (or down) to those expectations set for them by the teachers, adults, and parents who influence their lives.

Many classroom teachers who have low expectations for students tend to be more rigid in their own discipline style. Teachers with a more autocratic style of discipline tend to be the beginning and novice teachers. This discipline style tends to be less congruent with the learning styles of English Language Learners. When teachers are more concerned with order, control, and discipline, their students tend to become less motivated and less interested in the learning process. In some cases students give up, don't raise their hands, and assume that their personal effort does not matter (Curtin, 2005).

Under these circumstances, teachers often come to the wrong conclusion about their students, can attribute their behavior in the classroom to lack of concern about their work and to low aspirations, or they can even blame the student directly. Teachers may even relax requirements for students by setting lower expectations based on the well-intentioned premise that the teacher is actually doing the student a favor and helping him or her to pass (Curtin, 2005).

This strategy by the teacher, although well intentioned, may result in decreased feeling of self-worth, can lead to hostility and anger, and is not in the student's best interest in the long term. The message the student receives is that "I am not good enough" (Graham, 1991). The result of this misdirected strategy is a perpetuating cycle of failure.

Classroom Management

"Effective teaching requires a well-organized, businesslike classroom in which motivated students work diligently at their learning tasks free from distractions and interruptions. Providing such a setting for learning requires careful thought and preparation and is called effective classroom management" (Kellough & Kellough, 2007, p. 111).

There are many models of classroom management available for a new and beginning teacher. These models differ in their underlying psychological underpinnings and philosophies. Historically, classroom management tended to rely on coercion and fear. Students did as they were told and did not have a collective voice in classroom decisions. These classrooms tended to be autocratic in nature with the teacher in control (Dreikurs & Cassel, 1972). In this model the teacher would force his or her will on students to prove that he or she had control of the class. Students' motivation tended to be from outside pressure rather than from within. Silence was the predominant mode in the classroom with the teacher doing the majority of the talking.

Nowadays, discipline models and classroom management techniques tend to be what is termed more "democratic" (Dreikurs & Cassel, 1972). Here there are order and limits in the classroom and while there is firmness it is done with kindness and respect for students. Students tend to have more involvement in decision making, and cooperation is encouraged among students along with the creation of a sense of community.

What a new teacher should avoid is "permissive" classroom management where rules and orders are inconsistently enforced and where off-task behaviors are permitted. This is an ineffective classroom environment for all learners (Dreikurs & Cassel, 1972).

CLASSROOM APPLICATION STRATEGIES

Overview of Discipline Management Models and Practical Classroom Applications

It is impossible to do justice in just one chapter to the range of classroom discipline management models available. Following are three of the most commonly used and widely evidenced models of classroom management in K–12 classrooms today.

1 ASSERTIVE DISCIPLINE (LEE CANTER, 1993)

Basic Characteristics of Discipline Management System

Canter (Canter & Canter, 1993) believes that teachers have needs that must be met first and that students have the right to have a teacher who will ensure that inappropriate student behaviors are curtailed and punished as necessary in class. To ensure that the needs of both students and teachers are met, teachers must assert themselves.

Application in Classroom

Canter (Canter & Canter, 1993) advocates the use of the following steps for teachers when applying assertive discipline in the classroom.

STEP 1: *Develop Positive Student-Teacher Relationships*   Teachers must get to know all students as individuals, that is, to know students' hobbies and interests, and incorporate these in class. Teachers must teach students what they expect in terms of behavior and never assume that students know what is expected of them in class.

STEP 2: *Set Clear Rules and Expectations*   Rules should be clearly posted and known to all students. Here are some common rules that should be familiar to all students: rules in relation to assignments completed; doing own work; keeping hands, feet, and all objects to self. Canter recommends that teachers limit rules to only five or six.

STEP 3: *Monitor and Track Inappropriate Behaviors*   This is where the teacher must follow through and be very consistent with the enforcement of rules. Students must be aware of how their behavior is being monitored. Teachers can do this by marking a clipboard or a chart beside each student, marking appropriate/inappropriate behaviors. A teacher can utilize a color code system where a student's color changes if an infraction occurs and the student suffers consequences for each level of inappropriate behavior. Some teachers put the student's name on the board as a warning and keep tally marks. Each successive tally mark results in a behavioral consequence (punishment).

STEP 4: *Use Punishments When Rules Are Broken*   Following are examples of punishments supported by Canter: time-out, withdrawing a privilege, detention, student sent to principal's office, involving parents (phone call/letter/e-mail home), student sent to another class.

STEP 5: *Use Rewards for Appropriate Behaviors*   Canter supports the idea of catching children in the act of being good. Some examples of rewards for appropriate behavior supported by Canter (2002) include:

- ◇ Personal attention by teacher
- ◇ Awards—plaques, stickers, special rewards or tokens
- ◇ Certificates

◇ Special privileges
◇ Material rewards (tangible objects, stickers, books)
◇ Home rewards (teacher collaborates with parents and student earns extra time to watch TV or engage in an in-home activity agreed upon by both teacher and parent)
◇ Group rewards—the class earns a marble in a jar when groups exemplify appropriate behaviors, e.g., walking appropriately in line to another class, appropriate behavior in cafeteria or during recess.

STEP 6: *Get the Parents on Your Side*   Canter (2002) believes parents are paramount in helping teachers maintain classroom discipline. Following are some examples by Canter of how teachers can involve parents in discipline support:

◇ Send a postcard at the beginning of the year outlining your behavioral and academic expectations.
◇ Send a written explanation of rules and consequences (translated into home languages as much as possible).
◇ Have telephone conversations with parents early in the year and throughout the year at regular intervals.
◇ Schedule conferences with parents on a regular basis.
◇ Explain homework requirements to parents at the beginning of the year.
◇ Have back-to-school nights where parents are invited to attend school, meet the teacher, and attend a teacher-provided workshop on supporting students.
◇ Post a video on your Web site showing students doing exciting projects and being involved in learning experiences.

2 REALITY THERAPY/CHOICE THEORY (WILLIAM GLASSER, 2001)

Basic Characteristics of Discipline Management System

This discipline management system is inherently different from the one previously described. This system helps involve the student in making personal choices and decisions. The student is taught corrective actions and is involved in setting behavioral goals. The approach is to help students identify their inappropriate social behaviors, to accept and understand why they are inappropriate, and ultimately to replace the undesirable behaviors with ones that are more socially acceptable. Class meetings (Gathercoal, 2001) are used a lot as are one-on-one conferences with the teacher and individual students.

Reality therapy helps to develop a sense of belonging for students. Manning and Bucher (2007) provide the following examples of Reality Therapy for teachers to use in the classroom. Using these examples helps students feel a sense of belonging in the classroom.

1. Have students participate in developing the classroom rules. Have students determine appropriate and inappropriate behaviors.
2. Have students identify a name for their class or divide the class into teams and have students select names for the teams.

3. Use bulletin boards to highlight the work of all students, not just a few.
4. Encourage positive interdependence by having students work a lot in groups (Manning & Bucher, 2007).

The following five steps synthesize the tenets of Reality therapy/choice theory

1. **Students are helped to identify their inappropriate behaviors:** Ask students why they did the inappropriate behavior. Do not allow them to blame others; this will take time. Have them take responsibility for what they did. With older students you can have them "cool off" and write it out on a clipboard during recess, or at a time in the school day that is not devoted to instruction.
2. **Students identify consequences if their inappropriate behaviors continue:** Teacher has student identify the consequences of such behavior. There may be a specific classroom consequence already established or one he or she can create for self.
3. **Students evaluate their inappropriate behaviors and consequences:** Teacher gets students to evaluate the consequence and its appropriateness.
4. **Students create their own plan of action to eliminate inappropriate behavior:** Teacher helps student form a plan that will either signal or help preempt such behaviors in the future.
5. **Teacher supports students in their efforts to stick to their plan by enforcing the consequences if necessary:** Teacher reminds student of plan and consequences of behavior ahead of time (Edwards, 2004).

3 POSITIVE DISCIPLINE IN THE CLASSROOM

Basic Characteristics of Model

Nelsen, Lott, and Glenn (2000) believe that all schools should treat students with respect, and that students should never be ridiculed or humiliated. Their model of Positive Discipline offers a lot for teachers to consider as a classroom management option.

Nelsen, Lott, and Glenn (2000) help teachers to understand that students' inappropriate behaviors are defensive "barriers" that students use because underneath the students feel unworthy or incapable of succeeding. It is up to the teachers to create "builders" in the classroom. These "builders" must be initiated by the teacher. Essentially "builders" are skills that the teacher can teach students so they will be successful in school.

Nelsen, Lott, and Glenn (2000) advocate the use of "class meetings" where students have an opportunity to learn new skills, discuss inappropriate behaviors, and so on. The Positive Discipline model discusses five major barriers that educators need to be aware of when dealing with students. These five barriers are:

◇ **(1) Assuming That Students Know How to Behave (Barrier)**
◇ **Instead Checking (Builder)**

Teacher should always check with student's level of understanding and feeling about situations. Sometimes teachers expect more from students than they are capable of, for example, assuming students know how to line up in your classroom. A teacher should never assume that students know what is expected of them in terms of behavior but should instead ask and discuss with students and specify expectations clearly.

⬦ **(2) Rescuing/Explaining (Barrier)**
⬦ **Instead Exploring (Builder)**

Teachers should not do everything for students but allow them to learn from their own mistakes. For example, a teacher who is always lecturing to students about wearing their coats before going out should instead let students learn on their own by going outside without a coat and then suffering the consequence of being cold. This is a natural consequence that is more effective for the students and chances are they will not need to be reminded to wear their coat the next time.

⬦ **(3) Directing Students/Giving Commands (Barrier)**
⬦ **Instead Inviting/Encouraging (Builder)**

Many teachers forget to say "Please" and "I would appreciate it if . . ." Older students in particular will respond much better to being asked in such a manner rather than being ordered to do something. The goal should be to teach students to do the responsible thing and not to do it only when they are asked. Directing, say Nelsen, Lott, and Glenn (2000), only reinforces dependency and eliminates student initiative and cooperation.

⬦ **(4) Expecting (Barrier)**
⬦ **Instead Celebrating (Builder)**

Sometimes teachers fall into the trap of expecting too much from students in terms of maturity. A teacher who says, "I expected more from you than that" actually discourages students more and could make them more defiant or resistant. Instead the authors suggest praising a student who takes a risk and who suddenly does something in the classroom without being asked. Praise is more likely to cause the student to want to continue that behavior.

⬦ **(5) Adultisms (Barrier)**
⬦ **Instead Respecting (Builder)**

Language like "Why can't you ever___? How come you never___?" is what the authors term "Adultisms." Such phrases will only make the student feel anger, shame, or resentment and will not garner respect. Teachers who use this language forget that students are not mini-adults and expect them to act and think like adults.

The goal of this discipline model is to create a win-win environment. The authors stress the following as the rationale underlying their model: "Where did we get the crazy idea that to make people do better, we first have to make them feel worse? People do better when they feel better" (Nelsen, et al., 2000, p. 120).

HOLDING SUCCESSFUL CLASS MEETINGS (NELSEN, ET AL., 2000)

The following format is recommended:

1. Begin the meeting with compliments and appreciation.
2. Follow up on prior solutions.
3. Have an agenda and allow students to add to the agenda before the meeting:
   a. Share feelings while the other listens.
   b. Discuss without fixing.
   c. Ask for problem-solving help.
4. Discuss future plans and solutions (Nelsen, et al., 2007, p. 140).

For high school classes they recommend conducting the class meeting during advisor periods or alternating the class meeting in different subject departments. You may be tempted to say that you do not have time for this, but it will be worth it in the long run. Once students learn the format it goes faster. They caution that the process takes time.

Which Model to Choose?

This is going to be the most overwhelming choice at first for a beginning teacher. Marchesani (2007) recommends that a teacher who successfully implements a discipline system is aware of the following six factors when choosing a model to use (p. 78):

1. **What are the ages and developmental needs of my students?**

   High school student: need for autonomy; need for choice; need to save face in front of peers; more abstract in thinking

   Middle school student: still developing physically and emotionally; need structure; need to save face; peer pressure is very strong

   Elementary school student: need structure; need to feel secure; need to feel loved; short attention span; need a variety in choice of activities; become very restless

2. **What are the unique political characteristics of my school setting?**   What is the socioeconomic background of the school population? Is it Title I, middle class, or upper middle class? Is it an exemplary school or failing in terms of NCLB? Does it have a good or bad reputation?

3. **What is the principal's expectation in terms of discipline and classroom management?**   Is there a discipline management system already in place in the school? What is the climate of the school? Is the principal very visible? Does the principal deal with discipline issues in a fair and consistent manner?

4. **What is the physical environment of my school?**   Where are bathrooms located? Are there opportunity for students to get into trouble? Escape? Is the school new or old? Is there an intercom system? Is there a telephone? Or e-mail?

5. **What is the teaching and classroom management style of my teaching colleagues?** What is the system they use? Do I have to use the one already in use in the school or can I implement my own?

6. **What is my personal belief about classroom management?** Am I very structured? Do I like order and discipline? Do I tend to let the students have more control than needed? How can I teach my students not to abuse my limits if I am more relaxed in my discipline style?

The answers to all the above questions should help a beginning teacher decide which of the three discipline models presented in this chapter will best fit his or her needs. It is an important decision and one that should not be taken frivolously.

Creating a Classroom Management Plan

Once a discipline model has been chosen the teacher should observe the general guidelines suggested in Figure 9.1 for running a smooth and orderly classroom. The guidelines read like common sense but their implementation will ensure a classroom that is run smoothly and effectively for all students. All these guidelines are equally important. Failure in any one of these will result in disequilibrium in your class and lead to discipline problems. These guidelines are presented in question format to help a beginning teacher analyze what is happening in his or her classroom. These can be used periodically to reflect on classroom practice and to set goals for improvement as needed throughout the year.

Choosing a Discipline Plan: Importance of Knowing Your Students

Understanding the diversity of your students is a very important component when designing your discipline management plan. Manning and Bucher (2007) stress the importance of considering and understanding the following diverse differences in students:

1. **Cultural**
   ◇ Many students avoid making eye contact because they consider it rude and inappropriate.
   ◇ Some students feel threatened if their personal space is invaded.
   ◇ Calling attention to students through praise may cause older students to lose face as they do not want to excel at the expense of the group.
   ◇ Competition is not appreciated in many cultures that value cooperation over competition (Manning & Bucher, 2007).

2. **Linguistic**
   ◇ Many English Language Learners and culturally diverse students need to feel that they belong and that they can make language mistakes.

FIGURE 9.1   Self-Checking Guidelines for Maintaining an Orderly and Well-Functioning Classroom Learning Community

Use this checklist as a guideline before school begins or during the school year to help you pinpoint your areas of strengths and weaknesses. Ask your colleagues to evaluate you on these items and welcome their suggestions and feedback. These are only guidelines. Feel free to add additional ones in the spaces provided.

GUIDELINE 1: CLASSROOM ENVIRONMENT

Physical Environment
- ☐ How is the physical layout of the classroom?
- ☐ Is it warm and inviting?
- ☐ Is the furniture arranged so that all students are visible to you from any point in the classroom?
- ☐ Is the furniture arrangement conducive to cooperative grouping and pair work?
- ☐ Are student books and materials neatly organized, labeled, and within easy reach of students?
- ☐ Are all teacher materials clearly labeled and visible within easy access for a substitute teacher or colleague?
- ☐ Is the classroom colorful and inviting with lots of environmental print and posters depicting the content subject area?
- ☐ Are there quiet areas where students can work?
- ☐ Are the quiet areas at a distance from the noisy areas?
- ☐ Others _____
  _____
  _____

Psychological Guidelines
- ☐ Do you have a consistent procedure for students to do the following: enter, leave, go to restroom, seek help with assignments, take attendance, lunch count, get missed work if absent, make up work, turn in work, etc.?
- ☐ Do you have nametags for all students?
- ☐ Do students know what they are supposed to do when they enter the classroom?
- ☐ Do you have activities available for students first thing in the morning or when work is finished early?
- ☐ Do you stand and greet each student at the door at the beginning/end of period or at beginning and end of day?
- ☐ Is student work displayed around the room?
- ☐ Do you have assigned helpers and tasks for students so they contribute to the overall orderliness of the classroom?
- ☐ Others: _____
  _____
  _____

Routines and Procedures
- ☐ Do students know how to ask for help from you and each other?
- ☐ Do students know what to do when they finish their work early?
- ☐ Do you have centers for independent practice and make-up work if necessary?
- ☐ Do you have a procedure for saving assignments for students who are absent?

(Continued)

FIGURE 9.1   Continued

☐ Do you have a procedure for make-up work for absent students?
☐ Others: _____

_____
_____

GUIDELINE 2: LESSON PLANNING AND INSTRUCTION

☐ Have your lessons been planned according to guidelines in Chapters 4–6?
☐ Do you have resources and additional supplemental materials ready and organized?
☐ Do you have books, materials, centers ready?
☐ Do you reflect on how well your lessons go and make modifications as needed before, during, and after the lesson?
☐ How do you know if your lessons are engaging?
☐ Do you have a series of activities planned for students who finish early or who need extra time (see Chapters 5–7)?
☐ Do you have a backup plan if technology fails?
☐ Do you have a procedure for checking and grading homework?
☐ Do you have a fair and equitable grading policy that is clearly communicated to all students?
☐ When do you plan for the next day?
☐ Are you planning enough? Is it too much or too little?
☐ Are you spending too much of your personal time planning and wasting planning opportunities during the day?
☐ Others: _____

_____
_____

Lesson Instruction

☐ Do you spend some time on reviewing what was done yesterday or the previous lesson?
☐ Are you following a clear lesson cycle that includes whole group instruction, guided practice, independent practice, etc.?
☐ Are you including hands-on learning as much as possible?
☐ Do students have the opportunity to work in pairs and groups?
☐ Are you using assessment to gauge the learning of your students and adapting your instruction accordingly?
☐ Are your lessons engaging to students?
☐ Are your lessons too fast, too slow, or just right?
☐ Are your students allowed to speak and interact during the lesson?
☐ Are you doing too much talking?
☐ Are the students too passive?
☐ Others: _____

_____
_____

GUIDELINE 3: DISCIPLINE PLAN

☐ How are you going to teach your discipline plan to students?
☐ How will you communicate your discipline plan to parents?
☐ Have you posted the general rules and guidelines of the discipline plan for all to see?

☐ Is your discipline plan one that is congruent with your students, school, and community?
☐ How well do you know what will work with your students?
☐ Is your discipline plan appropriate for the developmental age of your students?
☐ How well do you know what discipline plan will work with your personality and emotional sensitivity?
☐ Is your discipline plan one that you are comfortable with and can implement without undue emotional demands?
☐ Will you be able to be consistent and follow through with your discipline plan?
☐ Others: _____

_____

_____

◇ The teacher needs to support the linguistically diverse students at whatever stage of English language development they exhibit, using Sheltered Instruction all the time.

◇ The teacher should build a sense of community that includes all students, "scaffolded" at their academic and language levels (Curran, 2003).

3. Socioeconomic: Ruby Payne (2005) is one of the lead researchers of how economic class affects behaviors and mind sets and why students from generational poverty often fear being educated. Within socioeconomic class levels there are "hidden rules" that teachers need to be aware of.

◇ Parenting styles are specific to each socioeconomic level and language registers vary.

◇ Many children from lower socioeconomic backgrounds come to schools that are run by members of the middle class. Because there are hidden rules inherent in how one acts in the middle class, children from lower socioeconomic backgrounds need to learn how to act and socialize within these new hidden rules.

◇ Teachers must be sensitive to the specific needs of poverty. They need to set high expectations for all students and understand why some students may behave in ways that appear different from the norm.

4. Developmental: Developmentally there are differences in how elementary students and high school students behave. For example, the use of external rewards like stickers is more suitable for the elementary level.

Students in older grade levels and high school have different social needs that the enlightened teacher needs to consider. Older students are more interested in what their peers think of them and so "saving face" is very important. Embarrassment or coercion techniques by the teacher eventually backfire in middle school and high school. A teacher must earn students' respect. Younger children in elementary school are very intent on pleasing adults and so will work harder for recognition. Very often this will not work in middle school and high school. Students in the older grade levels respond better to individualized or private praise. Having a relationship with significant adult role models is very important. It is also important for middle school and high school teachers to consider that teenagers:

◇ Do not like their bodies.
◇ Struggle with issues of self-esteem and appearance.
◇ Are coerced easily by peer pressure.
◇ Are at more risk of deviant behaviors like drugs and alcohol.
◇ Can have serious issues with violence or bullying.

5.   Challenges and Special Needs: The Individuals with Disabilities Education Act (1990) enables students with disabilities to get a free and appropriate public education. "Inclusion" is the policy term used to describe this process. Disabilities can be obvious, such as a student who needs a wheelchair, but many disabilities included in this law may be invisible, such as emotional or learning disabilities. In many cases, students with special needs will require individualized discipline plans and in many cases the classroom-wide discipline plan may have to be modified for their specific needs.

AUTHOR'S INSIGHT: Defining Limits in the Classroom and Other General Guidelines.   Teachers should post and explain classroom *rules and consequences* (natural consequences are best) that are fair and consistent, and should provide a daily activities schedule that is predictable and rewards positive behavior. Explain what you expect from students. For example, students should know:

◇ When talking is permitted
◇ The procedure for leaving one's seat
◇ When papers and assignments are due
◇ When and where to turn in homework
◇ The consequences of misbehavior

Establish a behavior management system by choosing a discipline management model.

AUTHOR'S INSIGHT: Check to see if your school or school district uses a particular behavioral management system. If so, find out as much as possible about it, and make sure you ask about its use prior to implementing it on your own.

Provide a cooling-off period by giving students time to "cool off" in a preestablished area. This is not to be considered punishment, but instead presents the student with a choice of "when you're ready to go back to work."

Do not embarrass any student, for any reason, and avoid sarcasm, especially with your older students. Always allow a student to maintain his or her dignity as much as possible, but do remain firm and assertive. When enforcing the consequences, do so without raising your voice or getting angry.

To extinguish behavior before it escalates and at the same time empower the student, say something like, "I notice you always get in trouble when you sit beside [name of student]. Who would you like to sit next to today?"

Use of Reinforcers

Major strategies used every day by teachers to positively motivate and encourage all their students are known as *concrete reinforcers*. Concrete reinforcers include tokens, stickers, daily behavior charts sent home for parental signatures, daily behavior calendars, "Happy Grams," certificates for doing exceptional work, positive phone calls to the parents (bragging opportunities), nods, smiles, winks, praise, special earned free time, a special bulletin board, and eating lunch one-on-one with the teacher are just a few such strategies.

Awards for Middle School and High School Students (Emmer, Evertson, & Worsham, 2003)

◇ *Awards and Recognition:* Give awards and certificates to students throughout the year; recognize students who make the honor role at the end of each grading period; awards can include those for most improved.

◇ *Competitions:* Spelling bee, math or science fair; these can be within the classroom and throughout the school.

◇ *Encouraging improvement:* Allow students to retake tests and redo assignments to bring up their grade to a B. Be careful of giving zeroes as students may never be able to bring up that grade and may become discouraged.

◇ *Extra-Credit Assignments:* These can be done at home or as extra work in school, an incentive to keep the grade high or to use if needed for lower grades.

◇ *Special Activities and Privileges:* Student of the week, student featured in class or school bulletin.

◇ *Weekly Point System:* Encourage students to keep track of their own work; students could earn up to 100 points weekly for turning in homework and work. Pass out a sheet at the beginning listing all assignments to be completed, and students earn so many points for completing each one for a maximum of 100. With older students this could be tracked for a grading period and then if completed becomes a grade, which can be averaged with other weekly test grades.

 AUTHOR'S INSIGHT: Problems with Rewards (Kohn, 1999).   Many researchers like Kohn caution that the use of rewards does not develop intrinsic motivation in students. These rewards work best only for short periods of time. Teachers who use rewards may find that soon they will have to increase the rewards to get the same effect. Critics of a discipline system based on rewards, like Kohn (1999), posit that students should not be rewarded for doing their work.

   If you decide to use rewards, then consider using them judiciously. Rewards should be given in a sporadic and unpredictable manner, ensuring students will not come to expect such rewards regularly. Keep in mind, however, that effective discipline management strategies "cannot override poor instruction" (Cipani, 2008, p. 25).

Additional Positive Reinforcement Ideas for the Classroom

◇ Nonverbal responses (the "OK" sign, the thumbs-up sign, a pat on shoulder, etc.)

◇ Classroom jobs and privileges

◇ Grab bag with coupons, cards with rewards, extra time on the computer, bonus points on a test, art supplies, extra free time, time in library, one night free from a homework assignment

◇ Marbles in a jar

◇ Gold at the end of a rainbow

◇ Class earns a popcorn party (Note: Individual rewards should be used most of the time to avoid having one or two students cost the class a reward. Don't punish the whole class for the misbehavior of a few.)

◇ No-homework night for the class

◇ Free-time passes

◇ White elephant gift raffle

◇ Bingo

◇ The right to borrow videos, comics, books, games

◇ Trading stickers

◇ Select a seat

◇ Decorate a window or bulletin board

◇ Happy squares—when the can is full it is turned in for a piece of candy or a sticker

Increase the response time for your English Language Learners by waiting an extra five seconds or so for an answer. Use visual response cards ("Yes," "No," "Thumbs up," "Thumbs down,"). Use a response board or slate. Use cooperative learning like, "Put on your thinking caps and tell me . . ."

Use language to encourage your students. Say things like "I am proud of you," "Well done," "Fascinating," "I like the way you . . ." but most of all be specific about what you like about their behavior. A casual statement like "You had a great day" doesn't mean as much as if you said, "You did great today because you followed directions," or "You had a great day because you turned in all your work." Personalized statements are much more meaningful to students and help students understand exactly what you expect from them.

Practice appropriate behavioral expectations (Girls and Boys Town National Research Institute, 2007) when students are misbehaving. Instead of punishing a student say, "I see we need some practice for this behavior" (e.g., not walking in line properly, talking out of turn, interfering with other students). Analyze the appropriate component of behavior that requires remediation and have students practice it. Write out on a poster the steps and components of a particular behavior, then practice it as a group. Students will learn to use the appropriate steps by practice and repetition. Students can have a lot of fun with this task if you permit them to model the inappropriate behaviors (but only if appropriate to do so and feasible). However, practice should only take place during a noninstructional time period (recess, free period, or on the student's own personal time). Remember, students are not "being punished" but instead are "practicing appropriate behavior." If you do this firmly and on a consistent basis, the students will know you mean business, and it will work.

Preferential seating. Pay close attention to how you design and configure your classroom, and consider the following:

◇ Designate a place where several students can meet to discuss what they are learning.
◇ Provide a well-lit, inviting reading area.
◇ Configure desks so the teacher can move with ease around the room and see what every student is doing.
◇ Ensure there are areas where students can work alone.

When All Else Fails—Specific Tips for Specific Problems

To Overcome the Difficulty of Getting Started

◇ Give a cue when work is to begin (approach students and ask "How can I help you get started?"); allow students to work with a partner.
◇ Divide work into smaller increments.
◇ Provide all the materials needed for a particular task or assignment so students don't waste time looking for materials. Use tote trays for writing materials, etc.
◇ Check on students' progress every few minutes by walking around the room observing and offering help if a student is having difficulty.

When Students Have Difficulty Keeping Track of Materials and Assignments

◇ Have students keep a notebook in which to file assignments and to be better organized.
◇ Check student notebooks often to ensure that papers are appropriately filed.
◇ Allow time in class for students to organize notebooks.
◇ Keep extra supplies or assignments so students are not punished for a lack of materials or assignments.

Dealing with Distractibility

1. Keep the student in close proximity so you can gently prod and provide cues without stopping your teaching (i.e., point to the place in the book if you are reading together, gently touch the student on the shoulder to regain his or her attention, or tap lightly on his or her desk).
2. Students need structure, so follow a set routine. Students should know what you expect and what comes next. (Don't feel tempted to change a routine that is boring for you as the teacher. This is what works for all students, so stick to it.)

3. Keep instructions short and concise. Write them on the board so students can refer to them when needed. Allow ELL students to ask other students for assistance without getting into trouble.
4. Give instructions one at a time. Then wait until the task is completed before progressing to the next one. This is very important with younger students.
5. Use a kitchen timer to establish a time limit that will help keep students focused.

Dealing with Student Frustrations

1. Be knowledgeable about each child's abilities.
2. Divide difficult tasks into smaller ones and provide instant feedback to students after each section is completed.
3. Encourage children to communicate their emotions. Use a chart with various emotional faces (happy, sad, angry) and have students point to it and tell you how they feel. Teach them it's okay to be frustrated but not to take it out on others.
4. Offer students an alternative means to expressing their negative emotions, such as drawing what they feel on paper, squeezing a ball, reading alone, or working away from the rest of the group in a quiet place in your classroom.
5. Provide for success on a daily basis. Remember that repeated failed experiences are never useful when it comes to learning. We all learn best through success and positive reinforcement.

Dealing with Hostile Behaviors

Hostile behavior is generally the result of student frustration, distractibility, and poor self-concept. Learn to recognize the onset or beginning signs of hostility so you will have a better chance of reducing the likelihood of an outburst or a physical or hostile confrontation. Children learn quickly to respect an adult who is firm and cannot be manipulated. Once this is established they will usually avoid situations that can lead to hostility. On the other hand, they also learn very quickly how to manipulate an adult, if they are allowed, and to get the results they want.

Strategies for Avoiding Emotional Outbursts

1. Watch for and learn to recognize symptoms that could lead up to an outburst and intervene immediately. Calmly say, "I notice something is bothering you. Would you like some time to cool off?" Let them respond but don't let them yell or shout.
2. "Drop that jump rope right now!" Don't get into a confrontation with students; they will always win if things get physical and you have to haul them kicking and screaming out of the classroom. Instead, calmly say, "I noticed you are really angry right now, and when you calm down, we'll talk about it." An angry or hostile student will try to engage you on the spot and goad you into an argument.

3. Reduce stress levels in the classroom by playing soft, instrumental background music.

4. If you need time to cool down, it's usually best to say, "Class, right now I'd like to take a moment to regain my composure. Please read silently, or put your head down on your desk for five minutes and take several deep breaths." This is preferable to "going off" on a tirade or visibly getting angry or upset with a student. It also allows for modeling appropriate emotional behavioral responses for your students.

5. Remove at-risk students from a stressful situation before it escalates too far. Send them on an errand, put them somewhere else in the room, or ask them a question in order to focus on something else.

6. Ignore minor behavioral traits of students if they are not really disturbing the class (i.e., whispering to another student during silent reading time is okay if it's not persistent, but address it if the whispering becomes a problem).

Steps in Negotiating a Behavioral Contract with Students

This can be used with individual students if needed. This is usually done with a parent's support and is an individualized behavior plan for one student.

1. Select one behavior the student needs to change.
2. Isolate the time when the problem seems to occurs the most.
3. Discuss the alternate behavioral approach the student will use when he or she encounters the situation again, and what is most likely to happen.
4. Discuss with the student and his or her parents what the consequences will be for not living up to the terms of the contract; and conversely, what the reward will be.
5. Write up the contract for both the student and the teacher to sign.
6. Establish a date to review the contract and to note any progress. If no progress is made, try something new.

CHAPTER SUMMARY

The links among motivation, learning, and self-efficacy were discussed at the beginning of the chapter. Students who possess high self-efficacy take responsibility for their own academic success by recognizing their own efforts or lack of effort and adjusting accordingly. Students who possess low self-efficacy do not recognize their own efforts. They give up easily and blame others, not themselves, for their academic failure. Teachers play a critical role in developing self-efficacious learners.

The chapter addressed both discipline and classroom management extensively. There are a myriad of discipline models, and many differ in their psychological and philosophical underpinnings. Regardless of which model a teacher chooses, it is imperative that there be a model in place to ensure an orderly classroom environment where learning occurs for all students.

When choosing a discipline model the teacher should keep the following factors in mind: (1) age and developmental needs of students, (2) political characteristics of the school, (3) principal's expectations, (4) physical environment, (5) teaching and management style of colleagues, and (6) one's personal beliefs about classroom management.

When choosing a discipline model teachers must have a thorough knowledge of their students and be aware of the following factors: students' cultural needs, linguistic needs, socioeconomic needs, developmental needs, and special needs.

Three discipline models were presented in this chapter. The characteristics of each were explained, as well as classroom application strategies and the advantages and disadvantages of each. The models presented were: (1) Assertive Discipline (Canter & Canter, 1993); (2) Reality Therapy/Choice Theory (Glasser, 2001); and (3) Positive Discipline in the Classroom (Nelsen, et al., 2000).

The chapter ends with a host of practical tips and guidelines for dealing with hostile behaviors, following directions, dealing with distractibility, staying on task, and so on.

REFLECTIVE CHAPTER QUESTIONS

1. How are motivation and learning linked?
2. Discuss the theory of self-efficacy introduced in this chapter. Reflect on times in your life when you experienced academic difficulties but did not give up. Does the theory of self-efficacy explain your own personal reasons for not giving up or were there other motivating factors that cannot be explained by this theory?
3. Using the discipline models presented in this chapter, which one or combination of models best fits your personality and your own belief about discipline? Explain why this is so.
4. Compare and contrast the discipline models presented in this chapter in terms of their philosophical and psychological underpinnings, belief about teacher's role, belief about role of student, and belief about who is in charge in the classroom.

SUGGESTED FIELD-BASED ACTIVITIES FOR PRE-SERVICE AND IN-SERVICE TEACHERS

1. Plan to visit a classroom and observe the classroom management skill being used by the teacher. Analyze what you are observing in the classroom, paying close attention to each of the following: structure and organization of desks; how students respond to teacher; degree to which autonomy is afforded students (i.e., can they get up and move about without seeking permission or are there clearly defined limits?). What do interactions between

students and teacher look like? How does the teacher redirect students who are off task? How does the teacher deal with interruptions?

2. Try out one of the discipline models with your classmates. Demonstrate the steps of each model. Discuss the advantages and disadvantages of your model.

3. Using the Web sites provided in the following section, research one of the discipline models discussed in this chapter. Present your findings in class.

ADDITIONAL RESOURCES

General Classroom Management Tips

1. *http://www.nea-org/websources/classmanagelinks.html*

2. *http://www.theteacherguide.com/classManagement.htm*

3. *http://www.disciplinehelp.com/parent/list.cfm?cause=ALL.*
This site provides a list of 117 misbehaviors ranging from minor ones to significant acts of violence and bullying.

Canter's Assertive Discipline

Canter, L. (2002). *Lee Canter's responsible behavior curriculum guide: An instructional approach to successful classroom management.* Los Angeles: Canter & Associates.

Reality Therapy/Choice Theory

http://www.ez2bsaved.com/Quality_Schools/index-qs.htm

Discipline with Love and Logic (Fay & Cline, 1998)

http://www.loveandlogic.com/pages/classroom.html.

REFERENCES

Bandura, A. (1985). *Social foundations of thought and action: A social cognitive theory.* Englewood Cliffs, NJ: Prentice Hall.

Brown, H. D. (2006). *Principles of language learning and teaching* (5th ed.). Upper Saddle River, NJ: Pearson ESL.

Canter, L., & Canter, M. (1993). *Succeeding with difficult students: New strategies for reaching your most challenging students.* Santa Monica, CA: Canter Associates.

Chamot, A. U., & O'Malley, J. M. (1994). *The CALLA handbook: Implementing the cognitive academic language learning approach.* Reading, MA: Addison-Wesley.

Cipani, E. (2008). *Classroom management for all teachers: Plans for evidence-based practice.* Upper Saddle River, NJ: Pearson Merrill Prentice Hall.

Curran, M. E. (2007). Linguistic diversity and classroom management. In M. L. Manning, & K. T. Bucher, *Classroom management: Models, applications, and cases.* Upper Saddle River, NJ: Pearson Merrill Prentice Hall.

Curtin, E. M. (2005). Instructional styles used by regular classroom teachers while teaching mainstream ESL students. *Multicultural Education Journal, 12*(4), 36–42.

Curtin, E. M. (2006a). Lessons on effective teaching from middle school ESL students. *Middle School Journal, 37*(3), 38–45.

Curtin, E. M. (2006b). *Overcoming the learning curve: The classroom perceptions of beginning teachers during their induction year.* Paper presentation for American Educational Research Association Annual Meeting. San Francisco.

Dreikurs, R., & Cassel, P. (1972). *Discipline without tears.* New York: Hawthorne Books.

Edwards, C. H. (2004). *Classroom discipline and management* (4th ed.). New York: Wiley Jossey-Bass Education.

Emmer, E.T., Evertson, C. M., & Worsham, M. E. (2003). *Classroom management for secondary teachers* (6th ed.). Boston: Allyn & Bacon.

Fay, J., & Cline, F. (1998). Discipline with love and logic. Golden, CO: Love and Logic Press.

Gathercoal, F. (2001). *Judicious discipline* (5th ed.). San Francisco: Caddo Gap Press.

Girls and Boys Town National Research Institute. (2007). Available online at: http://www.girlsandboystown.org/media/pros/research/2006FullVersion.pdf.

Glasser, W. (2001). *Every student can succeed.* Los Angeles: William Glasser Institute.

Good, T. L., & Brophy, J. E. (2007). *Looking in classrooms* (10th ed). Boston, MA: Allyn & Bacon.

Graham, S. (1991). A review of attribution theory in achievement contexts. *Educational Psychology Review, 3*, 5–39.

Kellough, R. D., & Kellough, N. G. (2007). *Secondary school teaching: A guide to methods and resources* (3rd ed). Upper Saddle River, NJ: Pearson Merrill Prentice Hall.

Kohn, A. (1999). *Punished by rewards: The trouble with gold stars, incentive plans, A's, praise and other bribes.* New York: Houghton Mifflin.

Manning, M. L., & Bucher, K. T. (2007). *Classroom management: Models, applications, and cases* (2nd ed.). Upper Saddle River, NJ: Pearson Merrill Prentice Hall.

Marchesani, R. J. (2007). *The field guide to teaching: A handbook for new teachers.* Upper Saddle River, NJ: Pearson Merrill Prentice Hall.

Nelsen, J., Lott, L., & Glenn, H. S. (2000). *Positive discipline in the classroom: Developing mutual respect, cooperation, and responsibility in your classroom* (3rd ed.). New York: Three Rivers Press.

Payne, R. K. (2005). *A framework for understanding poverty* (4th ed.). Highland, TX: Aha Process.

Rosenthal, R. (1987). Pygmalion effects: Existence, magnitude and social importance. A reply to Wineburg. *Educational Researcher, 16*, 37–41.

Schunk, D. H., Pintrich, P. R., & Meese, J. (2007). Motivation in education: Theory, research, and applications (3rd ed.). Upper Saddle River, NJ: Prentice Hall.

Stipek, D. J. (2001). *Motivation to learn: Integrating theory and practice* (4th ed.). Boston: Allyn & Bacon.

Woolfolk, A. (1999). *Educational psychology* (7th ed.). Englewood Cliffs, NJ: Prentice-Hall.

Facilitating School, Family, and Community Involvement for the English Language Learner

INTRODUCTION

One of the overarching beliefs about schooling in the United States is that teachers need and must have full cooperation and support from parents. Those of us in academics realize parents are an integral part of their children's educational success. Unfortunately, this is not always the reality. Speaking with new and experienced teachers alike reveals that maintaining home-school relations with families that do not speak English can be challenging, to say the least.

In many cases, this relationship with the family is the key to the successful functioning of English Language Learners in the classroom. Teachers who know the parents of their students and have established a good relationship from the beginning will have those same parents as allies in times of need. For the average middle school and high school teacher, maintaining a good level of communication with the parents of 120 students can be challenging and sometimes frustrating, however.

Chapter 10 will explore the importance and value of home-school relations. It will address these issues from the perspective of teachers and parents and will incorporate suggestions for parent-teacher conferences. This chapter will also include practical strategies for use with families that have been tested and proven in both research and practical application.

All the strategies suggested in this chapter are applicable for a K–12 setting. These strategies are effective for all parents, not just the parents of English Language Learners.

Focus Questions

- ◇ How can the school be supportive of the families of English Language Learners who do not speak English?
- ◇ How can community resources be utilized in the educational process of the English Language Learner?
- ◇ How do I conduct a successful parent-teacher conference?

Classroom Scenario

The following section illustrates the perspectives of actual administrators and teachers and the challenges they encounter in facilitating home-school relations.

Teacher's Perspective

Nolan, an elementary grade teacher, comments: "I think our campus has become an oasis for students and parents. In some instances teachers don't feel supported by the parents, but I feel differently because most of the time during open house my classroom is packed. At times I've even had families waiting in the halls because my classroom was so full of enthusiastic students and their parents that not everyone could get in. I attribute it all to the fact that I make them feel welcome but mostly because I try to communicate with the parents even though they don't speak English and I don't speak their native language. I use one of the parents of my students as an interpreter to meet with parents who are difficult to find, I try to visit their homes, and meet them in places in the community as much as I can.

"I feel like my job is as much about cultural relations as it is about teaching, and while I don't always agree with what parents may say or feel I am able to establish a connection directly with each of them and with their children. That bond is what the future of all my students, especially my ELL students, is built upon" (Curtin, 2006).

Parent's Perspective

Henry is an immigrant and a parent who serves non-English-speaking parents in the community in his role as school-home liaison and interpreter. Henry shares his perspective on home-school relations: "Inside our community the teacher holds a very high position culturally, which is essentially equal to that of a doctor or a priest. Our families are very close and whenever possible do everything together, even when just one of them needs to go to the dentist, everybody in the family goes—it is a cultural trait. . . ."

"Sometimes during parent/teacher conferences our parents don't fully understand what it is a teacher is trying to say or accomplish but most of the time parents are good about reading between the lines. Other times a teacher can be addressing a parent and that parent will turn to their child and say 'Are you listening to what your teacher is saying?' because parents want what is best for their children. Parents if they fully understand will accept and support what a teacher is trying to accomplish in class in order to improve their child's ability to learn and advance within the educational system. Parents in our community vest a lot of authority in the teacher. It goes back to what I said earlier about how powerful the teacher is in our community" (Curtin, 2006).

Role of Interpreters—Parent's Perspective

Henry shares his thoughts about the use of interpreters in parent-teacher communication: "We get the gist of what it is teachers are trying to communicate but we get very emotional when we talk about our kids. That emotion cannot be properly translated and therefore the message is incomplete and cannot be fully understood. In essence it is lost in the translation. Another thing I find that teachers don't fully comprehend that we do *not* consider e-mail as a form of communication. Less than 2% of this population has computers and of those that do, it's usually the kids who use them. Parents in our community are not going to sit down and send an e-mail to a teacher. They are going to drive to the school and wait until the teacher is free to meet with them face to face because only then can the emotions be seen. There are no emotions in an e-mail or on a piece of paper. There is little or no emotion in a telephone call, which is considered very impersonal within our community. Within our culture if there is a delicate issue we don't deal with it in an impersonal way, we deal with it in a very personal way" (Curtin, 2006).

Guiding Discussion Questions

◇ Compare the teachers' and parents' perspectives.
◇ What strategies did the teacher employ to connect with the parents of his students?

Author's Insight

These are real perspectives from actual individuals in schools today. All perspectives differ from the unique point of view of the individual. Nolan, who does not speak the native languages of his ELL parents, does not perceive his monolingual ability as a barrier to communicating with his parents. He reaches out to his community in other ways and gets them involved in his classroom. He sees part of his role as teacher as being involved in "cultural relations."

The parent's perspective was centered on the manner in which teachers communicate with parents. Henry's perspective provides an enlightening view that parents do care and that there are sometimes misunderstandings about what constitutes communication.

From my own 16 years of teaching grades K–12 I learned that being able to speak the native language of some of my English Language Learners and their parents, though helpful, was not the most important factor in forging successful home-school relations. In many instances I taught in schools with as many as 22 native languages spoken in the community. It is an impossible task, though well intentioned, for any teacher to think that he or she can learn so many languages.

I will say to you, whether you are a pre-service or an in-service teacher, that it is *how* you communicate with parents that matters. It is more important to understand the cultural mores of the family, understand where the family is coming from, understand that they do want a better life for their children, and that their values may not differ from yours as a teacher in respect to education, but they may be communicated differently. Pay attention to your body language and how you communicate, and if you build a good relationship with your students, the parents will come to school because they have respect for you as the teacher of their children. Teachers, however, can as easily win and lose the respect of parents. Tread carefully and always approach conflictive issues with an empathetic understanding. Be slow to rush to judgment and be slow to write parents off because they are not communicating with you. Gaining parents' respect takes time and commitment, but once it is earned you will have their full support.

WHAT RESEARCH TELLS US

The Importance of Family Involvement for Language and Literacy Development

Researchers now know that the literacy development that occurs between birth and five years of age, long before a child enters school, is paramount for cognitive development and key for successful literacy development (reading and writing). During this period a child who is furnished with books and toys, and interacts and uses language with a patient and literate adult, arrives in kindergarten understanding that print communicates meaning and already possessing an extensive range of vocabulary necessary for classroom literacy (Machado, 2007).

Researchers are also aware that families' socioeconomic status may account for their differences in literacy achievement (Snow, Burns, & Griffin, 1998). Illiterate parents or parents who do not read to their children or serve as literate role models can have a negative impact on the literacy development of their children.

The importance of the teacher's role in redressing literacy, linguistic, and language gaps that occur before the child enters school is paramount. The need to educate parents in their role in the literacy development of their children from birth is equally important (Hanson & Lynch, 2004a).

Attitude of Teachers toward Students' Home Environment

It is important for teachers to view all students' family and cultural backgrounds as an asset and not a deficit. Teachers can plan lessons that incorporate tools, symbols, and social relations that are familiar to the child (Gonzalez, Moll, & Amanti, 2005). Gonzalez and colleagues (2005) have worked extensively with groups of teachers to show them how to use information obtained from families' backgrounds and cultures to develop successful teaching units about plants, flowers and herbs, animals, music, and sound.

McCarthey (1999) found that when teachers believed students came from an impoverished background, they would not incorporate cultural background information about these students in the curriculum. In many cases these teachers did not appear to be knowledgeable or interested in the backgrounds and experiences of their students, but instead considered cultural and family backgrounds of children from diverse backgrounds as a deficit rather than an asset.

Accommodating Parenting Styles

Hones and Chao (1999) identified two types of parental involvement: structural (less hands-on) and managerial (more hands-on). When comparing families with Asian roots and European roots, Hones and Chao (1999) found that European American parents tend to demonstrate more managerial practices and Chinese American parents tend to demonstrate more structural involvement practices. A teacher might mistakenly misconstrue that a parent who is less visible in school is a parent who is not interested in his or her children's academic well-being.

Differences in parenting styles should be understood positively and should never be considered as a negative. Differences should be something exciting that schools are willing to embrace. Teachers unfamiliar with the cultural backgrounds of their students may assume and incorrectly assess the English Language Learner's academic challenges as being a lack of family support rather than being the teachers' own inability to connect the school's culture with those of the families (Hildebrand, Phenice, Gray, & Hines, 2007).

Practices That Promote Home-School Connections

Ladson-Billings (2001) proposes that facilitating connections between home and school is based on *culturally relevant teaching* practices. One of the tenets of this practice is via dialogue using the knowledge and backgrounds of the students first and then moving into more difficult knowledge and skills. Schools that have a heavy reliance on drill and practice, worksheets, and autocratic discipline create barriers to understanding for some English Language Learners.

Communication between home and school should be *preemptive rather than reactive*. Communication between home and school that tends to be for academic or behavioral problems only does not support positive home-school relations. It is reactive rather than preemptive. Reactive communication is more likely to be tense and to be difficult and psychologically uncomfortable for all involved (Allen, 2007).

Home-school *communications should be open and nonjudgmental*. It is important for a teacher not to assume parents of English Language Learners are not interested in their children's education because they are not visible in the school or classroom. In fact, many of these children have parents or older siblings who try to help them with their homework, and many receive incentives and rewards from their non-English-speaking parents for doing well in school. Many of them have parents who come to school instantly when they are requested to do so, and many have parents who show up just to keep "tabs" on them (Curtin, 2002).

CLASSROOM APPLICATION STRATEGIES

Strategies to Enhance Communication within School

The Building

The school building and the people in it communicate a very powerful first impression about the learning community. A building should be warm, welcoming, and inviting regardless of how old or new it is. A school that welcomes families of diverse learners should exhibit both the tangible and intangible aspects of the varying cultures the student body represents (Banks, 2006).

Tangible Aspects

A school that is clean, orderly, and decorated with pride communicates a strong sense of respect for the students in the school as well as the community surrounding the school. Following are some suggestions of how to communicate tangible respect for culturally diverse families:

- ◇ A map of the world indicating the cultural heritages of all students
- ◇ A slogan indicating that we are all part of "one world"
- ◇ Welcome signs in the native languages/countries of the community visible in the front office

◇ Art work representing other cultures visibly displayed throughout the school
◇ Bulletin boards displaying student achievement and student work
◇ Allocated section in the library carrying a host of books representing a wide variety of cultures
◇ Books in the library written in the native languages of the community
◇ School involvement in local community cultural fairs and events

Intangible Aspects

This encompasses the overall atmosphere and attitude of school personnel toward each other, toward visitors, and toward students. A school that is welcoming to immigrant and diverse families will display some of the following characteristics:

◇ Courtesy and respect toward all who enter the office area
◇ A staff member or interpreter present who has the ability to communicate with non-English-speaking parents and students
◇ A trained staff who deal empathetically with visitors and culturally diverse families
◇ Teachers and personnel who have respect for and understanding of cultural relations
◇ Ongoing cultural sensitivity training provided for teachers
◇ Availability of interpreters in students' native language

Strategies to Enhance Communication in the Classroom

The teacher sets the tone in the classroom. Following are some practical suggestions for teachers to ensure they are maintaining a classroom environment that is culturally inclusive.

Teacher's Classroom:

◇ Classroom is welcoming with student work visibly displayed.
◇ Classroom is decorated with culturally diverse materials that reflect the cultures of students in the class.
◇ Teacher has a welcoming packet for new students or students that enter the class throughout the year. This packet clearly explains classroom rules and procedures, attendance policy, late work policy, make-ups, how to reach the teacher, procedures for initiating a parent-teacher conference, as well as teacher contact information. If possible the teacher should arrange for the packet to be translated into as many languages as represented in the community.
◇ Teacher has access to interpreters when needed to conference with parents or communicate necessary information.
◇ Teacher knows the cultural traditions of all students.
◇ Teacher understands and has knowledge of cultural dos and don'ts, like: Is it appropriate to shake hands? How do I address parents?

◇ Teacher has ESL certification or some training in second language acquisition.
◇ Teacher plans lessons that incorporate tools, symbols, and social relations familiar to the children (Gonzales-Mena, 2006).

Understanding Parents' Perspectives

Figure 10.1 offers a summary of the cultural differences that may account for some possible *cultural mismatch/incongruences* (Nieto & Bode, 2007) between home and school for English Language Learners and their families. Understanding these cultural differences will help a teacher understand better why students may be exhibiting certain behaviors. A teacher who is culturally sensitive and aware of these underlying explanations for behaviors will be more

FIGURE 10.1   Examples of Possible Cultural Differences between Families Born in the United States and Families of English Language Learners

Cultural values in United States	Other possible cultural values
Competition	Cooperation
Individual	Group
Left brain	Right brain
Future—delayed gratification	Present—instant gratification
Value of education for future	Value of education only for present
Moving away from family once one leaves school—independence valued	Family always to be cared for and taken care of—dependence on family valued
Parents will question everything teacher and school do	Parents may not question the school or authorities
Parents will want to be involved in school	Parents may believe that the school does not want parents involved
Parental trust is high in school personnel	Parental trust may be low in school personnel for many reason (e.g., tenuousness of immigration status)
Parental educational attainment is high school or college level and thus parents will be more inclined to be involved with their children at the middle school or high school	Parental educational attainment is high school or less and thus parents will be less inclined to be involved with their children at the middle school or high school
Discipline style of parents will tend to be more permissive	Discipline style of parents will tend to be stricter

empathetic and understanding of the cultural needs of students. Figure 10.1 only provides some guidelines, and these are not meant to stereotype culturally diverse students and individuals. There are many exceptions and intragroup differences, and it is *not* the intention of the author to generalize and categorize particular groups of students.

Understanding the *circumstances that may prevent parents from active involvement in school* is important. Whelan-Ariza (2006) suggests the following as reasons why parents of English Language Learners may be unable to be more visible or actively involved with schools:

◇ Parents may not communicate with a teacher because they feel that their level of English is inadequate for communication purposes.

◇ Parents may not understand that they are supposed to visit the school, meet the teacher, communicate and initiate interaction, as this was not the case in the parents' native country.

◇ Parents may posses a low level of education and be unable to read or write.

◇ Parents may believe that teachers are the authority and may consider it disrespectful to question the authority of the teacher.

◇ Parents may have two or three jobs and may be physically or financially incapable of taking time off to come to school for a conference.

◇ Parents may not have access to transportation to school or may not be able to drive.

◇ Parents may not be able to come to school because they have no caregivers for younger children at home.

◇ In some come cultures it may be inappropriate for a female to leave the house without her husband.

◇ Parents may fear school authority figures due to their immigration status and may fear reprisal, i.e., deportation.

◇ Parents may not speak English and may consider it inappropriate for children to act as interpreters for older members of the family.

◇ Parents may be uncomfortable with people who do not belong to their own cultural group.

◇ Parents may not know that they have rights as parents and can make educational decisions on behalf of their children.

Planning Parent Night/Open House

A school that truly welcomes the involvement of parents in the educational process will provide nights periodically during the school year when parents are welcome to the school for events and to meet the teacher. Back-to-school nights are usually held at the very beginning of the school year. The purpose of this meeting is threefold: (1) to provide teachers the opportunity to meet the parents, (2) to provide parents the opportunity to meet the teachers, and (3) to provide teachers the opportunity to communicate their behavioral and academic expectations to parents.

Communicating Teacher Expectations

◇ Explain all policies concerning homework, behavior, classroom rules, consequences for misbehavior, late work, and so on.

◇ Let parents know how and when they can reach you and how long it takes you to return a call.

◇ If parents want to discuss something private with you concerning their child at open house, have them schedule an appointment with you.

◇ Have samples of student work on display.

◇ Be prepared to do a presentation such as PowerPoint that explains the curriculum, how parents can assist at home, and so on.

◇ Have a handout with helpful materials in folders for parents.

◇ Allow a question-and-answer session.

◇ Have a sign-in sheet for parents so you know who came and whom you need to contact later.

◇ Plan to have some food as an incentive for parents to come.

◇ Have volunteers available to provide babysitting during the open meeting.

◇ Do not let the meeting exceed an hour.

◇ Ask for parents to volunteer throughout the year.

Communicating with the Home

◇ It is recommended that schools try to send communications home to parents in as many languages as possible.

◇ Communication home should be daily or weekly in grades K–3. With younger children it is recommended that there be a daily folder where parents can see at a glance how their children performed behaviorally and academically in school. Parents can check this folder daily and sign that they saw it. This communication system is very immediate and keeps parents aware of the daily progress of their students. With older students a weekly or bi-weekly report is an excellent way of communicating grades, progress, and behavior.

◇ Send home a weekly newsletter or create a Web page with the current academic goals and objectives listed as well as homework guidelines; tips or materials you may need donated for class activities; general announcements; need for volunteers; news of upcoming events, and so on.

◇ Establish a reward system for students to bring back signed communications from parents.

◇ Be empathetic to the needs and concerns of parents. When a teacher negatively criticizes a child, the parent accepts that as personal criticism of themselves. Some immigrant children are socialized to behave by avoiding shame. Children who get into trouble in school for whatever reason may bring shame on the family. Be empathetic and understanding abut how you communicate negative news about students to parents.

◇ Consider asking for advice from members of the cultural community if you are uncomfortable or unfamiliar with certain cultural practices. Making the right impression on parents of culturally diverse students is critical if you wish to maintain a cooperative relationship with them.

Communicating Student Discipline Issues

A teacher should keep the following factors in mind:

◇ Do not be surprised if parenting or discipline philosophies differ from yours. You may find that parents of some of your students consider your discipline style to be too lenient, as many immigrant parents may have come from systems in their own countries where corporal punishment was the norm. You may witness parents harshly reprimanding their children in front of you and you might feel uncomfortable. Explain to parents what the behavioral and legal parameters are for teachers.

◇ Involve parents in ideas about how they can support your discipline management system at home. Ask the parents and get ideas about what works at home with their children.

◇ Explain school policies to parents. Include the dress code; chewing gum; school suspension; passing grades; high school graduation requirements; attendance. (It is not uncommon for some cultural groups to return to their native country for a month at a time and return to be served with papers to appear in court because of the truancy of their children. In some cases, parents were not aware of compulsory attendance laws.)

◇ Design homework activities that involve parents, such as having interviews with parents, TV programs parents and child can watch together, as well as looking on the Internet, and doing projects that are based on the family's culture and background. Also, the teacher can send home books the family can read together, and other items.

Strategies for Enhancing Community Relations

The following will assist in making the school a vital part of the community:

◇ Use of translators from the community.

◇ Active Parent-Teacher Association (PTA) that involves parents of varying cultural groups.

◇ Letters home to families that are translated into as many home languages as possible.

◇ Teachers initiating telephone calls or home visits on a regular basis to communicate good news with parents. Parents should not expect communication from the school to be only negative. Communicate as early as possible in the year when you have good reports of students.

◇ Back-to-school night and open houses organized on a regular basis.

◇ Home visits made on a regular basis.

◇ Family content subject nights—teach a math lesson, a science lesson, or a guided reading lesson. Invite the whole family; have food and concerts; create a carpool system for transportation.

◇ Organize ESL classes for adult English Language Learners in the community.

◇ Develop afterschool programs—use the library for bilingual story time, invite participants from the community.

◇ Use parent volunteers.

◇ Decorate the school and highlight cultural backgrounds of students.

◇ Organize a cultural fair with dances and celebrations, utilizing all the resources in the community. Make it an annual event.

◇ Provide resources for families and be familiar with community agencies and organizations that assist families in need.

Continuing Parent Education

It is not enough to increase the cultural knowledge and skills of teachers and school personnel. Parents must be educated. Immigrant families must understand that they need to be involved in the education of their children and they must know that firsthand. Some of the knowledge that parents need to know applies to their rights under NCLB (2001). Parents need to understand the following:

◇ Their children are being taught by a highly qualified teacher.

◇ Their children are getting English language support while learning grade-level academic content.

◇ The English language placement process and the role and function of the Language Proficiency Assessment Committee (LPAC).

◇ Availability of ESL assistance in the community and in school for their children.

◇ Community resources for homework assistance.

◇ Afterschool tutoring availability.

◇ Library resources available.

◇ Public recreational centers available.

◇ Available health programs for shots and immunizations.

◇ Employment opportunities.

◇ Available social services.

◇ It is important for parents to maintain the native language of their children. Many times, parents believe that knowledge of the native language will obstruct their children's English language development. Parents can inadvertently do a disservice to their children by refusing to have them placed in a bilingual program for fear of negative stigmatism. Many times, parents of English Language Learners do not understand the placement options and do not understand the difference between ESL and bilingual education.

◇ It is important to explain to parents how to be involved in homework and how to stay involved with school activities.

Developing a School and Parent Partnership

This model was developed by Joyce Epstein (2002) at John Hopkins University. It delineates six levels of parental involvement that need to be supported and developed by schools. Awareness of these levels will assist schools in planning appropriate strategies to encourage parental involvement. See Figure 10.2 for these levels of parental involvement and strategies and suggestions for implementation at the campus level.

FIGURE 10.2 Strategies for Developing Parent and Community Involvement

---

1. **Parenting:**
   - Helping families establish home environments to support children as students, e.g., parent education and training—GED; family literacy; ESL classes; family support programs in health and nutrition; home visits by personnel.

2. **Communicating:**
   - Frequent conferences with parents, e.g., language translator; regular notices; memos; phone calls; newsletters; and other communications between home and school.

3. **Volunteering:**
   - Recruiting and training members of the family to volunteer in school, e.g., school and classroom volunteers to help teachers; administrators; students and other parents; run a parent room or family center; volunteer for work meetings; provide resources for families; conduct annual postcard survey to identify talents, times, and locations of volunteers.

4. **Learning at home:**
   - Provide information to families about how to help children with homework and curriculum-related activities, decisions, and planning. Teacher can provide information on homework policies and how to monitor homework at school and at home; parent can participate in setting student goals each year with teacher as well as planning for college or work.

5. **Decision making:**
   - Parents can be helped to develop as leaders (parent as leaders) and representatives for other parents. Parents should be encouraged to be active in PTA and other parent organizations. Parents should be encouraged to be independent advocates for parent groups to lobby and work for school reform and improvement. Parents should be encouraged to network and connect all families with parent representatives; teachers should hold regular meetings and inform parents of how they can participate in decision making at the school.

6. **Collaborating with the community:**
   - Parents should be supported in linking with resources and services from the community to strengthen school programs, family practices and student learning and development. Parents should be provided with information for students on community health, cultural, recreational, or social support, and other programs or services, information on community activities that are linked to learning skills and talents, including summer programs for students, service to community by students, families, and schools, e.g., recycling, art, music, drama, and other activities for seniors and others.

Source: *School, family, and community partnership: Your handbook for action* (2nd ed., p. 165), by J. L. Epstein, M. G. Sanders, B. S. Simon, K. C. Salinas, N. R. Jansom, and F. L. Van Voorhis, 2002. Thousand Oaks, CA: Corwin Press. Used with permission.

Tips for Conducting Parent-Teacher Conferences
Initiating the Conference

Teacher Should:

◇ Have a form that can be sent home or call and schedule the conference with the parent. Use an interpreter if necessary or a member of the cultural community who is willing to initiate contact.

◇ Indicate to parents the purpose of the conference and that you are looking forward to their input and to meeting them.

◇ If the conference is parent initiated ask politely what their concerns are, pointing out that you would like to be prepared, and to have an agenda so that time is appropriately utilized.

AUTHOR'S INSIGHT: A conference can be nerve-racking for teacher and parents so it is important to be prepared for all eventualities.

◇ Collect as much data as you can; have grades, current work, test results, documentation of infractions, and so on. Procure the formal conference form required by the school. This form can be signed by all conference attendees, including the student (if the student is present). This provides you with a written record for documentation purposes.

During the Conference:

◇ Have the conference area ready. Have chairs ready, and make sure that it is in a quiet designated area without interruptions.

◇ Be on time.

◇ Greet parents and welcome them. It is very important to begin by listening. Thank them for coming. Always start by letting parents talk. Let them vent frustrations and listen empathetically to their concerns. Do not get defensive; say "I understand, I apologize if I offended you."

AUTHOR'S INSIGHT: Your goal as a teacher is to make sure that you get the parent on your side, working with you and not against you. You are all commonly united in that you are both interested in the well-being of the child.

◇ Accept criticism and be willing to admit you are wrong. From my experience, this works better. Focus on "What can I do to improve this situation?" With English Language Learner parents, do not be surprised if the whole family shows up. This is not uncommon in some cultures. Have toys available or puzzles for younger children the parents may have to bring with them to the conference, so the children will be occupied while you conduct the conference. Be flexible and willing to permit the whole family to come to the conference as that may be the only way you meet the parents on their terms.

◇ You may notice that in some cultures, mothers may defer control to their male children and the student may be in charge. Do not react negatively to this situation.

◇ If a parent becomes irate, stay calm. Never conference on your own with a parent that you suspect might be irate. Ask another colleague or an administrator or counselor to sit in with you.

Closing the Conference:

◇ Finish with a concrete plan of action that both teacher and parent (and student, if applicable) agree to.

◇ Have all present sign the conference sheet.

◇ Thank the parents for coming.

◇ Follow up with the plan of action agreed to and communicate the effectiveness of the plan to parents. Be prepared to reschedule another conference and proceed to the next level if necessary.

Conducting a Language Proficiency Assessment Committee (LPAC) Meeting

In this meeting the progress of the English Language Learner is discussed and placement is arranged for the coming year. This is a legal requirement as long as the student is receiving ESL services. A set procedure must be followed. Please defer to your state guidelines regarding this process. These guidelines may vary from state to state. In general the following people must be present to make placement decisions about the English Language Learner:

◇ A representative from the school administration

◇ ESL teacher

◇ Mainstream/regular teacher

◇ Parent (with interpreter) or a parent representative in case the specific parent is unable to attend

CHAPTER SUMMARY

This chapter discussed the importance of maintaining positive relationships with parents. The role the family plays in the literacy and language development of children was explained. All learners, but particularly the culturally diverse, need their cultural backgrounds viewed as assets they bring to the classroom rather than deficits.

Teachers who validate the cultural backgrounds of students, who incorporate it as part of their daily instruction, will better serve the learning needs of these students. A teacher who views the cultural heritages of families with respect and seeks to understand will forge successful home-school relationships.

Teachers who plan home visits and do everything possible to make contact with the parents are going to be preemptive rather than reactive when dealing with student and family concerns.

The classroom application strategies discussed in this chapter centered on creating a warm and welcoming school environment; a welcoming classroom; understanding why parents may be prevented from being involved in school; as well as tips for conducting successful parent-teacher conferences.

REFLECTIVE CHAPTER QUESTIONS

1. What is the role the family plays in early language and literacy development from birth to five years of age? How does lack of education and poverty interrupt this development in some children? How can society as a whole redress such trends of poverty and illiteracy?

2. What is the importance of viewing the cultural backgrounds of diverse students as an asset rather than a deficit? Reflect on examples of deficits and assets you have personally encountered or seen in schools or society in general.

3. What are the many factors that a teacher should understand about families of diverse students? Are there any additional factors other than the ones highlighted that may prevent a parent from being able to communicate with the school?

4. Using the tips for conducting a successful parent-teacher conference and with 2–4 other classmates, conduct a mock conference, utilizing the strategies provided in the chapter. Create different scenarios that you think you should be prepared to encounter as a classroom teacher. Take turns in the teacher's role. Engage the class in an evaluation of your teacher communication skills during the conference.

SUGGESTED FIELD-BASED ACTIVITIES FOR PRE-SERVICE AND IN-SERVICE TEACHERS

1. Ask permission to attend a parent-teacher conference. Observe how the teacher maintains open and positive communication with the parent. Discuss what strategies you observed the teacher utilize and discuss what you learned during the process. Conduct your own parent-teacher conference. Ask a teaching colleague to sit in on the conference and evaluate your teacher communication skills. Afterwards discuss with the teacher your strengths and weaknesses.

2. Visit a school that is in a culturally diverse area. Evaluate the buildings and the overall climate (atmosphere) for its tangible displays of cultural diversity. What do you see posted around the building? What is the message you are getting that represents the cultural community of the school setting?

3. Interview a parent and ask him or her to describe how the school and the teachers communicate in respect to his or her child's academic progress. Ask the parent to rate how well the school and teachers do to make him or her feel welcome. Ask the parent to make any additional recommendations that would enhance school-home relations in the community.

REFERENCES

Allen, J. B. (2007). *Creating welcoming schools: A practical guide to home-school partnerships with diverse families.* New York: Teacher's College Press.

Banks, J. (2006). *Cultural diversity and education: Foundations, curriculum, and teaching* (5th ed). Boston: Allyn & Bacon.

Curtin, E. M. (2002). *Students' and teachers' perceptions of culturally responsive teaching: Urban middle school case study.* Dissertation: University of North Texas. Electronic dissertation available at http://www.unt.edu/library.htm.

Curtin, E. M. (2006). *Overcoming the learning curve: The classroom perceptions of beginning teachers during their induction year.* Poster presentation for American Educational Research Association Annual Meeting. San Francisco.

Gonzalez, N., Moll, L. C., & Amanti, C. (2005). *Funds of knowledge: Theorizing practices in households and classrooms.* Mahwah, NJ: Lawrence Erlbaum Associates.

Gonzalez-Mena, J. (2006). *50 early childhood strategies for working and communicating with diverse families (50 teaching strategies series).* Upper Saddle River, NJ: Pearson Merrill Prentice Hall.

Hanson, M. J., & Lynch, E.W. (2004a). *Developing cross-cultural competence: A guide for working with children and their families.* Baltimore, MD: Brookes Publishing.

Hanson, M. J., & Lynch, E. W. (2004b). *Understanding families: Approaches to diversity, disability and risk.* Baltimore, MD: Brookes Publishing.

Hildebrand, V., Phenice, L. A., Gray, M. M., & Hines, R. P. (2007). *Knowing and serving diverse families* (3rd ed.). Upper Saddle River, NJ: Prentice Hall.

Hones, D. F., & Chao, C. (1999). *Educating Americans: Immigrants' lives and learning.* Mahwah, NJ: Lawrence Erlbaum Associates.

Ladson-Billings, G. (2001). *Crossing over to Canaan: The journey of new teachers in diverse classrooms.* Hoboken, NJ: Jossey-Bass.

Machado, J. (2007). *Early childhood experiences in language arts: Early literacy* (8th ed.). Clifton Park, NY: Thomson Delmar Learning.

McCarthey, S. (1999). Identifying teacher practices that connect home and school. *Education and Urban Society, 32*(1), 83–107.

Nieto, S., & Bode, P. (2007). *Affirming diversity: The sociopolitical context of multicultural education* (5th ed.). Boston, MA: Allyn & Bacon.

Snow, C., Burns, S., & Griffin, P. (Eds.). (1998). *Preventing reading difficulties in young children.* Washington, DC: National Press.

Whelan-Ariza, E. N. (2006). *Not for ESOL teachers: What every classroom teacher needs to know about the linguistically, culturally, and ethnically diverse student.* Boston: Pearson Allyn & Bacon.

INDEX